Multilingualism in the English-speaking World

THE LANGUAGE LIBRARY

Series editor: David Crystal

The Language Library was created in 1952 by Eric Partridge, the great etymologist and lexicographer, who from 1966 to 1976 was assisted by his co-editor Simeon Potter. Together they commissioned volumes on the traditional themes of language study, with particular emphasis on the history of the English language and on the individual linguistic styles of major English authors. In 1977 David Crystal took over as editor, and *The Language Library* now includes titles in many areas of linguistic enquiry.

The most recently published titles in the series include:

Ronald Carter and Walter Nash	*Seeing Through Language*
Florian Coulmas	*The Writing Systems of the World*
David Crystal	*A Dictionary of Linguistics and Phonetics*, Fifth Edition
J. A. Cuddon	*A Dictionary of Literary Terms and Literary Theory*, Fourth Edition
Viv Edwards	*Multilingualism in the English-speaking World*
Geoffrey Hughes	*A History of English Words*
Walter Nash	*Jargon*
Roger Shuy	*Language Crimes*
Gunnel Tottie	*An Introduction to American English*
Ronald Wardhaugh	*Investigating Language*
Ronald Wardhaugh	*Proper English: Myths and Misunderstandings about Language*

Multilingualism in the English-speaking World

Pedigree of Nations

Viv Edwards

Blackwell
Publishing

© 2004 by Viv Edwards

BLACKWELL PUBLISHING
350 Main Street, Malden, MA 02148-5020, USA
108 Cowley Road, Oxford OX4 1JF, UK
550 Swanston Street, Carlton, Victoria 3053, Australia

The right of Viv Edwards to be identified as the Author
of this Work has been asserted in accordance with the
UK Copyright, Designs, and Patents Act 1988.

First published 2004 by Blackwell Publishing Ltd

Library of Congress Cataloging-in-Publication Data

Edwards, Viv.
Multilingualism in the English-speaking world : pedigree of nations / Viv Edwards.
p. cm. — (The language library)
Includes bibliographical references and index.
ISBN 0–631–23612–0 (alk. paper) — ISBN 0–631–23613–9 (pbk. : alk. paper)
1. Multilingualism. 2. Language and education. 3. Linguistic minorities.
I. Title. II. Series.

P115.E285 2004
306.44′6—dc22
2004009039

A catalogue record for this title is available from the British Library.

Set in 10/12.5pt Galliard
by Graphicraft Limited, Hong Kong
Printed and bound in the United Kingdom
by MPG Books Ltd, Bodmin, Cornwall

The publisher's policy is to use permanent paper from mills
that operate a sustainable forestry policy, and which has been
manufactured from pulp processed using acid-free and elementary
chlorine-free practices. Furthermore, the publisher ensures that
the text paper and cover board used have met acceptable
environmental accreditation standards.

For further information on
Blackwell Publishing, visit our website:
http://www.blackwellpublishing.com

In memory of Hannah Davies,
Rachel Williams and Nicole Bérubé

Contents

Preface   viii

Part I The extent of diversity   1

  1 The myth of monolingualism   3
  2 Roots of diversity   13
  3 Language and the provision of services   48

Part II Language at home and in school   77

  4 Language in the family   79
  5 Language and education: a history   94
  6 Language and education in the modern world   105
  7 Minority languages and majority speakers   137

Part III Language in the wider community   147

  8 Language and the economy   149
  9 Language and the media   167
 10 Language and the arts   188
 11 Language, diplomacy and defence   207
 12 Is life really too short to learn German?   214

References   223

Index   241

Preface

Many people think of globalization as a recent phenomenon. In fact, the population movement we are currently witnessing is best seen as the second wave of a process that started several hundred years ago and became firmly rooted in the nineteenth century. Most people in the English-speaking world today can either trace their ancestry to another country or can name a member of their family who has embarked on the great adventure of migration.

In my own case, my great-aunt Rachel migrated from Wales to the USA in 1929. The farewell gift from the congregation of her chapel was a Welsh Bible with an inscription wishing her luck not in the 'new world' but in 'the other world'. Rachel did not return for 40 years, by which time both her parents had died. To all intents and purposes, the new world for which she departed might just as well have been the other world.

On one of many subsequent trips, she told us about a long-forgotten episode of family history. In the 1880s, her own grandmother had waited until her youngest son left school to start work at the age of 12, and had run away with the lodger to make a new life in the USA. The following year, she returned to her husband and the incident was conveniently forgotten. When asked at some point why she had decided to come back, she is reputed to have answered simply: 'The other one was even worse!'

This book has been inspired by a fascination with people like my great-aunt and my great-great-grandmother and the journeys they have made. It has also been moulded by my own childhood exposure to bilingualism in Wales and my work as an adult on the education of the 'new minorities' who have settled in the UK since the 1950s. It has provided an opportunity to weave the threads of my own experience into the much larger multi-lingual tapestry, which potentially enriches the lives of everyone in the English-speaking world.

My great grandparents wrote a weekly letter to Rachel, who loved receiving letters but was less enthusiastic about writing. She would, I am sure, have far preferred the electronic conversations I have been able to have with friends and colleagues in several continents as I have worked on this book. I owe a debt of gratitude to the many people who provided me with material or feedback: Stephen May in Aotearoa/New Zealand; Michèle de Courcy, Michael Clyne and Ian Malcolm in Australia; Nicole Bérubé and Jim Cummins in Canada; Jim Anderson, David Crystal, Mira Katbamna, Paddy Ladd and Chris Morriss in the UK; and Diana Eades, Susan Dicker and Anne Sienkewicz in the USA. Finally, my thanks to my husband, Chris Morriss, for his practical and moral support over several months of enforced house arrest with a prolapsed disc, which – ironically – allowed me to complete this book.

In keeping with the spirit of this book, and following the lead of Stephen May, I have deliberately departed from the publishing convention of italicizing non-English words, as a visual metaphor designed to make the point that minority languages are in fact a normal part of life in English-dominant countries.

Viv Edwards
University of Reading

Part I

The extent of diversity

1

The myth of monolingualism

In *Tour to the Hebrides*, Samuel Johnson remarks: 'I am always sorry when any language is lost, because languages are the pedigree of nations.'[1] Pedigrees are concerned, of course, with historical antecedents; but they are also helpful in interpreting the present and predicting the future. This book will venture well beyond the Hebrides to chart the influence of other languages on the English-speaking world. The aim will be to throw light on the social and historical complexities of relationships among the many different peoples who make up the English-speaking world, and the languages they speak.

Given the importance of English as a global language, this focus on multilingualism may seem perverse. English is used in some capacity by at least a billion people worldwide. Different people, of course, use English in different ways. In some countries, it is the majority language; in others, it is spoken as a second language for 'official' purposes such as education and government; in still others, it is learned as a foreign language in schools. The notion of concentric circles is useful in explaining these different patterns.[2] In the 'inner-circle' countries – the UK, Ireland, Canada, the USA, Australia and Aotearoa/New Zealand – English is the native language of the majority. In the 'outer-circle' countries, such as India and South Africa, English was introduced by colonial governments and remained an official language, alongside selected local languages, after independence. In 'expanding-circle' countries, such as China and Japan, English is a foreign language used for purposes of wider communication. The pre-eminence of English lies, in fact, in the combined numbers of native, second-language and foreign-language speakers.

In the inner-circle countries that will form the focus for this book, the ability to speak English is considered such an asset that many find it difficult to understand the need for other languages. This monolingual

The scale of linguistic diversity in the English-speaking world is greater today than at any point since the mass migrations of the nineteenth century. Photograph by Dave Andrews.

mindset can be traced to nineteenth-century Europe and the rise of the nation state, when one dominant group at the core achieved political and economic control of the periphery. Whereas the Greek, Roman and Austro-Hungarian empires were more concerned with collecting taxes than imposing a single language, nation states made systematic attempts to assimilate minorities and their languages.[3] European views on language were transported to the colonies, helping to perpetuate the monolingual myth. On a global scale, multilingualism remains the norm. And, even in the English-speaking world, an astonishing diversity of languages lies just beneath the veneer of homogeneity.

The extent of diversity

So how clear a picture, then, do we have of multilingualism in inner-circle countries? Sadly, the statistics that are often cited are seldom more than educated guesses, even in the case of the best-documented languages. Estimates of the numbers of English speakers in the outer-circle countries, for instance, range from 98 million to 518 million.[4] Estimates for expanding-circle countries are even more contentious: from 100 million to 1,000 million. Other languages face similar challenges.

Population censuses are an important source of information on language use. Some censuses, however, are more helpful than others: the UK collects data only on the Celtic languages; the Republic of Ireland covers only Irish. But even when the scope is much broader, the census is a blunt instrument. One problem is the compliance of respondents. In Ireland, the main purpose of early population counts was to gather information for taxation and military purposes. The census was predictably treated with extreme caution and it was not until the nineteenth century that the Catholic clergy encouraged the faithful to give accurate information.[5] More recently in the 2001 Canadian census, enumeration was not permitted, or was interrupted, on many First Nations reserves and settlements.

Questions are sometimes confusing or ambiguous. Many people who responded positively to an item in the 1991 census of Northern Ireland about 'knowledge of the language' may in fact have had only very limited fluency, thus creating a healthier picture than was actually the case. In other instances, ambiguity results in underestimates. There is a strong probability that some members of minority communities in Australia interpreted a question about languages spoken *in the home* too literally.[6] Many younger people who speak only English with their partner and children may use a different language when visiting other members of the family, or when taking part in community events. People living on their own may also have failed to report other languages. The fact that there are no explanatory notes means that responses to census questions are likely to be of the 'rough-and-ready' variety.

Indigenous languages

Putting to one side the problems associated with data collection, what general picture emerges of linguistic diversity in the inner-circle countries? An obvious place to start is with the languages spoken by the Indigenous peoples of the new worlds of North America and the Antipodes. These worlds were not, of course, new to the peoples who had inhabited them for millennia before the arrival of Europeans.

The impact of colonization was catastrophic. Populations were decimated by the introduction of new diseases and the genocidal impulses of Europeans. Attempts were made to assimilate forcibly those who escaped slaughter and disease by separating children from their parents in residential boarding schools where English-only policies were rigorously enforced. Indigenous people were denied full participation in mainstream society until the late twentieth century. Statistics for a range of indicators – over-representation in prisons, educational underachievement, unemployment, health, life expectancy – show conclusively that they remain more marginalized and disadvantaged than any other group. The social, political and economic pressures to abandon traditional languages are enormous, and the fact that the languages survive at all is a remarkable testimony to the cultural integrity of these peoples.

Indigenous peoples today make up varying proportions of the population of inner-circle countries – 14 per cent in Aotearoa/New Zealand, 3.3 per cent in Canada, 2.2 per cent in Australia, and 1.5 per cent in the USA. The languages they speak have several things in common. The first is the astonishing diversity that greeted Europeans on their arrival: well over 300 different languages in North America,[7] and between 200 and 250 in Australia.[8] Of these, fewer than 200 survive in North America and only 50 in Australia. Even the remaining languages are spoken by ever-decreasing numbers of people. Only a quarter of respondents who identified themselves as North American Indian, Métis or Inuit in the 2001 Canadian census – some 235,075 individuals – reported that they had enough knowledge of an Aboriginal language to carry on a conversation. According to the 2001 census, two of the most important Australian languages – Warlpiri and Arrente – had just 2,937 and 2,444 speakers, respectively.

Established languages

The situation in the British Isles is a little different. The distance between the languages and cultures of the original Celtic peoples and the English imperialists is far smaller than the distance between European colonists and Indigenous peoples. None the less, these 'established' languages – to use the terminology of Stacy Churchill[9] – occupy a similar niche and the health of Celtic languages is a matter of considerable concern.

With very few exceptions, extinction is for ever, although on rare occasions language decay has been reversed or at least delayed. Cornish revivalists, few but active, continue to promote the language, and over 1,000 people on the Isle of Man – some 2 per cent of the population – reported that they used Manx Gaelic in the 2001 census. Scottish Gaelic has a much more solid base but is none the less extremely vulnerable. In the decade between 1991 and 2001, the number of speakers dropped from 65,980 to 58,650, just over 1.2 per cent of the population of Scotland. Irish is much stronger. In Northern Ireland, 4.6 per cent are able to speak, read and write the language, but in the Irish Republic, this proportion rises to 43 per cent – just over 1.43 million people. However, statistics for frequency of language use suggest that Irish is less healthy than it might at first appear. Nearly two-thirds of those recorded as Irish speakers say that they never use the language or that they speak it less frequently than once a week. The most encouraging picture emerges from Wales, where the 2001 census reported the first increase in both the number and percentage of Welsh speakers since records have been kept. Almost 21 per cent of the population now speak the language.

Any discussion of established languages in the UK also needs to consider Scots, which has an estimated 1.5 million speakers in Scotland and a further 100,000 speakers in Northern Ireland.[10] The Scots battle for recognition centres on whether it should be considered a language in its own right or a dialect of English. Several other communities are involved in similar struggles, including speakers of Ebonics or Black English in the USA, Australian Aboriginal English and Hawai'ian Creole English.

Sign languages confront an even bigger obstacle: the battle for recognition as languages at all. Ignorance about sign is widespread. It is commonly assumed, for instance, that there is just one universal language. In fact, sign languages vary in the same way as their spoken counterparts. British Sign Language (BSL), the preferred language of the Deaf community in the British Isles, is distinct from the American Sign Language (ASL) used in North America. ASL, in turn, is distinct from Auslan, the sign language of Australia, and the closely related Aotearoa/New Zealand

Sign Language. Numbers are difficult to estimate: not all censuses collect information on sign languages and the accuracy of those which do is open to question.[11] It is likely, though, that BSL has well in excess of 70,000 users;[12] over 40,000 people in Canada and much larger numbers in the USA use ASL; Auslan is the preferred language of an estimated 15,400 people;[13] and a further 27,000 reported using Aotearoa/New Zealand Sign Language in the 2001 census.

Other languages might also qualify as established languages. French and Spanish, for instance, have a special status as colonial languages that arrived in North America at the same time as or earlier than English. The French presence on the continent extended at one point in an enormous arc from the Hudson in the north to the Mississippi in the south. Following defeat in eighteenth-century European conflict, France abandoned its colonies and large-scale immigration came to a halt. Some French-speaking strongholds, however, remained. At the beginning of the eighteenth century large numbers of Acadians – or Cajuns – who had been expelled from eastern Canada were resettled in Louisiana. French remained a supplementary language in the state until the 1920s and the French government continued to support the teaching of the language in secondary schools through much of the twentieth century. Over 1.6 million people reported themselves as speaking French, Cajun or Patois in the 2001 US census.

The main stronghold of French in North America is, of course, in Canada, where the 2001 census recorded almost 6.8 million Francophones, almost a quarter of the population. Of these, 86 per cent live in Quebec, and over three-quarters of the rest are concentrated in New Brunswick and Ontario. Two features ensure the continuing strength of this community: its sheer size and its concentration in and around Quebec. The fact that French is a world language also reinforces its position. But, unlike Welsh or Irish or Gaelic in the British Isles, if French disappeared from Canada or the USA, it would continue to be spoken in many other locations.

New minorities

After accounting for Indigenous and established languages, some writers group other languages together under the label of 'new minorities'. Yet this distinction is sometimes difficult to maintain. Take the case of Spanish. The first European settlers in North America were the Spanish and Spanish Mexicans who founded colonies in Florida, the southwest and California. Two factors – the special political relationship with Puerto

Rico and ongoing interaction with the peoples of Mexico – ensured a steady flow of new Spanish speakers throughout the twentieth century. Political crises and changes in immigration policy have swelled traditional Hispanophone communities with new arrivals from Cuba and Central and South America. Spanish is currently second only to English in the USA, with over 28 million speakers. It is a moot point whether Spanish speakers should be treated as an established or a new minority.

World War II was a watershed not only for the new worlds but also for the old. The UK, the most important source of migrants to the inner-circle countries, became a net importer for the first time when large numbers of outer-circle citizens began arriving from the British Commonwealth to help fuel post-war expansion. Ireland, for its part, remained an exporter of people until membership of the European Union transformed the economy in the 1990s. Countries which had traditionally depended on the British Isles – Canada, Australia and Aotearoa/New Zealand – needed to look elsewhere to supply their labour needs, and immigration in the late decades of the twentieth century reached levels very similar to those at the height of mass immigration at the beginning of the century.

Ironically, the same processes of globalization that helped establish English as the world's pre-eminent language have been responsible for the increasing linguistic diversity of inner-circle countries. In the 2001 Canadian census, one in every six people reported a mother tongue other than English or French; more than 100 different languages were recorded. The twentieth century saw the transformation of Australia from an overwhelmingly Anglo-Celtic population to one of the world's most multicultural societies. The 2001 Australian census reported that 142 languages, in addition to Aboriginal languages, were spoken by just over one in six of the population. According to the 2000 census, the equivalent proportion for the USA was even higher: one in five. Aotearoa/New Zealand is less diverse than the other inner-circle countries: about four-fifths are of European origin, mainly from the British Isles, but, even here, the population has become much more diverse in recent times.

The dismantling of 'Whites-only' policies in the 1960s means that the languages spoken by newer migrants are much more varied than in the past. Chinese, for instance, is currently the most common language after English in Australia, the most common language after French and English in Canada, the most common language after English and Spanish in the USA, and the most common language after English, Māori and Samoan in Aotearoa/New Zealand. Tagalog now appears in the top ten languages of the USA, Canada and Australia.

Table 1 *The other languages*[14]

Rank	UK	USA census 2000	Canada census 2001	Australia census 2001	Aotearoa/ New Zealand census 2001
1	Bengali	Spanish (28,101,000)	Chinese (872,000)	Chinese (386,000)	Samoan (81,000)
2	Panjabi	Chinese (2,022,000)	Italian (681,000)	Italian (354,000)	Chinese (70,000)
3	Gujarati	French (1,644,000)	German (636,000)	Greek (264,000)	French (50,000)
4	Hindi/ Urdu	German (1,383,000)	Spanish (611,000)	Arabic (including Lebanese) (209,000)	German (34,000)
5	Turkish	Tagalog (1,224,000)	Panjabi (339,000)	Vietnamese (174,000)	Dutch (26,000)
6	Arabic	Vietnamese (1,010,000)	Arabic (290,000)	Spanish (94,000)	Tongan (23,000)
7	English-based creoles	Korean (894,000)	Portuguese (265,000)	Tagalog (79,000)	Hindi 23,000)
8	Yoruba	Russian (706,000)	Polish (250,000)	German (76,000)	Japanese (20,000)
9	Somali	Polish (667,000)	Tagalog (245,000)	Macedonian (72,000)	Korean (16,000)
10	Chinese	Portuguese (565,000)	Hindi (227,000)	Croatian (70,000)	Spanish (15,000)

Despite issues of reliability, several observations can be made with confidence. Linguistic diversity is very much a fact of life in the inner-circle countries. The scale of this diversity is greater now than at any point since the mass migrations of the nineteenth century. The languages in question, however, originate from a much wider range of countries than the European nations, which fuelled earlier migrations.

Pedigree of nations

It is perhaps to be expected that any discussion involving large numbers of languages in six different national contexts over several centuries will generate some terminological confusion. The wide range of ways of referring to Indigenous peoples in North America gives a flavour of the complexity. The Canadian constitution, for instance, recognizes three distinct Aboriginal peoples: Indians, Inuit and Métis.[15] Many people today, however, prefer 'First Nations' to 'Indians', because of the colonial connotations of the latter term. Similar debates have taken place in the USA. 'Indians' was replaced in the 1970s by Native Americans. However, to avoid confusion with the indigenous peoples of Alaska, the legally accepted term is now 'American Indians and Alaskan Natives'.

Another area of confusion concerns the teaching of minority languages. In the UK, Australia and Aotearoa/New Zealand, most people talk in terms of 'community languages'; in the USA and Canada, 'heritage languages' are the norm; Australians also refer to 'languages other than English' or LOTEs. A further complication arises in relation to the target group for teaching. Most people think of heritage language programmes as designed for the children of recently arrived minorities; some writers, however, also apply this term to teaching that takes place in Indigenous communities.

Attempts to impose structure on such a complex subject inevitably involve some arbitrary decisions. Hopefully the decisions I have taken will assist – and not frustrate – the reader. In this first part of the book, I explore the extent of diversity in inner-circle countries. In the pages that follow, I trace the roots of diversity from the sixteenth century to modern times. I also look at issues of social inclusion: patients need to communicate with health professionals; defendants and witnesses with lawyers and the police; parents with their children's teachers. Although most minority-language speakers are bilingual, new arrivals need support to participate in the life of the wider community. The provision of services in other languages is also important for people who understand and speak English but none the less feel more comfortable using the heritage language.

In the second part of the book, I look at language in two very important domains: home and school. Parents, family and community play a critical role in passing minority languages from one generation to the next. I explore a range of reasons – social, intellectual and economic – for bringing up children bilingually, as well as the support structures that help families achieve this end. School has an important influence on language maintenance and shift. An historical overview – from pioneer days to World War II – provides a context for understanding a range of contemporary issues: is linguistic diversity a problem to be overcome or a resource to be nurtured? If other languages are to be used in formal schooling, which approaches produce the best results? What are the opportunities for English-speaking students to acquire other languages?

The third and final part of the book focuses on the role of other languages in the wider community: the economy, the media, the arts, and diplomacy and defence. I look at the benefits of other languages in business settings and at the double standards of the dominant English-speaking group. I consider the complex course which members of minority communities steer between minority and mainstream media in ways that meet their needs and interests. I examine the importance of traditional forms of artistic expression, as well as performances and creations which cross linguistic and cultural boundaries. I also look at the crucial role which competence in other languages plays in the post-11-September world, both in terms of intelligence gathering and diplomacy, and as a means of ensuring justice. Pedigrees are not only about looking back; they also help us to predict what might come next. I end by taking stock of the arguments for and against diversity and speculating on the future.

Notes

1   Boswell (1785).
2   Kachru (1985).
3   See, for instance, May (2001: 5–7).
4   Graddol (1999).
5   Ó Dochartaigh (2000: 7).
6   Clyne and Kipp (2002).
7   Francis and Reyhner (2002).
8   Romaine (1991).
9   Churchill (1986: 6–7).
10   Smith (2000); Kirk and Ó Baoill (2001).
11   Clyne and Kipp (2002).
12   McPake et al. (2002).
13   McPake et al. (2002).
14   The UK figures are based on a survey of London school children reported by Baker and Mohieldeen (2000: 5). Some sources give separate statistics for different Chinese languages, such as Mandarin and Cantonese; here all figures are conflated. Figures for all languages are rounded to the nearest 1,000.
15   The Métis people originated in the mid-1600s as children of Ojibway and Cree mothers and French and Scottish fur-trader fathers. Later, Scandinavian, Irish and English bloodlines became part of Métis heritage too.

2

Roots of diversity

The British Isles are the obvious starting point in a story of adventurism, colonization and empire, the first step in the journey which ultimately established English as a global language. The first casualties were the original languages of Ireland, Scotland and Wales but, with territorial expansion, the Indigenous languages of North America, Australia and Aotearoa/New Zealand were to sustain even greater losses.

The English were not, however, the only European power with colonial aspirations. They arrived in North America at the same time as or later than the Spanish and French, and the linguistic fate of the continent was unsettled for some time. As frontiers were extended in the USA and Canada, and Australia and Aotearoa/New Zealand were added to the British empire, an ongoing stream of Anglo-Celts was joined by settlers from other European countries as part of the unprecedented mass migration of the nineteenth and early twentieth centuries. A hundred years later, the forces of globalization had created a pool of labour from all parts of the developing world.

This chapter looks at the complex relationship of English with the other languages. Sometimes these languages have shown astonishing resilience and resistance; on other occasions, they have given way to English within the course of a few generations. In all cases, the past is the key to understanding the present.

British beginnings

The story of multilingualism in the English-speaking world today begins, of course, in the British Isles with the original settlers, the Celts. The linguistic landscape of the British Isles was further shaped by successive invasions of foreign powers – the Romans, the Angles, the Saxons and the Jutes, the Vikings and the Normans. Speakers of two different branches of the Celtic language family were pushed to the western fringes: Goidelic retreated to what is now Ireland, Scotland and the Isle of Man; Brittonic to Brittany, Wales and Cornwall.[1]

Dolly Pentreath, the last known fluent speaker of Cornish, died in 1777.[2] Against all odds, an estimated 800 or so people involved in language revival speak Cornish fluently and almost 3,000 are able to hold a simple conversation in the language. The situation in the Isle of Man is similar. Ned Maddrell, the last native speaker of Manx Gaelic, died in 1974 at the age of 97,[3] and the language survives only through the efforts of some 2,000 committed individuals who have learned it as a second language. The other Celtic languages have fared better. Although they have been in decline for centuries, they have not only survived but, in some cases, are regaining ground.

Ireland

In its heyday, a period stretching from the sixth to ninth centuries, Irish was spoken not only in Ireland but in the coastal areas of southern and northern Britain, and most of present-day Scotland.[4] By the eighth century it had even replaced Latin as the main medium of literacy and religion. The physical proximity of Ireland and England made economic and political links between the two countries inevitable. When England first laid claim to Ireland in the Middle Ages, the impact was minimal, partly because the incomers were relatively few in number and partly because they shared the same religion. Although English gradually became the language of public affairs in urban areas, Irish remained the main language of everyday communication. In rural areas, Irish was the most important language for all sectors of society.

The sixteenth century marked an important turning point in attitudes to the language when Henry VIII issued a proclamation discouraging the use of Irish. By the middle of the next century large numbers of Scottish and English Protestants had replaced Irish landowners, forming a power base for the English crown, particularly in Ulster, with long-term consequences for Irish language and culture. This religious overlay, of course, provides the historical context for the 'troubles' of recent times.

By the eighteenth century, Irish had retreated to the poor and under-developed rural areas of the west, as wealthy rural property owners and the urban population shifted to English. At the time of the Act of Union with England in 1801, Irish speakers made up only 3.5 million of a total population of 5 million. The great social crises of the nineteenth century accelerated this decline. Even before the potato starvation years of 1846–50, the New World was a magnet for small farmers eking out an existence on land rented from absentee English landlords. A million deaths later, emigration to Britain, Australia and the USA continued to offer an escape from abject poverty.

Mass migration inevitably affected the linguistic balance in Ireland. Although very large numbers of those departing were Irish speakers, parents tended to give higher priority to ensuring that their children acquired the English they needed to survive in their new homes. None the less, according to some estimates, Irish may have been the second most widely understood language after English in Australia in the mid-nineteenth century,[5] and evidence in the form of personal journals, letters and columns in newspapers suggests that the language also survived for many years in the USA.[6]

With the emergence of the Irish Free State in 1921, Irish was made the national language and a focus for cultural and ethnic loyalty. Policy moved forward on several related fronts. Areas on the western periphery, where Irish was still widely spoken, were designated as the Gaeltacht. Here Irish was the language of education and public administration in an approach summed up as: 'no jobs, no people; no people, no Gaeltacht; no Gaeltacht, no language'.[7] Considerable investment in the local economy was designed to ensure that the population stayed in place.

Outside the Gaeltacht, education was seen as the main tool in language revival. Irish was also used in public services. Yet, although Article 8 of the Constitution recognized both Irish and English as official languages, no provision was made for the exclusive use of either language, thus offering a convenient 'get-out' clause. Because high-ranking civil servants tended to favour English, the usefulness of Irish diminished as people made their way through the hierarchy.

This general approach had limited success. Census figures show an increase in the proportion of Irish speakers from 21.2 per cent in 1946 to 31.6 per cent in 1981. However, government policy failed to produce opportunities for speaking Irish in everyday life, leaving many people to conclude that time spent learning the language in school was, to some extent, wasted. Language promotion was left increasingly to voluntary bodies; the government pursued a course of benign neglect. Irish was no longer required to work in the civil service and only those wishing to teach in Irish-medium schools required a certificate of Irish competence.

Entry of the Republic into the EU in 1973 marked a new phase in official attitudes to Irish, redefined as a minority language, now promoted on a par with Welsh in Wales, Gaelic in Scotland and Catalan in France and Spain. The Official Languages Act 2003 provided the first statutory framework for the delivery of public services through Irish.

Scotland

Irish is closely related to Gaelic, the language spoken today in Scotland. Indeed, from the third century AD onwards, there was a steady migration from Ireland to Scotland, bringing with it the kilt, bagpipes and even the family-name prefix Mac.[8] In the Middle Ages, Ireland and much of Scotland shared a literary language, sustained by hereditary orders and travelling bardic schools. By the tenth century, the area had been unified into a mainly Celtic-speaking kingdom and, for several hundred years, Gaelic was the everyday language of most people throughout Scotland.

It was only in the twelfth century that Gaelic began to lose ground in southern Scotland, first to the Norman French and then to the English of the court. Over time, various acts of parliament promoted English-language education. The 1609 Statutes of Iona, for instance, were designed to Anglicize the Gaelic Highlands by making them more 'civilized'. Blame for Highland barbarity was placed firmly on the Gaelic language and clan chiefs were forced to educate their eldest sons in English. Hereditary literary orders, Highland dress and Highland music were all outlawed; the clans were disarmed and broken up. The Reformation in Scotland was also very damaging to Gaelic. Since the majority of Gaels were Catholic, Gaelic was seen as standing in the way of Protestant ideals and the government of the day made no secret of the fact that their aim was to destroy all traces of the language. By the seventeenth century, Gaelic had retreated to the Highlands and the Hebrides.

In the clan system, land was originally owned communally and passed down through the family. As the generations passed, the clan chiefs became more wealthy and detached, looking on their kinsmen as property rather than family. In the Highland Clearances of 1800–50, land overlords banished the Gaelic-speaking people of the Highlands and Islands to make way for Lowland sheep farmers who could pay much higher levels of rent. Tens of thousands of people were moved from their townships to poor, coastal plots and told to fish and work the kelp to pay the rent for their new homes.

When these areas failed to provide a living, people were forced to look further afield. Emigration to North America became a torrent, and by mid-century some 35,000 had made the journey to what became known as Nova Scotia – New Scotland. During the same period, a further 8,000

Gaelic speakers settled in Australia. As was the case in Ireland, mass migration had far-reaching implications for language. At the end of the nineteenth century, the numbers of Gaelic speakers had declined to just over a quarter of a million. Two world wars further hastened the shift to English and, a hundred years later, the 2001 UK census recorded just 58,650 speakers.

Gaelic is not the only established minority language in Scotland; so, too, is Scots.[9] When the Angles settled in the north in the sixth and seventh centuries, they brought with them a language known as Englisc ('Angle-ish') – the ancestor of both Scots and English – which developed over time into the everyday language of the Lowland Scottish people. Fourteen English-speaking settlements or burghs established in the twelfth century formed the stronghold of Scots, with the boundary between Gaelic and Scots forming along the edge of the Highlands. By the late fourteenth century, Scots had gained precedence over Latin as the language of state used in the royal council, parliament, burgh council and court of law. A hundred years later, it was spoken by everyone from king to peasant and was the medium of a burgeoning literature.

When James VI, king of Scots and himself a writer in Scots, succeeded to the throne of England in 1603, he moved his court to London. The Scottish aristocracy realized that they needed a command of southern English to make their way in society. In 1707, when Scotland joined England and Wales by the Act of Union to create Great Britain, Scots was downgraded to the status of 'provincial dialect'.

Scots is closely related to Ulster-Scots or Ullans. Because the Scots-speaking Lowland Presbyterians who migrated across the Irish Sea out-numbered the English by six to one, their linguistic influence was inevitably much stronger. Ulster-Scots remains a distinctive influence in Northern Ireland. Under the terms of the 2000 Good Friday agreement between the UK and Irish governments, it now enjoys 'parity of esteem' with Irish. The 2001 UK census of Northern Ireland, for instance, was available in Irish, Ulster-Scots and English. Questions included: 'Quhit sex ir ye?' (What is your sex?) and 'Quhitlike ir ye fur merryin?' (What is your marital status?).

Wales

The Welsh have been rather more successful in their attempts to preserve their language. In spite of successive invasions – first by the Anglo-Saxons and later by the Anglo-Normans – they were ruled by their own princes and governed by their own laws until the late thirteenth century. Latin and French became the languages of administration until English assumed this role in the fourteenth century. The Acts of Union of 1536 and 1542 officially made Wales a part of the kingdom of England. One of the consequences was the complete exclusion of Welsh from the public domain: 'no person or persons that use the Welsh speech or language shall have or enjoy any manor, office or fees . . . unless he or they use and exercise the speech or language of English.'[10] This legislation ensured the Anglicization of the gentry, who needed to abandon their mother tongue if they wanted to get on in public life, and Welsh came to be associated with the lower classes.

None the less, the language proved remarkably resistant. Returns on language use in church services show that, by 1750, Welsh had undergone very little displacement since the 1707 Act of Union.[11] However, Welsh was now used in a smaller number of domains and did not enjoy the same status. As a result, the language was in a much more vulnerable condition in the following century.

The first half of the nineteenth century saw the rise of religious non-conformity and separation from the Anglican church; the second half witnessed the industrialization of Wales. Both developments laid the foundations for a new Welsh nationalist movement and – ultimately – the re-establishment of separate Welsh institutions and legislation. It is ironic that the greatest assaults came when the language was numerically at its strongest, with the mass internal migration from rural areas to the industrial valleys of the south. In the closing years of the nineteenth century, three out of four people spoke Welsh as their language of choice.

Developments in the early years of the twentieth century reversed the fortunes of the language. Very large numbers of people arrived from England and Ireland. Railways increased mobility and reduced the isolation of rural communities. The great loss of life in World War I, together with the progressive decline in religious non-conformity, also reduced the numbers of Welsh speakers. Several events in the second half of the century, however, ensured that the language is now a great deal healthier. The 1967 Welsh Language Act offered status to Welsh in the legal system and allowed ministers to prescribe bilingual versions of official forms. A much stronger act passed in 1993 accorded Welsh and English equal status in public life and the administration of justice. The establishment of a Welsh Assembly in 2000 has also promoted the language.

England

The evidence for the roots of English – the Celtic languages, Latin, Anglo-Saxon, Norse and French – is clear for all to see in the place names and vocabulary of the modern language. English is a product of diversity. But while foreign invasions came to a halt with the Norman Conquest in 1066, the flow of human traffic from all parts of the world continued.

In the eleventh century, William the Conqueror encouraged a small community of French Jews to move to England and use their capital and experience to provide banking and financial services. From the four-teenth century, Dutch canal builders, printers, brewers and brick makers, French and Flemish weavers and German mining engineers brought new skills at a time when the only major British export was wool.[12] Africans were brought as slaves or servants in the seventeenth and eighteenth centuries. In the nineteenth and early twentieth centuries, refugees from various European countries sought a safe haven from revolution and persecution. In the same period, the Irish fled from poverty and famine to do the jobs that local people spurned. In the process they helped create much of the infrastructure of industrial Britain, building canals, roads and railways, and working in mines, docks and factories.

In good times, the new skills and muscle power of migrants are con-sidered valuable assets. In times of recession, the host country is often less generous. When James I appointed a commission to investigate immigration, the report complained of 'foreigners using machines' that could produce items faster and cheaper than English workers.[13] Similarly, in the economic slump of 1456–7, rioters accused the Venetians, Genoese and Lombards in London of causing English unemployment. This schizophrenic attitude towards 'outsiders' – openness in times of growth, hostility in times of recession – is, of course, by no means limited either to the British Isles or to the past.

Colonization and empire

While the British mainland has been a destination for immigrants for centuries, it has also been an important starting point for migration. As early as 1584, the English geographer and chronicler Richard Hakluyt was arguing that Elizabethan England could solve its vagrancy problem, create new markets for goods and increase employment at home by settling paupers in America.[14] A succession of conflicts – the Thirty Years War, the English Civil War, the rule of Oliver Cromwell, the English Revolution – had made seventeenth-century England a most unsettled place. The religious problems of Europe and the custom of deporting convicts also helped to foster the growth of new colonies. During this period, the English focused their attention on Hudson Bay and the

Atlantic coast. However, they were not the only ones – or even the first – to see the possibilities of migration.[15]

The Spanish – in search of gold – were the earliest arrivals in North America in the mid-to-late sixteenth century. After dominating three great empires to the south, they established settlements in Puerto Rico, Florida, the southwest, California and New Mexico. Traders followed hard on the heels of conquerors; so, too, did missionaries bringing the universalizing message of Christ to Indigenous peoples. The Spanish laid the foundation for a pattern followed by all later European colonists: the domination of strategic areas, the creation of settlements and plantations using slave labour, and the introduction of a legal system modelled on that of the mother country. Although Spain and Mexico lost their holdings in the nineteenth century, the continuing movement of Spanish speakers from Mexico and Central and South America has ensured that Hispanics continue to be the largest linguistic minority.

France was another great player in the colonization of North America, beginning in 1534 with Jacques Cartier's first voyage to present-day Canada in the search for gold. Within a relatively short time, it was apparent to all the would-be imperial powers that the future lay not in gold but in the pursuit of trade. When Samuel de Champlain founded New France at the beginning of the seventeenth century, he was attempting to discover a new route to the Orient, not to the elusive El Dorado. By the mid-eighteenth century, France had developed a strong relationship with a number of Indian tribes in Canada and along the Great Lakes, and taken possession of the Mississippi River. It had also established a line of forts and trading posts in a crescent stretching from Quebec to New Orleans. The British were confined to the narrow belt east of the Appalachian Mountains.

One hundred and fifty years of intense rivalry between France and England came to an end in 1759 with the defeat of the French on the Plains of Abraham above Quebec City. Events taking place in North America were, however, just one piece in a very complex colonial jigsaw puzzle. In 1763, the Seven Years War in Europe came to an end with the victory of Britain and Prussia over an alliance of France, Austria and Russia. Britain finally made the transition from colonial to imperial power in North America when France ceded vast stretches of land between the Mississippi and the Great Lakes as part of war reparations. However, the vanquished French considerably outnumbered the English in Quebec and continued to attach great importance to their cultural and religious rights. The French managed to win significant concessions from the English, including linguistic freedoms. None the less, Anglophones dominated

Francophones in every sphere of economic activity for the next two hundred years.

Quebec was not the only part of North America experiencing political unrest at this time. When the USA declared independence from England in 1776, many English-speaking colonists who had remained loyal to the British empire escaped to the areas adjoining what had been New France. The creation of Upper Canada (or present-day Ontario) and Lower Canada (Quebec) in 1791 was a formal recognition of the linguistic and cultural distinctiveness of the territories.

French influence was also strong in Louisiana. With the annexation of the territory in 1803, the express aim was to impose English on the Francophone majority; the governor spoke no French. When it became apparent that this policy was a failure, it was decided to appoint bilingual judges and keep public records in French and English, practices that continued into the twentieth century.

The American Revolution also had consequences for the southern hemisphere. A new destination was urgently required for convicts who previously had been sent to America. Captain James Cook claimed Aotearoa/New Zealand for England in 1769. In the following year, he raised the flag in eastern Australia, an area that, until that time, had appeared as a blank on European maps – the mysterious Terra Australis Incognita or Unknown Southern Land. Eight years later the first penal colony was established in Port Jackson, the site of present-day Sydney. In the fifty years that followed, whalers, traders, settlers and missionaries began to arrive from Britain and Europe.

One of the consequences of European competition was that bilingualism was the norm in all segments of society. The ability to speak other languages was a mark of refinement in both North America and Australia. The educated were expected to learn foreign languages through personal study or with the help of a tutor, and advertisements offering instruction were common in colonial newspapers.[16] Thomas Jefferson considered knowledge of both French and Spanish essential for diplomatic and other purposes and had taught himself Spanish by reading *Don Quixote* with a grammar and a dictionary. He encouraged his daughter to read French on a daily basis and recommended Canada as the ideal place to acquire the language. At the other end of the social spectrum, mid-eighteenth-century advertisements in US newspapers indicate that runaway slaves were often able to speak German, French, Spanish, Irish and Dutch. Bilingualism was also common in Australia: Arthur Philip, the first governor of New South Wales, came from a bilingual German and English background, and both French and English were used in the household of Charles La Trobe, the first governor of Victoria.[17]

The use of other languages was driven by pragmatism. At the end of the eighteenth century, German colonists made up a third of the European population of southeastern Pennsylvania and had also established a presence in the mid-west. German was used widely in proclamations, accounts and newspapers and in 1828 there was even an attempt – albeit unsuccessful – to elevate it to the status of second official language of the state.[18] On some occasions, the use of German served the interests of politicians. During the War of Independence, for instance, Congress printed a letter in German from the Lutheran and Reformed clergy of Pennsylvania to countrymen in North Carolina and New York appealing to them to join the cause of freedom. Australian politicians showed a similar pragmatism, using the German-language press to reach voters. Business transactions in Melbourne and Adelaide in the 1860s and 1870s also regularly took place in German.[19]

While multilingualism was the norm, linguistic imperialism was none the less alive and well. Benjamin Franklin, for instance, voiced concern that the German population of Pennsylvania would shortly be 'so numerous as to Germanize us instead of our Anglifying them'.[20] He was worried that the colonial Assembly would have to employ translators 'to tell one half of our legislators what the other half say'. Thomas Jefferson was also among colonial leaders who expressed the fear that the use of other languages would threaten civil society. None the less, the largely laissez-faire attitudes to language of the seventeenth and eighteenth centuries continued through much of the nineteenth century.

No man's land?

North America and the Antipodes were new worlds only for Europeans. Those who set foot on *terra nullius* were confronted with the inconvenient reality that 'no man's land' actually belonged to the Indigenous peoples. The European response was genocide, actual and attempted, which was justified in the name of racial purity, self-protection and civilization. Attempts to remove Indigenous peoples alternated with efforts to 'civilize' them, and the assumption that Europeans were ordained by nature to rule was never questioned. Such attitudes have proved remarkably persistent. It is ironic in the extreme that, when the Royal Commission on Bilingualism and Biculturalism was established in Canada in the 1960s, Indigenous peoples were excluded because, unlike the French and English, they were not considered to form part of the 'founding races' of the country. In Australia, Aboriginal peoples were not even included in the population census until 1967.

The linguistic consequences of colonization were evident to many from the start. When the linguist and cleric Antonio de Nebrija presented the first Spanish grammar to a somewhat perplexed Queen Isabella at the end of the fifteenth century, he explained that language was 'the perfect instrument of empire'.[21] His words were indeed prophetic. European empire building heralded the beginning of the end for hundreds of languages – and their speakers – in the inner-circle countries. The statistics speak for themselves. The American Indian population of the United States diminished from an estimated 10 million in 1492 to less than 250,000 in 1900. In Aotearoa/New Zealand the Māori, estimated at between 100,000 and 200,000 at the time of European contact, were in the minority within a hundred years. Australia's Indigenous population took two centuries to recover to levels similar to those at the time of early colonial settlement.

Several factors contributed to these disastrous falls in population. Epidemics of measles, smallpox, tuberculosis, typhoid and other diseases exacted a heavy toll. Firearms and warfare also depleted numbers. In order to open up the land for White settlers, Indigenous peoples were relocated on reservations far removed from their ancestral lands, often with dire consequences. A forced march dubbed the 'Trail of Tears', for instance, resulted in the death of several thousand Cherokees on the way to 'Indian territory' in Oklahoma. In all the inner-circle countries, dispossession increased mortality and decreased the fertility of Indigenous peoples.

The cumulative effects of centuries of oppression have inevitably taken their toll. Only 154 of an estimated 300-plus languages have survived in the United States; of these, only 20 are still being passed on to children from their parents and elders in the traditional way.[22] A further 30 languages are used by the parental generation; the rest are spoken by the middle-aged and elderly. The situation in Canada is very similar. Only three of the 50 surviving Aboriginal languages now have large enough populations to be considered secure. In Australia, between 200 and 250 distinct languages and approximately 600 dialects were spoken at the time of European settlement. Many were quickly lost as the local populations died or were displaced, and those that survive are spoken mainly in the sparsely populated areas of central and northern Australia. According to the 2001 census, fewer than 50 of the original languages now survive.

Early contact with the British gave rise to pidgins, simplified communication systems with limited grammar and vocabulary, which are formed when people from different language groups find themselves working

and living together. In two northern communities, the pidgin developed over time into distinct creoles, languages in their own right, which, unlike the earlier pidgins, fulfilled all the communication needs of their speakers. There are two large creoles in Australia.[23] Torres Strait Creole – also known as Broken English or, simply, Broken – developed from the varieties of Pacific Pidgin English used by marine workers of various nationalities across the Pacific. Kriol dates back to the early years of the twentieth century when 200 or so survivors of systematic massacres sought refuge in the Anglican mission at Roper River in the Northern Territory. The children from seven different language groups used Pidgin English for communication outside their families and, in the course of a generation, expanded the pidgin into a creole, which is now spoken from the Katherine region of the Northern Territory to the Kimberleys in Western Australia.

In other parts of Australia, Aboriginal English is spoken as a first, second, third or fourth language by an estimated 50,000 people. It differs from standard Australian English in accent, grammar and vocabulary and is best thought of as a continuum of dialects, with standard Australian English at one end and creoles at the other. Particularly in areas of Australia where the traditional languages are weak or have disappeared completely, Aboriginal English, Kriol and Broken are a vital part of Aboriginal identity.

Aotearoa/New Zealand, unlike Australia, has just one Indigenous language. According to the 2001 census, the Māori made up 14.3 per cent of the population – some 526,281 people. Of these, one in seven are fluent native speakers. Increases in the proportions of younger speakers of the language indicate that the rapid decline in the second half of the twentieth century has been slowed down for at least one Indigenous language.

The slave trade

Indigenous peoples were not the only ones to suffer at the hands of colonizers. In North America, the labour needed to clear the forests and tend the fields came at first from Europe, where rapid population growth had created unemployment and homelessness. In the seventeenth century, between half and two-thirds of all immigrants to the colonies came as indentured servants who traded up to seven years of labour for free passage, food and shelter. Within a relatively short space of time, indentured workers were free to farm their own land, and so the planters had to look for other sources of labour. Native Americans were unsatisfactory – they were susceptible to disease and unreliable, returning to their own people as and when they chose. An alternative solution was to use human cargo in the trade that brought 10 million Africans to the Americas.[24]

Although African captives were used initially as indentured servants, working alongside Whites, there was a gradual shift to slavery. The advantages were obvious: slaves were permanent, dependent and easily identifiable by race. Massachusetts was the first to recognize slavery legally, in 1641; other colonies soon followed. Blacks and Whites rapidly became enmeshed in a cycle of oppression and resistance. Slaves were denied freedom of movement and the right to earn money. South Carolina and Virginia passed 'compulsory ignorance laws', which made it illegal to teach slaves to read and write. The harsher the conditions, the more the slaves resisted, and rebellion was widespread. The planters responded with even greater brutality – whipping, branding, dismembering, castration and murder.

The linguistic situation of the slaves was complex.[25] They came mainly from West Africa and spoke many different languages – Ewe, Hausa, Ibo, Mende, Twi and Yoruba, to name just a few. The slavers operated a policy of divide and rule, and different language groups were deliberately separated on board ship to minimize the risk of revolt. On arrival in the New World, planters did not impose this practice to the same extent and, in much the same way as farmers prefer certain breeds of cattle or horses, the planters tended to select slaves from the same ethnic background. However, whenever demand exceeded supply, there was no option but to buy whatever cargoes were available.

The same processes that gave rise to Kriol and Torres Strait Creole in Australia were also observed on the plantations of North America and the Caribbean. In the absence of documentation or recordings, we can assume that, in early stages, a pidgin with simplified grammar and limited vocabulary emerged as a lingua franca. Over time the pidgin would have developed into a creole, a full-blown language that met all the communication needs of its speakers.

In 1776, some slaves bought their freedom after serving during the Revolutionary War; others were released by slave-owners, motivated by revolutionary ideals. However, the conditions enjoyed by free African Americans were only a little better than the conditions of those who remained in bondage. By the middle of the nineteenth century, slavery was causing serious rifts within the rapidly expanding nation. New immigrants from Europe tended to favour abolition, as did the northern industrialists, who believed that, if the slaves were freed, they would move from the south to supply the need for labour. Southern planters, in contrast, were very clear that their prosperity depended on the continuation of slavery. When Abraham Lincoln was elected president in 1860, with considerable support from the immigrant vote, he took the middle way. While he was happy for slavery to continue in the states where it was already operating, he was not prepared for it to spread to the new western territories. Southerners perceived this stance as a threat to their way of life, and slavery was a central issue in the outbreak of the Civil War in 1861. The final surrender of the Confederate Army in 1865 marked the end of 250 years of slavery with the granting of new rights for Blacks by the federal legislation. Hopes following Emancipation that African Americans would be able to compete on a more equal footing were short-lived. In 1877, a new Republican government returned power to White southern leaders, who proceeded to introduce racial segregation in public transport, schools, restaurants and hotels, and theatres.

Until the late nineteenth century, 90 per cent of the African American population had been concentrated in the south. However, two developments – the insatiable demand for labour in the factories and the devastation of cotton crops by the boll weevil – drove increasing numbers of Blacks to the urban cities of the north. Restrictive covenants and gentlemen's agreements between White home-owners and realtors effectively confined Blacks to ghettos where living conditions were appalling. It also reinforced the social separation of Blacks and Whites in recreation, worship and education. Segregated schooling was the norm for much of the twentieth century not only in the USA but also in Canada. The last separate Black school in Ontario was shut only in 1965.[26]

The origins and development of distinctively Black forms of speech have also been the object of White supremacist scorn. In the early 1920s, for instance, George Krapp speculated that Black American language had developed from the simplified English or baby talk used by 'white overlords' with their 'black vassals.'[27] In doing so, he conveniently overlooked eighteenth-century reports that White planters learned the language from their slaves and not the other way around. Other writers advanced physiological explanations for the assumed Black inability to gain control of English, including clumsy tongues, flat noses and thick lips.[28]

The language of most African Americans today is widely believed to exemplify decreolization, a process whereby the creole gradually converges with the dominant language. It has been called by various names over the years – Black English Vernacular, African American Vernacular English and, more recently, Ebonics. Its linguistic status is hotly contested, with some writers arguing that it is one among many varieties of English and others demonstrating its strong African underpinnings. The creole status of at least three other varieties spoken in the USA, however, is uncontroversial.[29] Gullah is used by up to 300,000 people whose speech ranges along a continuum from creole to standard English in coastal South Carolina, Georgia, parts of lower North Carolina and northern Florida. Speakers use more or fewer creole features according to the formality of the situation. Louisiana Creole, another legacy of slavery, evolved as the native language of descendants of West Africans brought to Louisiana by French colonists. Hawai'ian Creole also arose in a plantation economy, though much later and well after the abolition of slavery, in the late nineteenth and early twentieth centuries. With the annexation of Hawai'i by the US, English-speaking planters from the mainland supplemented the local population with contract labour from East Asia, the south Pacific and southern Europe. The resultant creole shows the influence of Japanese, Chinese, Hawai'ian and Portuguese as well as English.

Mass immigration

The eighteenth and, more particularly, the nineteenth centuries were times of very rapid growth in Europe.[30] The population of Manchester in northern England increased more than ten times in the nineteenth century. In the same period, the population of Odessa, one of the leading Russian ports, grew from 6,000 to 500,000. Changes in the organisation of farming increased productivity, accelerating the drift from the countryside to the industrializing towns where there was a greater demand for labour. The development of transport and communications also played a role in encouraging migration. Steam shipping greatly reduced the cost of travel while the flow of information about overseas countries gave many people the courage to leave home.

England was no longer the chief source of immigrants to North America, as thousands fled continental Europe to escape poverty and war. Discontent with political systems led first to revolution and later to the emergence of modern nation states. Since state and nation rarely coincided, discontented minorities were widespread and much of the continent was living in an armed peace. Catastrophic harvests, a slump in trade, poverty and unemployment all added to the attractions of neo-European destinations. Between 1821 and 1913 about 44 million emigrants left European countries for overseas destinations.

The German presence is of special note. The first German settlers on the east coast and in the mid-west were assimilated fairly rapidly into the English-speaking mainstream.[31] In the nineteenth century, however, these early groups were bolstered by large-scale immigration of new German speakers. In the 10 years following the failed revolution in 1848, the million-plus people who left for America formed the main language group after the English in many different states. By 1880 they made up 60 per cent of foreign-born people who spoke a language other than English in the USA. Around the same time, half of the non-British and non-French population of Canada also identified themselves as German. In Australia, too, there was a significant German-speaking community.

Anglo-conformity

Towards the end of the nineteenth century, there was a discernible shift in attitude towards minorities and their languages. In the USA, the Americanization movement argued that, in order to maintain stable government, immigrants needed to be assimilated rapidly into American culture. The ability to speak English was closely linked to patriotism and there was a widespread concern that 'new immigrants' from eastern and southern Europe were not learning English as quickly as the Germans and Scandinavians of the nineteenth century. Knowledge of English was made a basic requirement for naturalization.[32] English evening classes were set up in the cities by employers anxious to reduce compensation payments to workers involved in accidents because they could not read signs or understand instructions.[33]

Hostility towards recent settlers was high in all the inner-circle countries at this time. In Canada, there was a move to 'clean up' prostitution, crime and disease by limiting the numbers of foreign immigrants. A *Calgary Herald* article published in 1899 berates Sifton, the Canadian minister of the interior, for 'ignoring Britishers as desirable immigrants' in preference to 'a mass of human ignorance, filth and immorality'. Linguistic considerations were often paramount: 'This policy of building a nation on the lines of the Tower of Babel, where the Lord confounded the language so that the people might not understand one another's speech, is hardly applicable to the present century.'[34]

With the outbreak of World War I, xenophobia reached hysterical proportions. In the US, several states enacted statutes or issued emergency orders prohibiting languages other than English not only in public places but also on the phone, on the railroad and in schools. Church services in other languages had to be conducted in private homes. By 1921, nearly 18,000 mid-westerners had been charged under these laws abridging free speech.[35]

Expressions of xenophobia and linguistic intolerance were also common in Australia. During World War I, other languages were banned as the medium of instruction, non-English publications were prohibited and most German place names were changed. Telephone conversations were sometimes intercepted and refugees from Nazi Germany were advised not to speak German in public places: 'Do not make yourselves conspicuous by walking with a group of persons, all of whom are speaking a foreign language. Remember that the welfare of the old established Jewish communities in Australia, as well as every migrant, depends on your personal behaviour.'[36] Although the publication of German newspapers was allowed again in 1925, most English-only measures continued until after World War II, encouraged by bodies such as the Returned Sailors and Soldiers Imperial League of Australia.

Social Darwinism and eugenics

The influence of social Darwinism and the eugenics movement was very much in evidence in the early twentieth century and undoubtedly played a role in the development of tests that claimed to show a correlation between ethnicity and intelligence. In 1912, Henry Goddard chose to ignore the cultural bias of test items and low levels of English literacy and reported that 83 per cent of the Jews, 80 per cent of the Hungarians, 79 per cent of the Italians and 87 per cent of the Russians who had recently arrived were 'feeble-minded'.[37] 'Scientific' findings of this kind helped to shape the Immigration Act of 1924, which introduced a quota system for each nationality, based on its proportion of the US population. Since northern Europeans formed by far the largest proportion of Americans at this time, future immigration would continue to favour this group. With the demographic threat gone, people no longer perceived other languages as a threat and coercive efforts to teach English faded.

Because most unwanted immigrants had little or no formal schooling, politicians pushed for many years for a literacy requirement for naturalization. However, by the time this addition was agreed in 1917, levels of literacy in Europe had improved significantly, so that this measure was ineffective.[38] Tests were also used to exclude undesirable immigrants in the southern hemisphere. Aotearoa/New Zealand introduced a reading test for 'aliens', defined as non-British citizens, while in Australia, the main tool of the 'Whites-only' policy heralded by the 1901 Federal Immigration Act was a 50-word dictation test administered by customs officers. Applicants who failed the test were refused entry to the country; those already in the country were given six-month jail sentences and then required to leave. The passages were changed regularly to prevent cheating. In the first two weeks of January 1917, applicants were required to write from dictation:[39]

> We all call the lion king of the beasts, but compare the biggest maneless lion with the full-grown male tiger, and we see at once which is the mightier animal. The tiger does not look it, but he is really more terrible than the great maned lion. The lion looks, with his noble mane, as terrible as he is.

The test was extremely effective in controlling entry. In 1903, for example, only 3 out of 153 applicants were successful. The test was even used to exclude 'undesirables' with a good command of English, since it could be conducted in another European language at the discretion of a customs official. In one case, a German, also fluent in English and French, was made to take the test in Greek, and was sentenced to six months' imprisonment as a prohibited immigrant when he failed.

The influence of the eugenics movement permeated all sections of society in inner-circle countries. A speaker at the 1913 Presbyterian Pre-Assembly Conference in Toronto, for instance, proposed the following solution: 'Take all the different nationalities, German, French, Italian, Russian and all the others that are sending their surplus into Canada: mix them with the Anglo-Saxon stock and produce a uniform race wherein the Anglo-Saxon peculiarities shall prevail.'[40] In Canada, arguments of this kind remained at the level of rhetoric; in Australia, they were put into practice. In the 1920s and 1930s, the message of eugenics was that it was possible to improve a nation's racial stock. Mixed-race children, categorized with zoological precision as half-castes, quadroons and octoroons, were the object of special interest. The solution, endorsed by government, was to 'breed out' the Black blood: if half-castes mated with quadroons and octoroons, White blood would finally eliminate the Black colour within five generations. All states and territories passed legislation permitting policemen or other agents of the state to transfer children of mixed descent from their families to half-caste institutions or foster homes. Here they were taught to despise their Aboriginal heritage and forbidden to speak their own languages. The pain inflicted was enormous:

> When we left Port Augusta, when they took us away, we could only talk Aboriginal. We only knew one language and when we went down there, well we had to communicate somehow. Anyway, when I come back I couldn't even speak my own language. And that really buggered my identity up. It took me 40 odd years before I became a man in my own people's eyes, through Aboriginal law. Whereas I should've went through that when I was about 12 years of age.[41]

Tens of thousands of babies and children were subjected to this fate before being sent to work as domestic servants or station hands. The hope was that they would eventually merge into European society and marry out. In the inter-war years, two of the three most important administrators of Aboriginal affairs – Dr Cecil Cook and A. O. Neville – were enthusiastic converts to the policy of breeding out. Cook personally brokered sixty or so arranged marriages between inmates of the Darwin half-caste home and European men. Neville justified his policy in simple terms: 'Are we going to have a population of 1,000,000 blacks in the Commonwealth, or are we going to merge them into our white community and eventually forget that there were any Aborigines in Australia?'[42]

Procedures were even put in place to allow people who had been successfully assimilated to assume their place in mainstream society. Under the conditions of the Natives (Citizenship Rights) Act 1944, applicants needed to satisfy a magistrate that they had 'adopted the manner and habits of civilized life'; that full citizenship rights were conducive to their welfare; that they could 'speak and understand the English language'; and that they were 'not suffering from active leprosy, syphilis, granuloma, or yaws'.[43]

The Deaf were also a target for eugenicists. In the USA, campaigners who included Alexander Graham Bell succeeded in introducing legislation in 30 different states for the sterilisation of Deaf people.[44]

The 'Yellow Peril'

Another group subjected to widespread discrimination were 'Orientals': the Chinese and Japanese and, to a lesser extent, Indians were singled out as the objects of particular hostility. In the USA, immigration from China had begun with the California Gold Rush of 1849. Discrimination was in evidence from the outset, leading to the establishment of China Towns. Chinese immigrants were attacked, barred from employment, disqualified from owning land, and not allowed to testify against Whites in court or vote, due to English literacy requirements.[45]

Gold also lured the Chinese to Australia and Aotearoa/New Zealand.[46] When they began arriving in substantial numbers in the mid-1850s, antagonism from European and Australian diggers was immediate. European and Australian miners accused the Chinese of wasting water, reworking other miners' shafts, smoking opium and gambling. A series of riots in both Victoria and New South Wales led to restrictions on entry into Australia. The arrival of the Chinese in Aotearoa/New Zealand in the next decade led to similar resentment from the other settlers.

However, it was not until the late nineteenth century that dislike of Orientals assumed paranoid proportions. There was growing concern at the prospect of invasion from the East, the so-called 'Yellow Peril'. In response, head taxes on the Chinese were introduced to curb immigration in the USA, Australia and Aotearoa/New Zealand. Immigrant-carrying ships to Aotearoa/New Zealand were restricted to one Chinese passenger per 100 tons of freight and, when old-age pensions were introduced to the country in 1898, Chinese naturalized citizens were excluded.[47] In Canada, a 'continuous journey' clause in the Immigration Act of 1908 made it impossible for immigrants from India to land in the country legally, since there was an agreement that ocean steamers would not travel directly between the two countries.[48]

Resentment spilled over increasingly into civil unrest. In Canada, where large numbers of Chinese had come to build the railway, anti-Asian riots broke out in the recession year of 1907. In Britain, the majority of Chinese were employed initially as seamen, before moving on to laundry work, and, in the years before the outbreak of World War I, the newspaper of the National Sailors' and Firemen's Union makes frequent reference to Chinese strike breakers.[49] There are records of attacks on Chinese property in Cardiff, an important seaport during this period. The Union of Laundresses and Washerwomen also expressed concern about the employment of its members.

Like the Chinese, the Japanese started to settle in the US in the middle of the nineteenth century, mainly on the Pacific Coast and in California. However, they were not subject to the same levels of hostility. This may have been due partly to the military strength of Japan and partly to the Japanese desire to merge into the wider society. The Japanese Association of America, which controlled immigration to the US, encouraged compatriots to wear Western dress and educate their children in public schools. In Canada, a 'gentlemen's agreement' with Japan, Britain's ally, kept immigration in check. With the advent of World War II, however, anti-Asian sentiment throughout North America became increasingly ugly. Japanese property was confiscated and large numbers were interned in prison camps.[50]

The modern world

World war II was a watershed. The way the world conducted itself before the onset of hostilities was very different from the new order that emerged with peace. The rapid industrial expansion and falling birth rates in the post-war period had two main effects on the English-speaking world. First, large numbers of settlers from the British Commonwealth arrived in the UK to fuel industrial expansion. Second, fewer British and Irish people were interested in emigration to other countries, so that North America, Australia and Aotearoa/New Zealand needed to look elsewhere for the labour required for their economic growth.

The UK was faced with the massive task of reconstruction. The government encouraged immigration, first from European refugees displaced by the war, and then from Ireland and the Commonwealth. A loophole in the 1948 British Nationality Act meant that over 800 million Commonwealth citizens had the right to settle in Britain. Employers reliant on immigrant labour soon included the National Health Service, London Transport, and factories and mills in large industrial cities.[51]

The two main sources of immigration to the UK were the Caribbean and the Indian subcontinent. Many Indians and Pakistanis left their home countries to escape the aftermath of the 1947 partition of India, which had resulted in as many as 2 million deaths. Most immigrants came from areas with a long association with the UK. Azad Kashmir and the Northwest Frontier, for instance, were traditional recruiting grounds for the British army and the merchant navy. Large numbers also came in the early 1960s when villages in the Mirpur District were flooded for the construction of the Mangla Dam, displacing 100,000 people. Until 1952, the main destination for people from the former British West Indies had been the USA. At this point, the entry quota was reduced to 800 a year and attention shifted to the UK. Immigration rose sharply from around 3,000 in 1953 to 136,400 in 1961.

Most new arrivals in Britain came from the so-called New Commonwealth, a convenient euphemism distinguishing the White English-speaking countries of the Old Commonwealth from colonies populated by brothers and sisters of colour. In contrast, the other inner-circle countries continued to look to Europe. The 1952 US Immigration and Nationality Act followed policies that had changed little since the 1920s. The only difference was that quotas previously justified on the grounds of racial superiority were now promoted as preserving social and cultural balance.

In Canada, too, race continued to influence immigration policies, with a preference for northern Europeans. The prime minister, Mackenzie King, explained in a House of Commons debate in 1947 that large-scale immigration from the Orient would not be permitted 'to avoid altering the fundamental composition of the Canadian population'.[52] The Immigration Act of 1952 made it possible to exclude immigrants on the basis of 'peculiar customs' including habits, modes of life, or 'unusual' means of holding property; climatic, educational, economic or industrial suitability; and the likelihood of becoming rapidly assimilated in Canadian society. Public opinion polls at the time showed that most Canadians would rather allow German enemy aliens into the country than Mediterranean or Asian peoples.

The more favourable economic climate and falling birth rates finally paved the way for more expansive immigration policies; so, too, did the greater concern for human rights that followed in the wake of the civil rights movement. In the USA, amendments to national-origins quotas were replaced in 1965 with a system based on reunification of families and skill shortages. During the same period, Canada, too, began admitting immigrants according to skills and means of support, irrespective of national origins. And in Australia, the passing of the Racial Discrimination Act in 1975 prepared the ground for the admission of settlers from non-European countries.

One feature of the new policies is the sheer scale of population movement. In the last quarter of the twentieth century, the USA admitted approximately 17.1 million immigrants, almost as many as the 17.2 million admissions in the first quarter of the century when immigration was at its height. Canada also saw an increase in migration and federal quotas, for immigration nearly doubled in the early 1990s. There are, however, marked differences between contemporary and early twentieth-century migration.[53] At the earlier peak, 90 per cent of new arrivals in the USA came from Europe; today only 10 per cent have European origins. Previously, immigrants were concentrated along the northeastern seaboard and in the mid-west; today they are also settling in states or urban areas in the west, southwest and southeast. The 'huddled masses' of earlier times have been joined by well-educated newcomers who enjoy a high standard of living. Sixty per cent of immigrants from India, for instance, have university degrees, and poverty rates in this community are as low as 5 per cent.

Many of the changes have been driven by new trading patterns. Europe is now the main focus for the UK. Australia has finally accepted geographical reality and has developed extensive ties with other Pacific-region countries.[54] Canada has also undergone important changes. Its third-most important trading partner, after the United States and Britain, is Japan, while China and India also represent significant export markets.[55] At the same time, the forces of globalization have come into play.[56] As Western countries take advantage of raw material and cheap labour, patterns first observed in eighteenth- and nineteenth-century Europe are being repeated in the developing world. Low-skilled and female workers are migrating from the countryside, giving rise to underemployment in the towns. Because economic development has raised expectations about the standard of living, there is no shortage of potential emigrants, including highly qualified workers. A third of the shortages of engineers and doctors in the USA since 1980, for instance, have been filled by immigrants, frustrated by lack of economic development or repressive governments in the home country.

As the other inner-circle countries were liberalizing their policies, the UK was introducing its first restrictions on immigration. Increasingly stringent legislation enacted in the 1960s and early 1970s – and targeted specifically at non-Whites – brought immigration to a virtual halt. At the same time as Britain was closing the door on non-White peoples from the Commonwealth, it was opening its borders to nationals of European countries, when it joined the European Economic Community in 1973. Most immigrants to Britain today come from other parts of Europe, or are work-permit holders, mainly from the USA, India, Australia, Japan and South Africa. Much current public debate, however, focuses on asylum seekers and refugees, with a heavy emphasis on the number of 'bogus' and 'illegal' claimants who are allegedly 'flooding' the country. Yet immigrants make up only 3.8 per cent of the total population and asylum seekers represent only a very small proportion the immigrant population.[57]

Minority rights

The post-war world, then, was a very different place. As the drive for democratization gathered momentum, the accepted social order and its attendant inequalities were no longer acceptable. The spark that ignited the international fire is widely recognised as the US civil rights movement, spearheaded by the National Association for the Advancement of Colored People and by Martin Luther King Junior. Acts of civil disobedience finally succeeded in dismantling laws passed in the late nineteenth century to enforce racial segregation.

In the wake of these achievements, the plight of Indigenous people attracted increasing attention. Legislation from the 1970s onwards accorded special status to Native Americans in the United States.[58] After centuries of oppression, the right of Native Americans to separate identities was finally recognized. In a speech in 1971, the words of President Richard Nixon stand in stark contrast to those of the US peace commissioners who, in the previous century, had been severely critical of Indigenous languages and cultures:

> Both as a matter of justice and as a matter of enlightened social policy, we must begin to act on the basis of what the Indians themselves have long been telling us. The time has come to break decisively with the past and to create the conditions for a new era in which the Indian future is determined by Indian acts and Indian decisions.[59]

Unfortunately, appropriate levels of funding failed to accompany the political rhetoric.

In Aotearoa/New Zealand, the 1847 Treaty of Waitangi formed the focus for the Māori struggle for state recognition.[60] The Waitangi Tribunal was set up in 1975 with limited powers to hear Māori grievances. By 1984, however, the tribunal was given retrospective power to settle claims against the crown, and the centrality of Māori language and culture to life in Aotearoa/New Zealand was finally acknowledged. Māori enjoys much popular support for the role it now plays in national identity.[61]

In Australia, the conspiracy of silence surrounding the 'stolen generations' of children snatched from their families finally came to an end with a national inquiry in 1995, which examined the effects of separation on individuals, families and communities. The report of the inquiry, *Bringing them Home*,[62] is a testimony to the permanence of the grief that many Aboriginal mothers experienced. It tells, for instance, of a family that ritually mourned the loss of their daughter every sunrise and sunset for 32 years. The needs of victims had finally been placed on the national agenda.

Important gains for Indigenous peoples in Canada followed protest – violent and non-violent. The town of Oka, for example, was blockaded to prevent the expansion of a golf course on to ancestral territory, while the Oldman River was diverted by Peigan Indians in protest at the construction of a dam that would destroy their lands.[63] The most important recent development came in 1999 when Nunavut, a vast area in the central and eastern portions of the Northwest Territories, joined the Canadian federation. Inuktitut is one of Nunavut's three official languages (along with English and French) and is the working language of the government.

Although Indigenous languages other than Inuktitut have no official status, it is possible to interpret the 1982 Canadian Constitution Act as including Aboriginal language rights.[64] Several Supreme Court decisions support the view that the federal government has a duty of trust to protect the rights and interests of First Nations peoples, and hence their languages. The equality before the law guaranteed by the Canadian Charter of Human Rights also implies the protection of and access to services in their own languages. Somewhat belatedly, federal resources were allocated in 1998 to a four-year Aboriginal Languages Initiative (ALI) for the preservation, protection and teaching of First Nations languages, Inuktitut (the language of the Inuit) and Michif (a creole spoken primarily by the descendants of French traders and Cree Indians).

The UK has also seen significant gains for language minorities. In Wales, activists have finally succeeded in rehabilitating the Welsh language, banned from public life since the sixteenth century. A radio lecture by Saunders Lewis on the fate of the language is widely believed to have been the catalyst for more radical action, including attacks on TV transmitters, the painting out of English road signs and setting fire to holiday homes belonging to English incomers.[65] There can be little doubt that the publicity generated by these activities influenced the passing of legislation to strengthen the status of the Welsh language.[66] The setting up of a Welsh Assembly in 2000 has also helped create a more favourable climate, with growing financial support for initiatives and policies which promote the language. The overwhelming majority of English speakers in Wales consulted in a 1996 survey felt that the language was something to be proud of and supported its use.

Language activism in Scotland was less widespread than in Wales. Unlike Welsh, the language has no statutory legal status, but the partial devolution of power from the Westminster government to the Scottish Parliament in 2000 has helped to raise the profile of the language with the appointment of a Gaelic parliamentary officer, the identification of Gaelic education as a national Priority Action Area, and the setting up of the Gaelic Development Agency to direct and manage the National Plan for Gaelic.[67] There is also now provision for the use of the language in civil proceedings in areas with a substantial proportion of Gaelic speakers.

Scots, too, is enjoying more favourable conditions. The Scottish Parliament permits speeches in the language and motions may be lodged bilingually in English and Scots. Since 1996 Scottish Education Department Guidelines have allowed the study of Scots as an option within the 5–14 curriculum, reversing a long-term policy of discouraging the language. Courses on Scots language and literature are available in some universities and the language is also represented in the European Bureau for Lesser Used and Minority Languages.

The status of Irish varies between the Irish Republic and Northern Ireland. Irish has had official-language status in the Republic since its independence from Britain in 1921. It is also an official – but not a working – language of the European Union. However, the Irish language attracted little or no official support in Northern Ireland prior to the 2000 Good Friday Agreement between the UK and Irish governments. At this point, the work of the Irish Language Board in the Republic was extended to the whole island of Ireland under the aegis of a new body called Foras na Gaeilge; its function is to facilitate and encourage the use of the Irish language. The Ulster-Scots Agency was set up at the same time to promote the study, conservation, development and use of Ulster-Scots. The position of all the Celtic languages and Scots was further strengthened by the UK government's ratification of the European Charter for Regional or Minority Languages in 2001.

Throughout the inner-circle countries, mainstream politics – and public opinion – accommodated the new diversity in a number of ways. Assimilation gradually gave way to multiculturalism, which, in some cases, was used as the official underpinning for government. In Canada, the post-war period marked the beginning of a process that has sometimes been dubbed the 'Quiet Revolution', which transformed Quebec from a rural to an industrial society. In the early 1960s, Francophones found themselves blocked on the first rung of the economic ladder. Attempts to redress the balance led to the formation of a separatist movement, which used violent means to pursue its ends. The constitutional Parti Québecois, however, attracted far greater support and a new generation of political leaders set about wresting power from the Catholic church.[68]

Developments in Quebec forced the federal government to look seriously for the first time at the question of equal status for French at the national level, mindful of the fact that Francophones made up a quarter of the voters in federal elections. Two centuries after the defeat of the French on the Plains of Abraham, bilingualism assumed its place on the mainstream agenda. In 1969, following recommendations from the report of the Royal Commission on Bilingualism and Biculturalism, parliament adopted the first Official Languages Act, which recognized English and French as the official languages of all federal institutions. A delicate balancing act, requiring the recognition of the rights of other ethnic groups at the same as acknowledging the fears of Francophones that their language and culture would be relegated to the position of one among many, resulted in the framing of a policy of 'multiculturalism within a bilingual framework'. The position of French was further strengthened by the 1982 Canadian Charter of Rights and Freedoms and the 1988 Official Languages Act. The decision of the federal government to promote 'multiculturalism within a bilingual framework' was in response to pressure from Francophones, fearful in the context of immigration policies which were permitting entry to growing numbers of speakers of languages other than French or English.

There is evidence of considerable support for the government policy on French. In a poll undertaken by the Globe and Mail/CBC in 1991,

60 per cent of English-speaking Canadians and 75 per cent of French-speaking Canadians preferred the use of two official languages across Canada, rather than a territorial arrangement.[69] The 2001 census showed that English–French bilingualism is gaining ground and 17 per cent of the population – some 4.8 million people – are now able to speak both official languages. This news is clearly to be welcomed, though a note of caution should be sounded: the proportion of bilingual Francophones is almost five times that of Anglophones.

Australia has shown by far the most radical and progressive approach to multilingualism. A policy of 'unity within diversity' became the focus for a new national identity and, by the mid-1970s, all major political parties included language maintenance and the provision of services in other languages in their policies.[70] The 1987 National Policy on Languages represents the first serious attempt of any inner-circle country to recognize that other languages are resources that complement English.[71] The policy set out an ambitious programme with detailed guidance for implementation. In spite of important subsequent modifications to policy, aspects of Australian practice remain well in advance of that of many other countries.[72]

Aotearoa/New Zealand followed in Australia's footsteps, commissioning its own national policy of languages but publishing in the name of the author of the report rather than as an official document. In 1993, the National Languages Project was replaced with a number of more specific projects, including a programme for speakers of other languages and the encouragement of language learning at an earlier age. The shift in policy has been attributed to a range of factors. There has been some hesitation, for instance, over the place of te reo Māori in national life, with responsibility for the language passing from the Ministry of Education to the Ministry for Māori Development. The business world has shown a limited understanding of the importance of foreign-language capacity in international trade. Debate on language issues has also been taking place during a period of reduced government spending.[73]

The USA, like Aotearoa/New Zealand, has no national languages policy. None the less, important gains have been made.[74] The 1964 Civil Rights Act requires physicians and others who accept federal funding to ensure that individuals with limited English proficiency can access programmes and services. Since 1973, bilingual ballots and voter information have been provided in jurisdictions where speakers of Spanish, Native American and Asian American languages number more than 10,000, have below average rates of voter turnout and English proficiency, or exceed 5 per cent of the population. The 1978 Court Interpreters Act requires simultaneous interpreting for any party to judicial proceedings in federal courts and consecutive interpreting for witnesses.

New minority languages have no official status in the UK. Their presence is recognized in a range of settings, though the issues that they raise tend to be related more to *access* than *identity*. The government recognizes that members of ethnic minorities have the right to use their minority language 'freely and without interference'.[75] In public administration, the government's policy is to 'deal with non-English speakers on a basis of courtesy and respect for their linguistic preference'. Users of public services have access to translation services, as do those not able to understand or speak English in criminal proceedings.

The Deaf community has also made significant advances. Deaf activists have campaigned for the recognition of sign languages in education and the media and for control of organizations, such as the British Deaf Association and Gallaudet University, which are directly concerned with Deaf people. Auslan was included in the Australian National Policy on Languages in 1990, although the UK government took the formal step of recognizing British Sign Language (BSL) as a language in its own right only in 2003.[76]

The monolingual backlash

Minority rights activists encountered resistance from the start, although it was not until the 1980s that opponents began to organize more formally. In Canada, the rights offered by the Official Languages Acts have been contested by the Alliance for the Preservation of the English Language, which campaigns with the motto: 'One language unites, two divide.' Canadians for Language Fairness opposes the requirement to learn a second language for federal service employment, arguing that bilingualism is an affirmative-action programme for Francophones, which discriminates against Anglophones. These concerns appear to be unfounded. A survey of 20,000 public servants in the year following the second Official Languages Act found that only 2 per cent identified skills in the other official language as the most important factor in appointment to their current position. Another survey undertaken in 1990 by the Professional Institute of the Public Service of Canada showed that only 6.6 per cent of its members felt that the language policy had a negative effect on their ability to get a first job in the Public Service.[77]

Immigration has always been a hotly contested issue, though the nature of debate has tended to change over time. In the past, the focus was on which immigrants should be allowed to enter. Currently, much

On 18 March 2003, Andrew Smith, the secretary of state for the Department of Work and Pensions, and Maria Eagle, the minister for disabled people (pictured here with Alan Murray of the British Deaf Association), announced that the UK government had formally acknowledged British Sign Language as a language in its own right.
Photograph by Mark Wheatley. Reproduced with permission of the British Deaf Association.

discussion centres on whether immigration should be allowed to continue at present levels. There also seems to be a greater polarization within host populations. Migration is very much an urban phenomenon, concentrated in large gateway cities like London, Sydney and Vancouver and giving rise to tensions between urban and rural populations.[78] In Australia, for instance, where urban ethnic organizations and political parties shaped the multicultural policies of the 1980s, there was always the danger of resistance from the rest of the population. Significantly, the strongholds of the One Nation Party which influenced the Howard government to reduce immigration and limit the multicultural programme are suburban, small-town and rural. Public opinion in Aotearoa/New Zealand has followed in the same direction, with the introduction of random checks on Pacific Island immigrants to catch overstayers, and changes to immigration law, designed to allow faster removals of people unlawfully in Aotearoa/New Zealand.

In the US, widespread misunderstanding about the flow of immigration has fuelled considerable public hostility. While new admissions increased from the late 1970s onwards, the rate remained constant until 1989, at which point – and for the next three years – they reached the million mark.[79] Although the actual number of new immigrants remained at similar levels, the statistics were greatly inflated by the amnesty offered to undocumented immigrants already living in the country. Media campaigns that overlooked the reasons for the increase helped to make immigrants – documented and undocumented – the target of populist attempts to cut public welfare benefits and end the granting of automatic citizenship to anyone born in the US.

Language has played a prominent role in the debate. Ronald Reagan continued a presidential tradition of intolerance, condemning the maintenance of other languages as 'un-American' and cutting the federal budget for bilingual education in 1983.[80] The same year witnessed the founding of an organization called US English, following the failure by Senator Hayakawa to introduce a constitutional amendment making English the official language. US English and various other groups campaigning on language issues have experienced some degree of success. Although attempts to amend the constitution were unsuccessful, a number of states have declared English the official language.

While there would appear to be a good deal of popular support for measures of this kind, there is also a great deal of opposition. The pressure group English Plus has proposed its own constitutional amendment, the Cultural Rights Amendment, which would give legal backing to the preservation and promotion of ethnic and linguistic diversity.[81] Some observers have imputed racist motives to the English-only movement. US English, for instance, has been linked to funding agencies with a history of racism, including the Pioneer Fund, founded in the 1930s to promote 'racial betterment' through eugenics. The writer James Crawford sums up the situation in the following terms: 'For many supporters of Official English, there is no sinister, hidden agenda. But for others, the campaign for Anglo-conformity functions as a surrogate: a way to vent racial hostilities, to limit immigration from the Third World, to preserve the supremacy of white Americans, and to do all these things while wrapping themselves in the flag.'[82]

Reactions in the UK have followed a similar course. The 2003 manifesto of the far-right British National Party (BNP) sets out its determination to:

> campaign to end, or oppose the introduction of, the teaching of Asian languages to classes containing any native British children . . . If minorities want to teach their own children their native languages, they should do so in their own time and at their own expense. Where foreign pupils have not achieved a satisfactory standard of English, they should be taught separately rather than being allowed to drag down standards and hold back native English-speakers.

Mainstream politicians have sometimes responded to growing popular opposition to asylum seekers. David Blunkett, the home secretary, advocated that British Asian parents speak English to their children at home to help 'overcome the schizophrenia which bedevils generational relationships', thus linking the use of minority languages in the family setting with a form of mental illness.[83] Those who suggest that members of minority communities need to choose between English and other languages, however, show a wilful disregard for the evidence. Census data from the US and Australia suggests that the increase in the numbers of people who speak English 'very well' or 'well' is keeping pace with the increase in numbers who speak other languages at home. The importance of English in the inner-circle countries is plain for all to see: political intervention is not required to make the point. What can and should be disputed, however, is the assumption that other languages are obstacles to achieving this end.

The new minority languages are not, of course, the only targets for dissenting voices. The tabloid newspaper the *Welsh Mirror* has led a vitriolic campaign, the general thrust of which is that the protection of a minority language is in some way detrimental to monolingual English speakers.[84] The Scottish Parliament's Gaelic officer, Alex O' Henley, resigned in 2002 citing a calculated prejudice against Gaelic among senior civil servants as the reason for his decision to leave.[85] In Ireland, any gains for the Irish language are closely monitored by speakers of Ulster-Scots, which, under the Good Friday agreement, is granted 'parity of esteem'.

The Deaf community has also needed to engage with significant obstacles. The increasing medicalization of deafness during the course of the twentieth century has meant that children who are born profoundly Deaf are grouped with elderly people who have become hearing impaired. It is symptomatic of this general trend that the use of cochlear implants – electromagnetic devices fixed inside the cranium – has been extended from adults to children, despite the fact that any residual hearing is destroyed and young children are unable to make informed decisions which will affect the rest of their lives.[86] Deaf activists challenge audio-centric assumptions that Deafness is a medical condition, and see themselves instead as a linguistic and cultural minority.[87]

Looking forward, looking back

'The past', according to British novelist L. P. Hartley, 'is a foreign country: they do things differently there.'[88] Or do they? Several patterns emerge from this rapid overview of the other languages of inner-circle countries. The first concerns the use of language as a tool for the subjugation and assimilation of other peoples. There is an unnerving similarity between the call of the US peace commissioners to blot out the 'barbarous dialect' of the Indians as they attempted to bring the frontier wars to a halt and the Australian entreaty to Aboriginals to 'build huts, wear clothes and be useful . . . love God . . . love white men . . . learn to speak English'.[89]

The next concerns the remarkable resilience of oppressed peoples. Language is a powerful symbol of identity, a wisdom neatly encapsulated in proverb. According to the Welsh, 'Heb iaith, heb cenedl' (No language, no nation). The Māori express a similar sentiment: 'Ka ngaro te reo, ka ngaro taua, pera i te ngaro o te moa' (If the language is lost, we are lost, we will become extinct as has the moa). The fact that Indigenous languages have survived at all is an impressive testimony to their cultural capital. So, too, is the fact that enthusiasts are fighting to revive Cornish over two centuries after the death of the last native speaker.

Attitudes towards other peoples are essentially pragmatic. At various points in history there has been an urgent need for human resources:

to extend frontiers, to fuel the Industrial Revolution of the nineteenth century, to fulfil ongoing needs for economic expansion in the modern world. In order to satisfy these demands, governments are easily persuaded to suspend feelings of 'us and them'. When northern Europeans were no longer available in sufficient numbers, efforts were made to attract southern and eastern Europeans. When economic development in Europe was such that emigration was no longer an attractive option, Whites-only policies were dismantled. Yet, as soon as the achievements or the sheer numbers of newcomers threaten the power of the dominant group, forces of reaction come into play. Language is often the focus for hostility. The same xenophobia that led to the banning of other languages in public places in the early twentieth century is now a feature of movements like US English or the One Nation Party in Australia.

History allows us to discern patterns of behaviour; it also points to incremental advances. In the wake of the civil rights movement, governments made unprecedented concessions to minority languages. French, Welsh and Māori are now co-official languages in Canada, Wales and Aotearoa/New Zealand. Inuktitut is one of the official languages of Nunavut. The UK has ratified the European Charter for Regional or Minority Languages, which recognizes Irish, Gaelic and Scots as well as Welsh; it also accepts BSL as a language in its own right. While activists still feel that the support they are receiving is too little, too late, the achievements of the last few decades are none the less remarkable. The future, however, is difficult to foresee.

Notes

1   Price (2000: 4).
2   Payton (2000: 115).
3   Romaine and Nettle (2000: 2).
4   Ó Dochartaigh (2000) is a useful source on the history of Irish in Ireland; Ó Riagáin (1997: 11–23) and Ó hIfearnáin (2001) on language planning; and Guinnane (1997) on Irish migration.
5   Jupp (1988).
6   Smith (1997).
7   Commins (1988: 15).
8   MacKinnon (2000).
9   See, for instance, Smith (2000) and Kirk and Ó Baoill (2001).
10   Cited in May (2001: 258).
11   Jones (1998: 8).
12   Holmes (1988: 5).

13 Malchow (1979: 3).
14 Armstrong (2001).
15 Pagden (2001) offers an overview of European colonization.
16 A useful discussion of language in this period is contained in Read (1937).
17 Clyne (1991: 7); Ager (2001: 96).
18 Kloss (1998).
19 Clyne (1991: 8); Ozolins (1993).
20 Read (1937).
21 Pagden (2001: 77).
22 Francis and Reyhner (2002: 29–31).
23 Shnukal (1991); Harris (1991).
24 Useful histories of African enslavement include Thomas (1998) and Kolchin (1995).
25 For an historical overview of the linguistic history of African Americans see, for instance, Dillard (1972) and Smitherman (1986).
26 Cummins and Danesi (1990: 11).
27 Krapp (1924).
28 Gonzales (1922).
29 Nichols (1981).
30 A wide-ranging discussion of European migration during this period can be found in Glazier and De Rosa (1986) and Casles and Miller (1998).
31 See, for instance, Kloss (1988) and Dicker (1996).
32 Lund (1994).
33 Higham (1988).
34 Cited in Palmer (1975: 45).
35 Rippley (1976); Crawford (1990).
36 Cited in Clyne (1991: 15).
37 Kamin (1977: 55).
38 Del Valle (2003: 89–92).
39 www.abc.net.au/federation/fedstory/ep2/ep2_institutions.htm
40 Cited in Cummins and Danesi (1990: 10).
41 HREOC (2002).
42 Manne (1998).
43 Beresford and Omaji (1998: 29–60).
44 Mirzoeff (1995).
45 For a discussion of voting restrictions, see Del Valle (2003: 89–93).
46 Markus (1979); Place (1969).
47 New Zealand Immigration Service (undated).
48 Whitaker (1991: 13).
49 Holmes (1988).
50 Crost (1994).
51 Peach (1978).
52 Applied History Research Group (1997).
53 Zhou (2001).

54 Herriman (1996); Ozolins (1993).
55 Applied History Research Group (1997).
56 Zhou (2001).
57 For discussion of asylum seekers in the UK and Ireland, see IRR (2000); for an Australian perspective, see Kilner (2003); and for an international perspective, see Stalker (2002).
58 Indian Education Act (1972); Indian Self-Determination and Education Assistance Act (1975); Native American Languages Act (1990).
59 Nixon (1970: 564).
60 Benton (1996); May (2001).
61 Nicholson and Garland (1991).
62 HREOC (1997).
63 Links North (undated).
64 Burnaby (1996).
65 Davies (1993).
66 May (2000).
67 Taskforce on Public Funding of Gaelic (2000); www.bord-na-gaidhlig.org.uk
68 Burnaby (1996).
69 Canadian Heritage (1999).
70 Herriman (1996); Ozolins (1993).
71 Lo Bianco (1987).
72 Herriman (1996); Malcolm (2002).
73 Benton (1996).
74 Del Valle (2003).
75 UK Government (1999).
76 Department for Work and Pensions (2003).
77 Canadian Heritage (1999).
78 Ley and Murphy (2001).
79 Zhou (2001).
80 Cummins (1996: 40).
81 See, for instance Adams and Brink (1990), Baron (1990) and, for up-to-date information, the James Crawford website: http://ourworld.compuserve.com/homepages/JWCRAWFORD
82 Crawford (1990).
83 Hinsliff (2002).
84 See also May (2000) for a discussion of less strident expressions of dissent.
85 *West Highland Free Press* (2002).
86 Ladd (2003).
87 See chapter 6, pp. 131–2.
88 Hartley (2000: 1).
89 Broome (1982) cited in Romaine (1991: 6).

3

Language and the provision of services

The numbers of people in inner-circle countries who speak other languages at home are growing. The concern expressed at these developments by groups such as US English or the One Nation Party in Australia is unfounded, since census data makes it clear that the proportion of the population that speaks English 'well' or 'very well' is increasing even more rapidly. Yet even though most speakers of minority languages are bilingual, the fact remains that large numbers experience communication difficulties while they are learning English, which make it difficult to take part in the life of the wider community. In the USA, close to 2 million people over the age of 5 report that they speak English 'not at all well'. In Canada, almost half a million people speak neither French nor English. Over 370,000 Australians are unable to speak English well, if at all, and many more cannot read and write the language. And, according to one estimate, as many as 1.5 million people in the UK lack the skills in English necessary for employment.[1] New arrivals clearly need support: workers need to understand their rights; patients need to communicate with doctors; defendants and witnesses need to know what is happening in police interviews and in courtrooms; parents are anxious for their children to make the most of educational opportunities.

The issues around service provision in Indigenous and new minority languages are different. Sometimes people speak English but feel more comfortable using their first language. In a study of Bethel in Alaska, for instance, 85 per cent of the Yup'ik community said that they would understand better if court proceedings were conducted bilingually, even though most of the respondents also spoke English.[2] In other cases, speakers who demand services in minority languages are asserting their political rights. In Wales, the demand for banking in Welsh, for instance, may seem perverse, given that only a minority of the population speak the language. However, Welsh speakers are making an important point, since the survival of the language depends on its use in an ever-widening number of domains.

The financial implications of multilingualism often attract an adverse press. While it is certainly more expensive to offer services in two (or more) languages than in one, the costs are likely to be offset by longer-term social and economic benefits for minority groups. Most people, it would seem, are persuaded of the need to provide services in other languages for people in the process of learning English. The growing emphasis on other languages in inner-circle countries is not, of course, entirely altruistic. The marginalization of large numbers of people who cannot speak the language well carries costs of its own. There is a great deal of support for bilingual services in other contexts, too. In a 1991 Globe and Mail/CBC poll, for instance, 60 per cent of English-speaking Canadians and 88 per cent of French-speaking Canadians agreed that public services should be offered in the minority language.[3] As former Canadian prime minister Pierre Trudeau once commented: 'Of course, a bilingual state is more expensive than a unilingual one, but it is a richer state.'[4]

In this chapter we look at service delivery in multilingual settings. Bilinguals are the linchpin: they mediate between English and minority-language speakers, providing translation of the written word and interpreting in face-to-face situations.

Interpreting and the spoken word

The history of interpreting is long, but not always illustrious. When Jacques Cartier claimed the area around the St Lawrence River for France in 1535, he sanctioned the kidnapping and transportation of two Iroquois to France, where they spent eight months learning the language. On their return, they served as interpreters and, when conflicts of interest arose, they sided – somewhat predictably – with their fellow Iroquois. The French responded by returning them to France, where they died in exile.[5]

Joseph Nicholas became the first recorded interpreter in the US when he orally translated the 1785 Treaty with the Cherokees. He was just one of many bilinguals who played a key role in the unfolding of American history. Sacajawea (or Bird Woman), the Shoshone wife of a French Canadian fur trader, served as interpreter to Captains Lewis and Clark on the long trek to the Pacific in the early years of the nineteenth century.

She has the distinction of having more statues erected in her honour than any other American woman. Other interpreters have received less recognition but have none the less played a vital role in mediating between incomers and established populations. Very often they are the product of their own family circumstances. In Aotearoa/New Zealand, for instance, many sons of early settlers and missionaries began a career in Māori administration as interpreters to the courts. Many sign interpreters are the hearing children of Deaf parents.

Meanwhile in Europe, French was widely accepted as the language of international relations, and it was not until the entry of Americans into World War I that interpreting became an issue. Bilingual military officers were used at the Versailles peace conference and went on to form the nucleus of a corps of interpreters that served the League of Nations and other international meetings. The growth of organizations such as the United Nations and the European Union greatly increased the number of multilingual meetings and conferences and led to a considerable expansion of the profession.

Technological advances have played an important role in shaping practice. The use of headphones made it possible to receive the interpreter's message without delay or repetition, and led to the birth of simultaneous interpreting. The capacity to transmit a single interpretation to many people has been beneficial not only in international meetings but also in a range of other settings. At one time in California, for instance, the entitlement of all non-English speaking defendants to their own interpreter used to result in a distracting level of noise in the courtroom.

The very large population movements that followed World War II created a different challenge for interpreters. Away from the controlled environment of the conference, large numbers of non-English-speaking people required help with communication in immigration centres and hospitals, and with the police, social services and housing departments. Here the need was for what has variously been described as 'liaison', 'community', 'public service' and 'dialogue' interpreting: three-corner situations where the interpreter conveys messages in both directions between the two parties. In the vast majority of cases, people serving as de facto interpreters had no formal training; many were thrust into the role simply by dint of the fact that they knew more English than the person for whom they were interpreting. A survey of Sydney hospitals in 1978 found that all except two relied heavily on their domestic, clerical, medical and paramedical staff for their interpreting needs; in Scotland, over 90 per cent of health authorities were making similarly informal arrangements for interpreting as recently as 2000.[6] There are also reports of janitors, secretaries and clerks being used on some occasions as court interpreters in both Australia and the USA.[7]

Family members or friends are also widely used, and child interpreters have received particular attention. Sukhwant Kaur, a British Sikh, writes of the heavy responsibilities which fall on children as they accompany their mother to the doctor's, negotiate rental agreements, and handle bills or even the sale of a house.[8] Vasilia Kazoulis, the oldest child of an American Greek family, talks in similar terms of her own experience of becoming the family interpreter at the age of 5: 'I carried out all the bank transactions, escorted my parents to the physician, attended the parent–teacher meetings at school and basically made all the major decisions that had to be made.' However, children also develop important skills: maturity, self-reliance and astuteness. As Vasilia Kazoulis explains: 'I could enter an environment, immediately calculate the demands of that environment and act accordingly.'[9]

The level of sophistication shown by young children was demonstrated very clearly in a simulation where 9-year-old Urdu speakers were asked to act as interpreters for a non-English-speaking mother wanting to enrol her child in school. The children often modified what the other two participants said. For instance, at one point the mother was not impressed with the teacher's explanation of what her child would be doing in school:

MOTHER: *What do they do in school?*
CHILD: What do you do in school?
TEACHER: When the children are young we like them to play a lot.
CHILD: *When the child is young they make them play.*
MOTHER: *Not playing! Do we send our children to learn to read and write or play?*
TEACHER: What's she saying? What's she saying?
CHILD: She doesn't want him to play a lot.
TEACHER: Don't worry it's playing with things to help them to learn.
CHILD: *They learn him something. They learn through play, then they learn something.*
MOTHER: *Oh, all right then.*[10]

The child glosses over the mother's annoyance and thus side-steps the problem of having to explain to one adult that another adult disagrees with them.

Some London schools have found a way of giving formal recognition to children's bilingual skills on occasions such as parents' evenings, since professional interpreters are expensive and are often not available for all the languages required. North Westminster Community School has responded imaginatively to this challenge with an ongoing training programme for its 17–18-year-old students, which looks at ethical issues such as confidentiality and impartiality and practical issues such as specialist vocabulary.[11] Students who successfully complete the course are responsible for contacting parents by phone to let them know about parents' evenings and to offer their services as interpreter. They are not, of course, used for any sensitive matters.

From the 1960s onwards, concern for social justice has expanded the role of the interpreter to that of advocate or cultural mediator. In medical encounters, interpreters often feel the need to explain choices to clients, or to advise health-care professionals on factors that might affect patient compliance. In contrast, in interviews with the police and in the courtroom, intervention on the part of the interpreter is constrained by law, and advocacy is inappropriate.

The professionalization of interpreters

Academic institutions have been slow to respond to the needs of interpreters and, in many cases, training is provided on an ad hoc basis. In the US, the North Virginia Area Health Education Center puts bilingual members of the community, preferably with some medical background, through a 40-hour training programme. The Community Interpretation Services Program (CIS) in Seattle offers a different model, with at least 12 hours in the classroom and on-the-job training where new interpreters are paired with more experienced colleagues.[12]

Where training takes many different forms, accreditation and the monitoring of standards assume particular importance. Australia has been very active in this area. The National Accreditation Authority for Translators and Interpreters (NAATI) recognizes five different levels of competence.[13] Level One is aimed at low-level aides – hotel staff, telephonists, airline clerks, and other personnel who come into contact with non-English speakers in carrying out their duties. The second level is targeted at 'advanced language aides' who need to deal with more complex texts in the same domains as Level One. Level Three is the basic professional level for a full-time interpreter or translator. Level Four covers advanced interpreting assignments such as higher courts, international meetings and conferences, while Level Five is designed for international conference simultaneous interpreting.

Other countries take a more piecemeal approach. Aotearoa/New Zealand has its own official accreditation system for Māori, but uses

NAATI for other languages. UK sign interpreters are registered with the Council for the Advancement of Communication with Deaf People, while interpreters working in courts and police stations are selected from the National Register of Public Service Interpreters, a non-profit-making subsidiary of the Institute of Linguists (IOL).[14] The IOL also provides a range of public examinations from post-beginner to professional translator or public service interpreter in nearly 40 languages. The Canadian Translators and Interpreters Council (CTIC) serves a similar function, providing examinations and certification for translators, conference interpreters, court interpreters and terminologists.

Although the professionalization of interpreters is welcome, there are serious shortages of qualified interpreters and insufficient funding to employ them. In Australia, the dearth of Aboriginal interpreters has been a matter of particular concern and, at the turn of the century, there were no professionally accredited NAATI court interpreters for any of the Aboriginal languages. In the UK, difficulties in finding good legal interpreters are widely acknowledged.[15] There are, for instance, fewer than 300 trained BSL interpreters, making access to public services and information very difficult for the Deaf. In the USA, courts in areas of high immigrant settlement such as California have their own staff interpreters; elsewhere courts often rely on non-certified interpreters and translators.

Telephone interpreting

One of the responses to the shortage of interpreters has been to develop telephone services. Again Australia led the way, establishing the Telephone Interpreter Service (TIS) in 1974. Groups eligible for fee-free services include doctors, not-for-profit community-based organizations, local government services, parliamentarians, trade unions and emergency services.[16] In the UK, telephone services developed somewhat later. Language Line was established in 1992 and is used by a wide range of government bodies and voluntary organizations. The US Court Telephone Interpreting Project has been offering services to courthouses in remote locations since 1990. In the fiscal year 1996, over 400 federal court hearings and 200 off-the-record events were interpreted over the telephone.

Telephone interpreting offers an attractive solution for many different problems. Projects such as TIS and Language Line make it possible to provide a professional service when there are no competent local interpreters. These services are very efficient in situations where immediate action is required; for instance, when a non-English-speaking victim of domestic violence seeks a restraining order. They are also cost-effective. If there is no federally certified Spanish interpreter in Alaska, the judge is more likely to use a qualified telephone interpreter than to fly in a certified interpreter at considerable cost for a 10-minute hearing.

But telephone interpreting is also viewed with scepticism, if not outright hostility, particularly in legal interpreting, where the consequences of mistakes can be very serious.[17] Critics argue that it is not simply a matter of choosing between two equally good alternatives, one of which costs more. Many interpreters dislike the fact that they miss non-verbal information when they are at the end of a telephone line. They also have concerns about the reliability of equipment. The worst-case scenario would be a poorly trained interpreter dealing with a difficult case over the telephone with inadequate equipment.

Videophones, another technological advance, overcome some of these disadvantages and are of particular interest in medical and sign interpreting. They make it possible to provide a real-time interpreting service via a personal computer with a digital camera and ISDN link. Doctor and patient, equipped with headphones, both speak through an interpreter at a remote site.

Medical interpreting

Access to health services is protected by several kinds of legislation. The rights of Deaf people are covered by disability legislation. In the UK, for instance, Section 21 of the Disability Discrimination Act requires service providers to ensure 'reasonable access to services'. Under Title II of the Americans with Disabilities Act and Section 504 of the Rehabilitation Act, doctors are obligated to provide auxiliary aids and services not just to patients with disabilities, but also to family members with disabilities.

In most settings, equal access to health care for non-English speakers is ensured through international human rights legislation or international charters. The US is an important exception to this general trend. Title VI of the 1964 Civil Rights Act, better known for prohibiting discrimination on the basis of race, colour or national origin, requires physicians and others who accept federal funding to ensure that individuals with limited English proficiency can access programmes and services. The type of assistance depends on the size of the facility, the size of the population to be served and the resources available. Options include hiring bilingual staff or on-staff interpreters, contracting for services as needed, using trained community volunteers or a telephone interpreter service. Responses to the legislation are often both flexible and imaginative. The CIS in Seattle, for instance, uses a shared service approach. A pool of four full-time, salaried family health workers, who together speak eight Southeast Asian languages, rotates through the clinics on a regular weekly schedule depending on a clinic's need for a specific language. Over the years, as the language needs of the clinics have diversified, the programme has added on-call, contract interpreters.[18]

Debates on health care tend to focus on who pays, rather than on the need for services. Yet the cost of failing to take correct patient histories or make accurate diagnoses is likely to be much greater than the bill for providing interpreters. An analysis of hospital records in the London Borough of Waltham Forest showed that people from the Asian sub-continent were more likely to be misunderstood and misdiagnosed. They were also more likely to be prescribed drugs and electroconvulsive therapy rather than 'talking' treatments such as psychotherapy and counselling. Mental distress was more likely to be detected at a later stage, with a low take-up of services until the point of crisis.[19]

When patients misunderstand information about treatment options or fail to follow instructions, the consequences can be serious. In a survey undertaken by the Royal National Institute for Deaf People (RNID), one in four reported leaving a doctor's appointment without knowing what was wrong with them.[20] One in six admitted that they did not go to the doctor when they were ill because communication was such a problem. Communication difficulties also have implications for the cost-effectiveness of treatment. Patients may not, for instance, be able to explain that they have already had the same series of tests that another clinician is about to prescribe.

The complications of ageing mean that elderly patients make disproportionately high use of medical services. In the case of speakers of minority languages, communication problems greatly exacerbate problems of access. Many of the settlers who arrived in English-speaking countries in the years following World War II are now in their seventies and their eighties. Inevitably, they are coming into increasing contact with the medical profession and their encounters are often complicated by language barriers. Unlike their children and grandchildren, these elderly patients may not have achieved high levels of fluency in English. For some, the ageing process also involves the loss of English and a reversion to the first language.

Language and communication barriers affect not only patients but also their carers. In the UK, many Asian carers complain that their consultations with health professionals are rushed, and that explanations are either poor or omitted altogether. These carers are often unable to ask for information, advice and services, and dependent on family members to act as interpreters. A Bangladeshi mother caring for an adult son with mental and physical impairments explains her frustration thus:

> The problem is, because I cannot speak their language, I go with my son and I can't actually ask the questions that I want to ask or I don't know which questions I should be asking. So I don't think we're getting the full benefit of that meeting that we should be getting. And if I take my daughter, you know, she's young, she doesn't want to ask too many questions, she gets embarrassed, she thinks I'm being awkward when I say, ask this question, ask that and she doesn't ask everything that I want her to ask.[21]

This situation, it would seem, is common. A 1996 study of almost 7,000 children in the USA points to the critical role that language barriers play in determining access to care. Forty per cent of the Hispanic families in the study needed their interviews to be conducted in Spanish, which suggests that that they would probably require interpreters in health-care settings. The children in these families were found to be at a substantial disadvantage compared with Anglo children, even when health insurance and socioeconomic status were taken into account. However, when parents were able to speak English, the differences between Hispanic and Anglo children were negligible.[22]

The cultural construction of health

Cultural issues also play a role in access to health care. The cultural construction of health and illness varies a great deal from one community to the next, but the distance from the European model is particularly great in Indigenous communities. A handbook for health professionals working with rural Australian Aboriginal peoples makes this point very clearly.[23] The handbook offers a series of episodes or scenarios; the health carer is then invited to pick one of four possible responses.

Episode 16
One of the things that puzzled Jo after she had worked at the clinic for several weeks was how inaccurate the people were. This made her work rather difficult because it was often most essential that the accurate amount of medicine was taken. On a few occasions when Jo had asked a patient

how much there was left in a bottle of medicine the answer had been 'half' and the bottle should have been almost empty or only a little bit should have been gone. This was worrying. By making a sign with her fingers she had indicated to these patients the amount that should still be in the bottle. They would look rather puzzled and said 'Yes'. Jo had also noticed that whenever she let a mother make up her own food mixture for her baby, her instructions about the quantities of ingredients would hardly ever be followed accurately. In order to do something about it, Jo felt it was necessary to find out first why her patients were inaccurate.

What was the reason for the people's inaccuracy with regard to quantities?

A)   They had little understanding of our concepts of quantity such as half and quarter.
B)   In Aboriginal society traditionally 'near enough' has always been 'good enough'. There was no concern for accuracy.
C)   They are not as concerned with their health and the health of their babies as we are.
D)   They have never had to concern themselves with making up delicate mixtures and their movements are still somewhat awkward and uncoordinated.

You chose (A). They had little understanding of our concepts of quantity such as half and quarter.

This is the best alternative. In the Pitjantjatjara language there are no words for such concepts as 'half' and 'quarter'. In their culture there has been no need for this type of mathematics. It would thus be extremely difficult for the people to grasp these concepts. We take them for granted because we use them every day, but maybe you can remember how difficult it was when you first learnt about divisions. To Jo's patients 'half' meant anything between empty and full, and it could mean that a little bit was left or a little bit had gone. This does not mean that they can't ever be expected to learn about these things, it just means that you have to start right from scratch with a lot of patience. If you begin to lose your patience just think how difficult it is for you to learn about some of the things in their culture. This is because even though you live close to it, you don't live right in it, doing what they do every day. Similarly, they only have marginal contact with our culture. The best thing for Jo to do would be to indicate, by showing the level in the bottle or containers, how much is to be taken out or put in. She would probably have to repeat this patiently and for a long time.

You chose (B): In Aboriginal society traditionally 'near enough' has always been 'good enough'. There was no concern for accuracy.

This is an unjustified generalization. Just because the Aborigine does not show the same concern for accuracy in the things that we think important you can't assume that he has a general lack of concern for accuracy. Think how accurate a boomerang has to be. Although, in choosing this answer, you have shown that you are trying to think in terms of the foreign culture, you are still generalizing in terms of your own culture.
Please re-read the passage and make a better choice.

You chose (C): They are not as concerned with their health and the health of their babies as we are.

This is not true. Why would the people come to the clinic in the first place? It may appear to us that they show less concern, but this is because they often show their concern in a different way than we do.
Choose again.

You chose (D): They have never had to concern themselves with making up delicate mixtures and their movements are still somewhat awkward and uncoordinated.

There are two points made here, both of which are incorrect. Firstly Aborigines did and still do make up delicate mixtures for their own use. Ceremonial paints had to be mixed although they use mostly chalk now, and also Pitjuri has to be carefully mixed. But they don't do this by measuring half an ounce here and half an ounce there. Secondly Aborigines are very skilled craftsmen as can be seen from the way they make their tools. There is no reason to believe that their movements are awkward and uncoordinated.
Re-read the passage and choose again.

Although the authors caution against applying the lessons learned here in other settings, they suggest that time spent considering Aboriginal responses to health care will help doctors and nurses be more human in any cross-cultural situation.

Language and the law

The law is another area where access to interpreters is vitally important. People come into contact with the law in many different roles – suspect, victim, defendant, witness – and in a variety of settings, from police stations to courtrooms. The failure to provide interpreters threatens the integrity of the justice system; so, too, do poor standards of interpreting.

Traditionally, it was the decision of the court whether there should be an interpreter. Today, agreements such as the International Covenant on Civil and Political Rights enshrine the right of individuals to be informed why they have been arrested and what they are charged with in a language they understand, and to be provided with an interpreter without charge to themselves. The willingness to recognize these principles has varied from country to country and legal rights to interpreting have often expanded in a piecemeal way.

In the USA, it was not until 1978 that pressure from the civil rights movement led to the passage of the Court Interpreters Act, which requires simultaneous interpreting for any party to judicial proceedings in federal courts and consecutive interpreting for witnesses.[24] In the years since its enactment, the number of cases conducted with the aid of interpreters in federal courts has increased more than five-fold, reflecting the growth in the immigrant population during this period. Although the act applied only to federal courts, it has had the effect of increasing the use of interpreters in state and municipal courts.

In countries where English is a co-official language, the situation is more complex. In Aotearoa/New Zealand, the Māori have traditionally enjoyed greater rights and privileges than other non-English speakers.[25] From 1882, the law required documents served on Māori people to be translated into Māori; a licensing system for Māori interpreters has been in operation since 1909. But by far the most important development was the recognition by the Waitangi Tribunal in 1986 that the crown has an obligation to protect the language. One of the recommendations of the tribunal was the introduction of legislation making it possible to use the Māori language in all courts of law.

In the UK, the twentieth century witnessed a slow but steady series of concessions in the rehabilitation of the Welsh language in public life. The Welsh Courts Act has permitted the use of Welsh in law courts since 1942. While the 1967 Welsh Language Act offered 'equal validity' for English and Welsh in Wales, its impact was limited in practice. In contrast, the Welsh Language Act of 1993 gives Welsh speakers an absolute right to speak Welsh in court; cases where the Welsh language is used are heard, wherever practicable, before a Welsh speaking judge, and in a court with simultaneous translation facilities.

In Canada, either English or French can be used in proceedings before federal courts, orally or in writing. As in Wales, judges assigned to the case must be able to understand the proceedings in the official language chosen by the parties without the assistance of interpreters. Simultaneous interpretation must be provided where necessary so that witnesses are heard in the official language of their choice. The Criminal Code gives the accused the right to be tried in a criminal court before a judge (or judge and jury) that speak the official language of the accused. Provision is also made for the Deaf and for witnesses who do not speak or understand the language of court proceedings to have the assistance of an interpreter.

Equal before the law?

Awareness of the rights of speakers of other languages is arguably more acute today than at any point in history. Yet in practice, shortages of suitably qualified interpreters and inadequate levels of funding lead to patchy provision.

Indigenous groups throughout the world find themselves at a particular disadvantage within the criminal justice system. In Australia, high levels of unemployment, poverty and ill-health are reflected in crime statistics, especially for males. Aboriginal people make up 80 per cent of the prison population in the Northern Territory, in spite of the fact that they make up only 30 per cent of the population. They are also over-represented in prisons in other parts of Australia. In southwest Alaska, legal professionals report disproportionately high rates of confession and guilty pleas in Yup'ik people. The Deaf are another group that has been poorly served by the legal profession. An appreciation of the part that language plays in this process, however, is relatively recent.

There is no shortage of cases to illustrate the unfortunate consequences of failure to provide interpreters. Take Ronald Chisolm, a profoundly Deaf American who communicates in ASL, and whose story begins in 1994 when an open bench warrant was issued for his arrest, in another state and without his knowledge. Mr Chisolm was held at Mercer County Detention Center in Trenton, New Jersey.[26] Despite state law requiring a telecommunications device for the Deaf and prohibiting the incarceration of a Deaf person before the arrival of an interpreter, he was allegedly denied access to an interpreter and was unable to make phone contact with family, friends or a lawyer. He allegedly could not understand the charges against him, or the reason for his arrest. To compound the problem, he was classified as an unemployed vagrant, resulting in an increased level of security, although he had in fact been employed by the same company for 13 years and had lived at the same address for three years. Some days later, Mr Chisolm was brought before the County Court, where he was remanded back to the Detention Center for an additional six days, pending the arrival of an interpreter. He was finally released when an attorney, contacted by a friend, intervened on his behalf.

The nature of the task

Although there is unanimity about the importance of interpreters, many legal professionals have a limited understanding of the complex nature of the task. It is often wrongly assumed that the interpreter acts as a simple conduit between the English-speaking court and non-English-speaking defendants or witnesses in what is essentially a mechanical process. There is also an assumption that, simply because a person is bilingual, they will be able to function in both languages and in all settings with equal ease. The reality is rather different. The linguistic requirements of the court-room are highly sophisticated. At the formal end of the continuum, the characteristics of legal English include a high incidence of technical terms (often Latin, French or Old English in origin), polysyllabic words and long sentences. At the informal end of the continuum, lawyers often use colloquial speech to show solidarity with jurors, and witnesses may use strong language in their testimony. The task of the interpreter is to convey subtle differences in meaning and shades of speaker intent. Stylis-tically inappropriate translations may influence the jurors' perceptions of the speakers in many subtle ways; so too can the addition or omission of information.

Haydee Claus, a certified interpreter for the federal court system and the California state system, sums up the task of simultaneous inter-pretation thus:

> In a typical trial a judge may read the jury instructions at more than 120 words a minute. The interpreter must hear the English, grasp each idea, and transform the English ideas immediately into the words and grammar of the second language. She must do this continuously and almost simul-taneously, usually lagging behind a few words. She must perform a careful balancing act of intense concentration. If she focuses too much on what she hears, she loses track of what is coming out of her mouth and she runs the risk of stuttering, making grammar errors or leaving sentences unfinished. If she focuses too much attention on her delivery, she can miss

what is being said in court. She must have a broad enough educational background and language proficiency to understand and simultaneously interpret testimony, whether the witness is a forensic doctor, a fingerprint expert or a ballistics expert.[27]

Consecutive interpretation, provided when a speaker has finished an utterance or paused, can be equally taxing. It requires the same levels of proficiency and attention to detail, but the demands on memory are particularly strenuous. The interpreter is expected to retain long stretches of speech and render them accurately into the other language. Again, Haydee Claus neatly encapsulates the complexity of the task:

> Try reading the following sentence and simply repeating it in English to yourself, without looking at the text: 'Well, uh, the thing is, like I told you, me and Joe and Rick had a couple, well maybe more than a couple, say four, I guess, beers apiece before the cops got there but that was after we had had two scotch and sodas and two, no one, or was it two, well, a couple of Margaritas at the bar on 5th and Folsom.'

In a highly stressed situation such as the courtroom, the potential for making serious errors is very real, as illustrated by actual instances provided by interpreters from the Yup'ik Language Center:

ATTORNEY: Why did you leave home?
INTERPRETER: *He asked why you left your village?*
WITNESS: *I never told anyone that the person was doing anything to me.*
INTERPRETER: She never told anyone what he was doing to her.
WITNESS: *I can't answer that question. [It's too difficult.]*
INTERPRETER: She won't answer that question.
ATTORNEY: In what condition was your mother in?
INTERPRETER: *Your mother wasn't there. Where was she?*
ATTORNEY: Did he use anything else to touch you – other than his hand?
INTERPRETER: *Did he touch you only there or did he touch you somewhere else, too?*[28]

Cultural challenges

The challenges for interpreters are not simply linguistic; they are also cultural. Colonial legal systems pose a direct challenge to many of the most basic tenets of Indigenous culture, as illustrated by the following examples from peoples on different continents, separated by thousands of miles.

The Innu of Eastern Canada are egalitarian, consensual and far more tolerant of 'aberrant' behaviour than Europeans.[29] Thus drunkenness is seen as symptomatic of a far more general malaise, rather than as a 'crime' to be punished. The Innu resent the interference of the law in traditional activities such as hunting and fishing. They are also bewildered by the apparatus of police, courts and jails.

The Alaskan Yup'ik have similar attitudes towards the law. Their very different world view makes the task of translating European legal concepts extremely challenging for even the most gifted interpreter, a point made very eloquently in the following transcript from a Yup'ik court case:

ATTORNEY FOR THE APPELLEE:	Now here finally is my question. Did you consider it fair for you to claim 160 acres in a village where other families who were also living in that village had no land claims?
[Pause]	
ATTORNEY FOR THE APPELLEE:	Is there a word for fair in Yup'ik?
TRANSLATOR:	That's what I'm groping for.
ATTORNEY FOR THE APPELLANT:	Well, may I suggest that –
COURT:	Well, just a minute let's – let's try and deal with this and –
ATTORNEY FOR THE APPELLANT:	Okay, he can go.
COURT:	– then if we can't it – can it – is it untranslatable?
TRANSLATOR:	It's – I – I don't know if it's untranslatable. Perhaps someone else may be able to translate it although I'm –
ATTORNEY FOR THE APPELLEE:	Is there no concept –
TRANSLATOR:	– although I'm fluent Yup'ik speaking Native I have never encountered such a word in –
ATTORNEY FOR THE APPELLEE:	Do the Natives not have a concept of fairness?
TRANSLATOR:	Are you asking me or him?
ATTORNEY FOR THE APPELLEE:	I'm asking you.
COURT:	How about –
TRANSLATOR:	Well, I'd have to give you a – a history and the cultural value system we have –

ATTORNEY FOR THE APPELLEE:	Let me ask you this.
TRANSLATOR:	– in our –
ATTORNEY FOR THE APPELLEE:	Do you consider that to be an unfair question?
TRANSLATOR:	I don't –
ATTORNEY FOR THE APPELLEE:	You don't know what fair means?
TRANSLATOR:	consider that to be an unfair question. It's just that I'm unable to come up with a word to translate the word fair.
COURT:	Well, if you know the concept of fair and I take it that you do understand the English concept of fair?
TRANSLATOR:	Yes.
COURT:	How would that concept – what type of word would you use in Yup'ik to convey that concept?
TRANSLATOR:	I'd have to make an analogy and use the word fair to – to make that distinction.
ATTORNEY FOR THE APPELLEE:	Can I ask this question? Can we ask Mr. A if he understands the word, fair, in English?
TRANSLATOR:	Can we ask this question?
COURT:	Do you have the – the witness has asked for a translator. Unless Counsel for Mr. A agrees I'm not going to require him to answer in English.[30]

The frustration and bewilderment experienced in this Alaskan courtroom is by no means limited to the Yup'ik. Similar examples have been reported in cases involving Indigenous peoples in many parts of the world.

Silence is another area perceived and treated very differently from one culture to the next. Australian Aboriginal peoples, for instance, value silence and spend lengthy periods of time thinking about what they want to say. Unfortunately, non-Aboriginal police, lawyers, judges and juries often interpret such silences as insolence or guilt. The Yup'ik have a similar relationship with silence and it is probably no accident that the Yup'ik word for court is 'a place to be made to talk' (qanercetaarvik), and not 'a place where you bring problems to be solved' or 'a place where justice is administered to wrongdoers'.[31]

There are also differences in the use of questions. The entire legal system in many countries is based on the assumption that asking questions is the most effective way of establishing what has happened. While this assumption is deeply rooted in many Western societies, it is by no means universal. The Yup'ik, for instance, generally steer clear of direct questions and answers: the more formal the relationship between speakers, the more people take care to be indirect. This pattern can make court-room exchanges confusing for everyone involved. Contrast the responses of two jurors when asked if they thought they could evaluate their level of intoxication on a scale of, say, one to ten. While the Euro-American juror simply answered, 'Yes', the Yup'ik juror responded: 'I wouldn't – I've never thought about it in those terms. If you could be more specific on what you want me to say, then I could tell you, but I've never thought about it.' When asked questions designed to elicit their opinions, the normal Yup'ik answer is, 'I don't know.'[32]

Australian Aboriginal people also prefer more indirect ways of seeking information. When bombarded with yes-no questions – a common feature of police and courtroom interviews – many agree with the questioner, irrespective of whether they have understood the question, or accept the truth of the proposition, a strategy that has been called 'gratuitous con-currence'.[33] Unfortunately, if suspects later change their position, they are deemed unreliable witnesses.

Legal challenges to interpretation

Legal interpreting is something of a minefield. Critical details may be misinterpreted. Suspects, witnesses and defendants may be too intimidated or embarrassed to admit they can't understand the interpreter. There are even documented cases of bilingual jurors correcting court interpreters. On some occasions, the interaction of legal and linguistic issues becomes extremely complex. For instance, in one case where interpretation was provided for a Spanish-speaking witness, a judge disqualified jurors who were Spanish/English bilinguals on the grounds that bilingual jurors would necessarily hear both the Spanish and the English interpretation, and that the Spanish testimony had to be based entirely on the English record. This case raises questions of possible discrimination against His-panic jurors. But, equally important, it highlights the court's ambiguous stand. On the one hand, it accepted the adequacy of interpretation by using an interpreter. On the other hand, it assumed that the English interpretation would not be equivalent to the Spanish.[34]

Legal challenges are becoming more frequent. In some cases, objections are based on the linguistic competence of the interpreter; in others, on their failure to observe the high ethical standards expected of court inter-preters. Take the case of a Roma family from the Czech Republic whose applications for refugee status in Aotearoa/New Zealand were declined in 2001.[35] At appeal, their counsel formally objected to the interpreter appointed by the authority, the same person who had been used at the initial interviews on entry. It was alleged that the interpreter had challenged the evidence of the wife in an English 'editorial comment', which was not translated into Czech. The interpreter was also alleged to have made prejudicial comments about Roma, thus bringing into doubt his independence.

A murder suspect's rights were seriously violated in a US case where a bilingual police officer served as interpreter. When left alone with the suspect, the police interpreter assumed the role of interrogator, thus violating the suspect's constitutional rights. The suspect was subsequently found guilty of murder. However, at appeal, the murder conviction was reversed, in spite of overwhelming forensic evidence pointing to his guilt.[36]

While speakers of languages other than English are routinely provided with courtroom interpreters, the situation is much less clear-cut for speakers of English-lexicon creoles. Although creoles share much of the vocabulary of standard English, there are many subtle but important differences in syntax and morphology which could conceivably result in misunderstanding. The Jamaican expression, 'Mind you don't', for instance, corresponds to standard English, 'Be sure you do.' The potential for miscommunication has been demonstrated experimentally. Re-enacted audio-taped exchanges in Caribbean creoles from the transcripts of court proceedings in New York City were played to speakers of standard English. When given four or five alternative interpretations of each extract, incorrect interpretations were made in just under half of the cases.[37]

Similar issues affect speakers of Aboriginal English. As in Caribbean creoles, the grammatical differences between standard English and Australian English are relatively small, but pragmatic differences are much larger. Examples of the different meanings attached to silences and questions have already been given for speakers of Aboriginal languages. These differences apply not only to Aboriginal languages but also to Aboriginal English.

The case of Robyn Kina highlights the unfortunate consequences of the failure to recognize Aboriginal ways of speaking.[38] Robyn Kina was found guilty of stabbing her common-law husband to death and sentenced to life imprisonment in 1988. Her lawyers were unaware that, as an Aboriginal woman, she would feel uncomfortable about disclosing important personal information to people she did not know very well. Crucially, they had mistakenly believed that her silence meant that she had nothing to say. It is also probable that they had misunderstood her 'yes' answers as indicating agreement with their suggestions. Poor skills in intercultural communication had effectively prevented them from uncovering the details of the tremendous provocation that led to the stabbing. Five years later, she successfully appealed against the conviction, on the grounds that her lawyers had been unable to present an adequate defence.

The Pinkenba case was another landmark, not only in the sensitization of the legal profession to the importance of linguistic differences, but also in the cynical manipulation of this knowledge. Six police officers were charged with the unlawful deprivation of liberty of three Aboriginal boys aged 12, 13 and 14 who had allegedly been taken in separate vehicles late at night and abandoned 14 kilometres away in an industrial wasteland at Pinkenba. The boys were witnesses for the prosecution in a committal hearing where the case centred on whether or not they had gone against their will.

At the hearing, a handbook for lawyers on *Aboriginal English and the Law*[39] was clearly visible on the defence counsel's bar table. Although this publication was designed to help law professionals to be more sensitive to the needs of Aboriginal peoples, there is compelling evidence that, on this occasion, it was used against them. On some occasions, the time between initial and follow-up questions was so short that the witness could not think about the question. On other occasions, uninterrupted silences were followed with some form of harassment. Repeated direct questions were used to make a witness agree that his silence showed he was unreliable. Predictably, the linguistic and cultural manipulation of the boys' evidence ensured that the charges against the police were dropped.

To understand what was happening in this courtroom, we need to look not only at the details of the case, but at the wider institutional and societal struggles. The witnesses were powerless on several counts: they were children in an adult court; they were participants in a legal system that systematically oppresses Aboriginal people; and they had no experience of the language of the courtroom. In this particular case, Aboriginal Legal Services and the Criminal Justice Commission were challenging the police. The defence counsel were among the top criminal lawyers in Queensland, and had far greater experience than the prosecuting lawyer. In this struggle of David and Goliath, David was unfortunately vanquished.

Room for improvement

When service providers and clients come from different language backgrounds and have different cultural understandings, there is a very real possibility that levels of service will be unsatisfactory. The need for education – for all parties – is urgent and new ways of reaching target populations must be found. Suggestions for improving knowledge about the legal system in Indigenous communities, for instance, might include the staging of mock trials to allow discussion of cultural issues and the consequences of confession. The legal profession, for its part, needs to develop alternative strategies for eliciting and communicating information. It also needs to be alerted to language issues. As part of Victorian bar courses in Australia, participants who speak another language – usually Greek or Italian – act as magistrates and barristers; others assume the part of the accused and give evidence or make statements with the assistance of an interpreter.[40] The experience works well as a means of sensitizing barristers to the vulnerability of non-English-speaking witnesses and defendants.

The legal profession is taking the first faltering steps to accommodate cultural difference. The Waitangi Tribunal in Aotearoa/New Zealand, for instance, developed a range of new procedures for hearing evidence and argument in hearings on marae (Māori cultural centres used for community gatherings).[41] Because marae etiquette does not permit the speaker to be interrupted, the interpreter kept a written note of what was said, to be delivered later. Members of the claimant tribe familiar with both the nature of the claim and the people giving evidence were allowed to serve as interpreters. They were also permitted to hold discussions with the witnesses to clarify both meaning and intention.

Adaptations have also been made in Aboriginal Land Claim proceedings in the Northern Territory of Australia. Anthropologists are used as a bridge between Aboriginal people who often have little knowledge of Western law and lawyers who may not understand what the Aboriginal witnesses are trying to tell them. Interested parties visit the places cited in the claim and evidence is taken in situ.[42]

Another way forward is to encourage bilingual-bicultural individuals to enter the legal and medical professions. A small number of specialist programmes is being targeted at Indigenous peoples. Red River College in Manitoba, for instance, offers training for fluent Algonquian speakers in translating and interpreting in a variety of settings, but focusing initially on legal and medical areas. Some discussion has also taken place in the USA about lowering entry requirements for prospective Hispanic candidates for medical school.[43]

Various quite simple, low-cost procedures also have the potential to improve the quality of services. For instance, translations in the main minority languages of the caution and other relevant information can be tape-recorded and played to suspects before starting a formal record of the interview; and audio-tapes explaining commonly used legal forms, rights and procedures can be made available to people seeking legal services. Hawai'i offers many examples of good practice.[44] Translation is under way of the state Bar Association brochures on subjects such as *I've been in an auto accident! What do I do?* The public can consult Lawline, a 24-hour recorded information service with messages in seven different languages. Two videos dubbed into Korean and Ilocano – one on what happens when you file a small claims case or are sued, the other on what happens when you receive a traffic citation – are free through local libraries and have also been broadcast on public-access television. And Korean-speaking lawyers appear at 'Meet a Lawyer' meetings in shopping centres and other locations as part of annual Law Week activities organized by the state Bar Association.

Translation and the written word

Translation is in many ways a less glamorous occupation than interpreting. Removed from the immediacy of interpersonal encounters, the translator has time to make considered judgements about the best ways of rendering one language into another while remaining as faithful as possible to the original.

Although most people agree about the usefulness of translation, there are none the less dissenting voices. For some people, translation is a convenient opt-out: it is all too easy to feel that obligations to non-English speakers have been fulfilled by translating the relevant information when, in fact, considerably more support may be required for people unfamiliar with the new culture to understand their rights and obligations. The case of an Italian traveller's struggles with his landing card on his arrival in Australia clearly illustrates this point.[45] Despite the fact that the cards were available in several languages – including Italian – he needed help in understanding what the questions *meant*. In a valiant attempt to find a solution, he addressed all those around him in Italian. They, in turn, guessed at what he was asking and answered in English and with gestures. It finally required the intervention of an Italian speaker to negotiate the successful completion of the form.

For others, translation services are often an unnecessary extravagance. Money spent on providing a Welsh version for people quite capable of understanding the English, it is argued, would be better used elsewhere. Similar arguments might be made of translations into languages such as Urdu in the UK, since literacy levels in the Pakistani community are relatively low.[46] Counter-arguments for both Welsh and Urdu centre on the importance of translation in making other languages more visible and hence raising their status in the wider society.

In certain circumstances, however, the need for translation is uncontentious. Immigrants may need English translations of documents such as birth certificates, marriage certificates, education qualifications and employment references. The Australian government has been particularly responsive, providing a free translation service for documents relating to settlement in the first two years of arrival or after being granted permanent residency. Since the introduction of cost-recovery policies in the mid-1980s, however, private rather than government agencies have played an increasingly important role not only in Australia but throughout the English-speaking world.

Information is a vital aspect of service provision. Large numbers of government departments produce information leaflets in minority languages. For example, the UK Department for Education and Skills publishes information leaflets on school attendance for parents, and the Department of Health produces leaflets on pregnancy, maternity services and cot deaths. Sometimes, information is provided by non-government organizations such as the Refugee Service Center, which specializes in materials on various aspects of life in the United States, from housing to transportation, from employment to cultural adjustment.

The standard of translation is sometimes an issue. For instance, a leaflet on the home care of AIDS patients translated into Italian in Australia was ineffective on a number of fronts.[47] The Italian version was linguistically demanding and, possibly, beyond the reach of many Italian Australians. It also overlooked the different customs relating to home deaths and funerals by directly translating advice aimed originally at the Anglo community.

The Internet offers opportunities for both disseminating information and sharing experience. The Babel Tree project in Australia, for example, acts as a repository for translated material on a wide range of health issues and in many different languages, which users can download.[48] Australia has also developed the world's first multilingual news and community information portal.[49] The site has an emphasis on older people with links to online resources for 16 community language groups and a multilingual directory of government and community services. It also features multilingual email, message boards and chat rooms with simple instructions, for each of the 16 languages, on how to view non-English websites. Similar initiatives in the private sector include a booklet and CD-ROM on Internet access for Panjabi and Urdu speakers, produced by Barclays Bank working with the UK charity Age Concern.[50]

Visible language

Bilingual signage is another important area of work for translators and terminologists. Signs in other languages have two quite distinct functions. They offer valuable information to non-English speakers on where to go and what to do; at the same time, they draw the attention of English speakers to the rights and needs of other language communities. The invisibility of other languages has been a recurrent irritant for language activists; so, too, has their visibility. Benjamin Franklin was among the first to complain about bilingual street signs in Philadelphia.

Sometimes irritation gives way to action. During the 1960s, the Welsh Language Society painted out English-only road signs across Wales, as part of a campaign for bilingual signage. Welsh is now used routinely alongside English on public notices, road signs, street names, automatic teller machines and cheque books. Gaelic and Irish have also become more visible in recent years. Environmental print sends clear messages about the relevance and legitimacy of minority languages, often serving as a rallying point for much wider issues. It frequently provokes an emotional response. The addition of the words 'Fàilte gu Cathair Inbhir Nis' (Welcome to the City of Inverness) to signs at the entrance to the city triggered a heated exchange between Clí, an organization for new speakers of Gaelic, and the city council.[51] Although welcomed in principle, the decision to use small letters and a 'strange' font as part of the design attracted bitter comment from the Gaelic learners.

In Aotearoa/New Zealand, signage in both official languages is commonplace, acknowledging the status of Māori, and signalling a message of welcome.[52] Many Native American and First Nations people are also recognizing the importance of print in the environment as part of their efforts to revitalize Indigenous languages. A large billboard at the entrance to a Navajo reservation, for instance, asks: 'Did you speak Navajo with your child today?'[53] Attempts are also being made to use traffic and street signs in Navajo within the community and reserve, as well as signs and labels for locations such as washrooms and kitchens.

However, the most hotly contested example of bilingual signage comes from Canada. Attempts to win greater visibility for French have a long history. In Quebec, the Lavergne Law of 1910 required tickets for buses, trains and trams to be printed in both French and English, but it was not until the 1969 Official Languages Act that provision was made across Canada for bilingual signage in federal government buildings and for bilingual labelling on food packaging.[54] The 1977 Charter of the French Language, designed to protect and promote the French language in

The Swedish company IKEA cooperated with the Welsh Language Board in producing trilingual signs – Welsh, English and Swedish – when its first store was opened in Cardiff.
Reproduced with permission from the Welsh Language Board.

Quebec, took matters one step further by effectively banning the use of English in signs. Anglophone opposition to this measure was fierce. Morton Brownstein, the owner of a Montreal shoe store, took his case all the way to the Supreme Court of Canada, which ruled that the sign law violated freedom of expression: the 'greater visibility' or 'marked predominance' of French on signs in Quebec was permissible, but English could not be prohibited altogether.[55]

A new bill was passed allowing English inside commercial establishments, though still requiring only French on exterior signs. Angry Francophone demonstrations soon followed. By way of compromise, the 'notwithstanding' clause was invoked to override the Charter of Rights and Freedoms on which the Supreme Court judgement was based in order to avoid any further legal challenges.[56] A 1993 United Nations Human Rights Committee ruling led to yet another amendment. Quebec's sign laws were deemed to contravene an international covenant on civil and political rights; other languages would be permitted on exterior signs, but only if the French lettering was at least twice as large as the English. Some Anglophones remained defiant. In 1999, the owners of a small antique store near Montreal contested a fine imposed because the English and French on their sign were the same size. The Quebec court ruled that the province could only continue to impose restrictions on the use of languages if it could prove the fragility of French in Quebec society. However, the Quebec Superior Court overturned this ruling in the following year, citing Quebec's unique geographical situation as an enclave of French speakers on an English-speaking continent.

Bilingual signage has polarized Anglophone and Francophone Canada. Four members of the new English-rights Equality Party were elected to the Quebec National Assembly in 1989. A vocal Anglophone minority has waged a relentless battle against the 'language police' in the media. They have focused on the absurdity of attempts to dub 'Kentucky Fried Chicken' as 'Poulet frit Kentucky', and have conveniently overlooked the issues behind the original language policies. An equally vocal Francophone minority in the guise of the Brigade d'Autodéfense du Français (French Self-Defence Brigade) has conducted a firebombing campaign on 'Second Cup' coffee shops in the name of linguistic purity.[57] But although the vast majority of Francophones condemn terror tactics, there is no doubt of the continuing symbolic value of this issue for large numbers of people.

Bilingual signage is not, of course, the only option. Multilingual signs are now commonplace in public buildings such as hospitals and council offices in many cities. In schools, welcome notices raise the visibility of the languages spoken in the community, and signs (head teacher's office, library, staff room, reception, etc.) help visitors to find their way around.

Conclusion

Debates surrounding the provision of services in other languages give clear indications of both the aspirations of minority-language speakers and the attitudes of English speakers. People in the process of learning English are dependent on interpreters for access to medical and social services, and for equal treatment under the law. The role of language in miscarriages of justice is now well documented; there is also a better appreciation of the cost-effectiveness of providing interpreters in medical encounters. Awareness of the need to translate public information and bilingual signage has also grown. Interpreting and translation, however, require high levels of skill, and the availability of qualified professionals falls well short of actual demand.

Language learners are not, of course, the only ones with an interest in bilingual services. Speakers of Indigenous and established languages may be able to speak English but none the less wish to use their preferred language, particularly in high-stress situations such as job interviews or court appearances. Alternatively, language activists may feel the need to assert their right to speak their language in the widest possible range of contexts; by achieving greater visibility and audibility, they are helping to resist the shift to English. Significant gains have been made in recent decades, particularly by minorities whose languages have achieved official status.

The gains of any minority are inevitably contested by the dominant group, hence the violent opposition expressed by Anglophones in Quebec to legislation concerning signage, and the cynical manipulation by Australian barristers of their knowledge of Aboriginal English to defend the police. On balance, however, most English speakers are sympathetic to the needs of minority speakers for services in other languages.

Notes

1   Schellekens (2001).
2   Morrow (1994).
3   Canadian Heritage (1999).
4   Branswell (2000).
5   Colin and Morris (1996).
6   Ozolins (1998); SASLI (1997).
7   Del Valle (2003); Ozolins (1998).
8   Kaur and Mills (1993).
9   Kazoulis (2001: iii).
10   Hall (2003). Translations of the Urdu are italicized.
11   Edwards (2000).
12   www.diversityrx.org/HTML/MOBISE1.htm
13   www.naati.com.au
14   www.iol.org.uk
15   Auld (2001: ch. 11); Runciman (1993: chs 3 and 8).
16   Ozolins (1998).
17   Mintz (1998); Vidal (1998).
18   www.diversityrx.org/HTML/MOBISA.htm

19 Wilson (1993).
20 RNID (1999).
21 Katbamna et al. (2002).
22 Weinick and Drauss (2000).
23 O'Brien and Plooij (1973).
24 Del Valle (2003).
25 Lane et al. (1999).
26 NAD (1994).
27 Claus (1997).
28 Morrow (1994); italics indicate the meaning conveyed in Yup'ik; Roman text, the meaning conveyed in English.
29 Samson et al. (1999: 26–7).
30 Morrow (1994).
31 Morrow (1993).
32 Morrow (1993).
33 Eades (1992).
34 Del Valle (2003).
35 Refugee Status Appeals Authority (2001).
36 Berk-Seligson (2000).
37 Hutchins (1999).
38 Eades (2002).
39 Eades (1992).
40 Gobbo (2000).
41 Lane et al. (1999).
42 Walsh (1999).
43 Carreira and Armengol (2001: 122).
44 Hawai'i State Supreme Court Committee on Equality and Access to the Courts (2001).
45 Michèle de Courcy (personal communication, 2002).
46 Bowes and Meehan Domokos (1997).
47 Saini and Rowling (1997).
48 www.adec.org.au/babeltree
49 www.multiculturalaustralia.com.au
50 Age Concern (2003).
51 www.cli.org.uk/cgi-bin/main?action=full_statementands_id=6
52 Department of Education (1987).
53 Ignace (1998: ch. 6.1).
54 Burnaby (1996: 165–8).
55 O'Malley and Bowman (2001).
56 Bélanger (2000).
57 O'Malley and Bowman (2001).

Part II

Language at home and in school

4

Language in the family

Despite the myth of monolingualism, large numbers of people in the inner-circle countries are bilingual and, in some cases, multilingual. Responsibility for passing languages from one generation to the next starts in the home. Families can be the vehicle for maintenance and growth, or for the decay and death of languages.

Bilingual families come in many different shapes and sizes. Since the beginning of time, trade, conquest and marriage have brought different people into contact, creating the need to speak other languages. Contact in modern times, however, is arguably far greater than at any point in the past. More and more people find themselves in relationships where their partner speaks another language, thanks in no small measure to ongoing developments in transport – bicycle, train, steam ship, car, plane. Workers have become more mobile in the wake, first, of urbanisation and, later, of globalization, making it possible to form relationships further and further afield. Tourism has also increased the probability of partnerships and marriages involving other languages.

A losing battle?

Which factors, then, determine whether a family follows a bilingual course or shifts to English? Decisions are not always easy to predict.[1] For instance, there may well be more opportunities to use the language if you belong to one of the larger minority communities. But, on the other hand, small groups can be more cohesive and focused. In some cases, parents with little education and minimal knowledge of English continue to rely heavily on the first language; in others, they make an all-out effort to learn English. Similarly, refugees react in different ways: on some occasions, they reject the language of the oppressive regime; on others, the first language remains a key element of their identity.

Parents are often plagued with doubt. They may mistakenly believe, for instance, that early exposure to two languages results in confusion and interference between the languages.[2] Alternatively, if they decide to use only the minority language, they may worry about what will happen when the child arrives in school with little or no knowledge of English. Other languages and accents can be ridiculed or ignored, making children feel that there is no value in being bilingual. Popular prejudice can also be undermining. Take the case of Samuel C. Kiser, a district court judge in Amarillo, Texas, who accused Martha Laureano of child abuse for speaking Spanish to her 5-year-old daughter in a 1995 custody suit. He warned that if she failed to speak English only, the girl would be condemned to a life as a maid. Judge Kiser later responded to protests about his stance by apologizing to maids, but refused to move on his English-only order.[3] This is not an isolated example. In 2003 Judge Ronald E. Reagan ordered a Hispanic father in Papillon, Nebraska, to speak mainly English to his daughter as a condition for his visitation rights.[4]

For many families, a cost-benefit analysis, conscious or otherwise, leads to the decision to shift to English, a process which is often complete within two or three generations. Most Hispanics in the USA today, for instance, speak English as their usual language by the second generation, and as their *only* language by the third.[5] Recently arrived immigrants or refugees are likely to be more concerned with day-to-day survival than with cultural and linguistic issues, especially if they work in jobs with long, anti-social hours. By the time the parents realize that English has become their children's dominant language, it is usually too late to reverse the process.[6] As English becomes the dominant language, children may lack confidence in their ability to speak the other language and may fear criticism or teasing from fluent speakers.

The speed of language loss often comes as a shock for established minorities, too. In Scotland, fewer than one in three Gaelic speakers now live in neighbourhoods where Gaelic is the majority language or in households where both parents speak the language. The use of Gaelic is standing up to some extent among neighbours and in pubs but is declining rapidly in shopping and at church.[7] The situation is complicated by the different rates of migration between men and women. Young women are more likely to remain within the community and tend to be less supportive of Gaelic. Men, on the other hand, are more likely to leave and may not find Gaelic-speaking partners. All of this bodes ill for the future of the language. Welsh researchers have also drawn attention to the consequences of 'mixed-language' households.[8] When both parents speak Welsh, there is an 82 per cent chance that a child will be Welsh speaking. However, if only one parent speaks Welsh this percentage drops dramatically, to 40 per cent.

Language loss is also a pressing issue for Indigenous communities. An unexpected consequence of new housing on North American reservations has been an increased rate of language shift. Although conditions have improved, three-generation families no longer live under one roof, reducing children's exposure to the Indigenous language. In Nunavut ('our land'), the new Canadian territory, many people consider that the first sign of decay is when the children play in English. The second is when the parents speak in Inuktitut and the children reply in English. And the third is when the language of the home is English, except for the elders in the corner, a generation cut off from their grandchildren.[9] Very often attitudes towards the Indigenous languages are positive but complacent, and it has become an urgent priority to educate parents about their responsibilities. The linguist Clifton Pye, for instance, describes his frustration in trying to record a 3-year-old girl in British Columbia in order to find out how much Chilcotin she knew:

> Her mother helped me by telling her, 'Say *naslhiny*. Can you say "naslhiny,"' using English to coax her daughter into producing the Chilcotin word for horse. This was interrupted when the grandmother came to the back door to find out what I was doing there. The mother and grandmother entered into a long conversation in Chilcotin. Yet, when the mother returned to her daughter, she continued the conversation in English.[10]

One thing is clear. When other languages are in competition with English, the decision to use another language in the home requires particular commitment. English is, after all, the language of power and glitter – Coca-Cola, Bill Gates, MTV and the mass media. In comparison, minority languages can seem old-fashioned and unglamorous. Given the odds, it is perhaps surprising that anyone should contemplate a struggle against the English-speaking tide.

Reasons for being bilingual

Parents are only too aware that English will rapidly become the dominant language for their child. They are also aware that the presence of older school-aged siblings makes it even more difficult to pass on the minority language. Yet in spite of the overwhelming pressures to switch to English, many families decide to use other languages in the home. This decision is not taken lightly. Young adults who retain fluency or near fluency in their native tongue are likely to come from families who have agreed very consciously on a policy of speaking the minority language in the home.

Family relationships

Reasons for making this choice are many and varied, but the desire for meaningful communication is usually a high priority. Communication is crucial to family relationships. When grandparents' or parents' English is limited and children have difficulty with the minority language, neither generation can make itself understood to the other. Language autobiographies written by Asian American college students in California give interesting insights into the attendant frustration. A Chinese student highlighted the 'shallowness' of everyday conversations:

> [I] do not have enough of a vocabulary to have meaningful talks with [my parents]. Such was the case just the other night when they asked me what my major at Berkeley was but I did not know the phrase for 'Biology,' much less, 'Molecular and Cellular Biology.' The best I could manage was 'science' in Chinese and explained the rest in English; I could not communicate to them why I selected this major, what I was going to do with it, and so forth – we ended the discussion by changing the subject.[11]

Lack of fluency has an impact on many social situations. Children feel humiliated, for instance, when they can't relate to others of their own age on visits to the home country, or when they can't join in conversations with visitors. Many young people reject the language in adolescence but bitterly regret this decision as they grow older. 'I noticed that I began to think more and more in English', wrote one of the students in the California study. 'Now, the only thing that is still Chinese in my mind is the multiplication table.' A poignant postscript reads: 'I wish I had kept up with my reading skills in Chinese. It felt as though my Chinese heritage was fading away with my Chinese literacy.'

For parents and grandparents, the failure to pass on the language to the next generation is equally painful. An Innu from northeastern Canada explains the dilemma thus: '[Young people] ask us "What are you saying? What does that word mean?" And we can't translate into English because we don't understand English . . . I wonder what's going to happen in the future, when the kids don't understand us and we don't understand

Communication between grandparents and grandchildren has become an issue in many Indigenous communities, including the Innu of northeastern Canada. Photograph by Serge Jauvin. Reproduced with permission from Survival International (www.survival-international.org).

them. Next thing, our grandchildren will be putting words in our mouths.'[12] In contrast, fully bilingual children not only tend to remain closer to their elders but often provide essential services as 'language brokers', helping them negotiate difficult situations in English.[13]

Language, culture and identity

Closely linked to the question of communication in the family is the role of language in personal identity. Each language is imbued with cultural values that shape self-awareness, identity and relationships. On the level of the individual, young people who speak the heritage language are able to explore their roots – literature, art, music, history – and have a firmer sense of who they are. On the level of the community, when languages are lost, generations of wisdom and knowledge go with them. In the words of a member of the Navajo tribal council: 'Once we lose our language, we lose our culture and we're just another brown-skinned American.'[14] Bilinguals – and biculturals – are privileged in knowing at first hand that there are many ways of being and doing, not just one, and that the sum of human knowledge is much greater than its component parts.

Many established and new minority families also have strong views on this matter. In a study of a predominantly Mexican community in California, a Mexican-born mother summed up the situation thus: 'It's a shame if they forget their Spanish, because you carry your roots in Spanish . . . It's important for them to continue their roots, the culture and that they feel proud of us and of themselves because they are Mexican.'[15] Many people in this study were very critical of parents who abandoned the use of Spanish in the home: 'I know many men at work and I tell them, "Listen, mister, your daughter is Spanish. How shocking. Teach her. Some day she will thank you."'

Children respond to the tensions between parental and mainstream views in many different ways. Some express considerable frustration at the attempts of parents to enforce the use of the minority language, and resolve to use only English when they have children of their own. Others feel the same level of commitment as their parents to bringing up their own children to speak the minority language. Still others initially rebel against the minority language only to rediscover their identity in late adolescence or early adulthood, as part of a conscious rejection of attempts by English speakers to disparage them and their culture.

Religious observance

Many languages enjoy a close relationship with religion. In Scotland, Gaelic literacy was traditionally associated with Bible reading, home worship and the singing of metrical psalms.[16] In Wales, when Elizabeth I authorized a translation of the Bible into Welsh in 1563, the aim was to assimilate the Welsh and hasten the acquisition of English. Ironically, this development had the opposite effect. It prevented the fragmentation of the language into different dialects and helped ensure an enduring national identity.[17] Language and religion were also intimately linked in the New World in Francophone resistance to the British. Following the conquest of New France in 1759, the church was responsible for education and remained the main defender of French language and culture in Canada until the Quiet Revolution of the 1960s.[18]

Other languages continue to play an important role in religion, even in families that use English as the main language of communication. The Jewish meal on Friday evenings to welcome the Shabbat, or holy day, is a case in point. When everything is ready, the mother lights the candles, covers her eyes and says a blessing in Hebrew: 'Blessed are you, Lord or

God, King of the universe, who has sanctified us with his command-
ments, and commanded us to light the Shabbat candles.'

The ritual significance of language is also a central feature of Muslim
family celebrations. Many Muslims in the Pakistani diaspora speak Panjabi;
many Indian Muslims speak Gujarati; many Bangladeshis speak Sylheti or
Bengali. Yet for all these groups, Arabic remains the language of religion
and important family rites of passage. Babies are welcomed, either by the
Imam or by the head of the family, who takes them in his arms and
whispers in Arabic the Adhan, or call to prayer, in their right ear: 'Allah
is great, I bear witness that there is no God but God, I bear witness that
Muhammad is the Prophet of God. Come to prayer, come to success.
God is great. There is no God but God.' After the Adhan is whispered in
the right ear, the Iqamah, or command to rise and worship, again in
Arabic, is whispered in the left ear.

Participation in the religious life of a community is usually a family
affair. Attendance at a Catholic mass in a Spanish community involves
not only participating in Spanish masses but also socializing with other
Spanish speakers before and after. Sikhs worshipping at the gurdwara or
temple find themselves in a comparable Panjabi-speaking atmosphere.
The church, mosque and temple have also traditionally played a key role
in teaching the language and literacy of the community in question.
Interestingly, the new self-confidence engendered by multicultural policies
is reflected in religion. Many churches where previously only English was
spoken, or which used other languages as a transitional measure, are now
openly designated as multilingual.

Intellectual benefits

Myths about bilingualism abound. For many years researchers claimed
that children who speak two languages find themselves at an intellectual
disadvantage, performing at a lower level than monolinguals on a range
of tasks. These claims, however, have not stood up to close scrutiny.[19]
On some occasions, researchers were comparing middle-class monolinguals
with working-class bilinguals, raising the possibility that differences in
performance might be explained in terms of social class. On other occasions, researchers failed to take into account that they were comparing
monolinguals with bilinguals working in their weaker language. Discrepancies in performance were often explained with the image of the
brain as a receptacle with a finite capacity: because two languages were
assumed to take twice the space of one, bilinguals could not be expected
to do as well as monolinguals.

More recently, however, the receptacle metaphor has been replaced with the double-peaked iceberg.[20] The two peaks showing above the water represent the relatively automatized surface features – basic grammar, vocabulary and phonology – of the languages in question. The shared base lying below the surface represents the common underlying proficiency involved in cognitively demanding tasks. Children who, for instance, learn to read and write in Spanish do not simply have skills in Spanish; they also develop skills related to literacy which they are able to transfer to the task of learning to read and write another language. Psychologists point to the greater mental flexibility of bilinguals, and speculate that this may be because control of two symbolic systems offers more than one way to approach a problem.

Career advantages

Globalization and increasing diversity of populations means that the ability to speak, read and write in other languages is a skill in increasing demand by employers. Bilinguals bring considerable linguistic and cultural 'capital' with them to the job market.[21] In addition to the opportunities in international business, they have a growing edge in the domestic market in areas such as tourism, social services and education. In Australia, a Linguistic Availability Performance Allowance (LAPA) was introduced in the 1970s to encourage bilingual federal officers in public contact work to use their languages.[22] In some parts of the USA, bilingual Hispanics can earn up to 50 per cent more than those who speak only English.[23] Bilinguals in Canada command higher salaries on average than monolingual English speakers.[24] The range of career options, then, is much greater for bilinguals; so, too, are the financial rewards.

Patterns of language use

Decisions about language use in the home are complex. Where parents speak little or no English, there is clearly no alternative to using the minority language. If partners come from different backgrounds, the initial language of communication may become the home language. If one partner speaks the second language more confidently than the other, this may also determine language choice. Status issues affect decisions, too. Parents may be more prepared to make the necessary effort to transmit a high-status international language like French than a language spoken by a small number of people or in a country with little political power. The presence of older family members inevitably increases motivation to use the other language, especially when their English skills are limited.

The arrival of the first child is often an important turning point. When parents decide they want their child to be bilingual, there are several possible routes. Some families adopt a 'one person – one language' policy where each parent speaks their own language to the child from birth.[25] Sometimes one of these languages is English, in which case the child will be bilingual. On other occasions, it is not, in which case they will become trilingual. This policy seems to work best when parents use their 'designated' language consistently with their children and when other relatives, neighbours and friends support the parents' efforts. So far, the focus has been on two-parent families. It is, of course, possible to achieve bilingual children in one-parent families.

No two bilingual families are the same, although it is possible to detect certain patterns. In a study of a Puerto Rican neighbourhood in New York, for instance, some caregivers spoke Spanish among themselves and addressed children in Spanish.[26] The children answered adults in Spanish but spoke Spanish and English to each other. In other cases, caregivers spoke both Spanish and English among themselves and to the children, but the children replied mainly in English and usually spoke English to each other. In still other cases, the caregivers spoke English to each other but one parent used Spanish with the children while the other used Spanish and English. The children used Spanish and English with their caregivers and each other. These were by no means the only permutations.

The code-switching behaviour of Puerto Ricans in New York is neatly encapsulated in the title of an article by Shona Poplack: 'Sometimes I'll start a sentence in English y termino en español' (and finish in Spanish).[27] Code-switching is not, of course, limited to this particular community, as is demonstrated by the use of labels such as Tex-Mex, Spanglish and Hinglish (Hindi-English). Attitudes to code-switching vary. In families – or communities – where code-switching meets with censure, children rapidly learn to separate their languages. In families where this behaviour is the norm, children learn to make the same creative use of language as their parents. Code-switching is triggered by social and psychological factors. As in the case of the Puerto Rican families, children are more likely to use English with each other and the minority language with parents and older relatives. The topic of conversation also helps determine language choice. Thus, a conversation about something that happened in school may well be recounted in English; an incident that takes place in a community setting such as the church or mosque will be reported in the minority language. Identity is not a unitary concept: it is more accurate to think in terms of multiple identities. In the case of bilinguals and multilinguals, each change of language stresses one set of values or ideas over another.

The situation in families with Deaf children is rather different. Between 5 and 10 per cent of Deaf children are born to Deaf parents, who play a critical role in passing sign language from one generation to the next.[28] From the late nineteenth century, pressure was put on parents to avoid the use of sign in order to give their children the best chance of acquiring spoken English. The research evidence, however, suggests that this advice was ill conceived: the cognitive development of profoundly Deaf children who are not exposed to sign in the early years may be impaired.[29] Ideally, hearing parents and siblings decide to learn sign language themselves at the earliest opportunity, and classes are now widely available. However, children also need the active input of native 'speakers'. Deaf peers in school provide invaluable support in the early stages; later, national networks of Deaf clubs forms the focus for Deaf people's social and cultural lives.

The hearing children of Deaf parents play an important role as intermediaries. Membership of both Deaf and hearing communities brings many benefits, but also heavy responsibilities. Organizations such as CODA (Children of Deaf Adults) in the USA and HMFD (Hearing Mother-Father Deaf) in the UK have emerged to support children who find themselves in this role.

Support for families

As attitudes towards bilingualism have changed, institutional and other support for bilingual families has grown.[30] The nature and extent of this support varies a great deal from one country to the next, and also according to the kind of bilingual family.

Aboriginal peoples are developing a wide range of support strategies for the family. In Canada, for instance, the Aboriginal Language Initiative is designed both to increase the number of speakers and to expand the domains where Aboriginal languages are spoken. The focus is on community-based projects that preserve, protect and teach Aboriginal languages within Aboriginal communities and homes.

Where numbers have fallen to crisis level, the challenges have been described by one language activist as 'like trying to stitch together the fragile threads of a special cloth that is coming apart in your hands'.[31]

In California, where none of the 50 Indigenous languages is spoken as a mother tongue by children, some groups are developing master–apprentice programmes. Native-speaking elders work with young apprentices over a period of months and even years on everyday activities where all communication is in the Indigenous language. In a variation on this theme, Hinono'eitiit Hoowu' – the Arapaho Language Lodge – teams mothers with an Elder woman who teaches them traditional language used in caring for children, so that by the time children start pre-school class they already speak Arapaho.[32]

There is no shortage of ideas to encourage the use of Indigenous languages. In North Eastern Quebec, an Innu community has developed a system of buttons: fluent speakers wear a blue button; learners wear a red button. People wearing blue buttons make a commitment to use the language with both blue and red button wearers.[33] Strategies suggested by grassroots organizations for revitalizing the language include making a point of using it at meal times or on other regular occasions during the day; encouraging grandparents to use the language with their grandchildren; and getting together with other families with the same objectives.

The family is also an important focus for policy makers in established communities. In Wales, the relative health of the Welsh language at the start of the twenty-first century owes much to the efforts of the school. There is, however, concern that the gains attributed to Welsh-medium education are being eroded by the decisions of growing numbers of bilingual parents to transmit only English to their children. In 2001, the Welsh Language Board launched the Twf (Growth) project to address this issue. A national network of project officers works with midwives, health visitors and early-years organizations, offering information on the benefits of bilingualism, and directing parents to organizations which give practical support, such as the Cylchoedd Ti a Fi (You and Me Circles), which allow parents and toddlers to socialize in Welsh, and the Mentrau Iaith (Language Initiatives),[34] community-based organizations which work with individuals, groups and businesses to promote the language through social and leisure activities. The team has developed a wide range of materials, including CDs of Welsh nursery rhymes for parents to sing with their children, bilingual activity books, and newsletters which tell the story of how different families have gone about the task of bringing up their children bilingually.

Similar initiatives can be found in other Celtic nations. In Ireland, Comhluadar provides an information service and opportunities for families to meet others in their area who are using the language with their children.[35] Glór na nGael is an annual competition to reward those communities that have been successful in stimulating the use of Irish, with some 140 local entries throughout the country.[36] In Scotland, the Gaelic in the Community Scheme is responsible for setting up Gaelic Energy Centres, where everyday business is conducted in the language.[37]

Among the most urgent challenges for more recently arrived minorities is the provision of culturally and linguistically sensitive childcare. A study undertaken by California Tomorrow found that only 55 per cent of childcare centres had staff that could communicate with Spanish-speaking children and less than a third of centres serving Asian children employed someone who could speak Chinese, Vietnamese, Tagalog or Korean.[38] The monolingual ethos of most formal childcare provision not only undermines the efforts of parents to transmit other languages to their children; it also has practical implications. Take the case of a baby that has been pulling on its ear and may well be developing an infection: the caregiver will need to communicate what has been happening so that, if the child develops a fever, parents know they should see a doctor straight away. Similarly, parents might want feedback about how their child behaves in the day-care setting to establish whether their concerns about bullying or shyness are well founded. If parents' English is limited and no caregiver speaks the parents' language, it is simply not possible to share important information.

Isolated families

In the case of Indigenous communities like the Innu and the Inuit, or established communities like the Welsh and Irish, we are dealing with relatively large numbers of people with a territorial base. In many other cases, bilingual families are isolated; they experience problems and challenges similar to those of other groups, but rarely have access to the same level of support. The Grover family is a good example. Mike is an English speaker, Marjukka is Finnish. They live in Clevedon, in the west of England, where there is only one other Finnish speaker.

As publishers of books on language, they have been particularly well placed to offer support to other isolated bilingual families. The need first struck them in the early 1980s when a book which they had just produced on family bilingualism was reviewed in a national newspaper. Very soon they started receiving a flow of letters from worried parents asking for advice. The Grovers related only too well to these concerns and responded by setting up the *Bilingual Family Newsletter*, which currently has a circulation of well over a thousand.[39] According to Marjukka, the issues that preoccupy parents have changed over time. In the early stages, there was a great deal of scepticism as to whether family bilingualism could really be achieved, and anxiety about whether it would in some way harm the child. Today, information is more readily available and attitudes towards bilingualism are a great deal more confident.

With the advent of the Internet, isolated families have access to advice and information from international networks. Nethelp, for instance, identifies two main problems in bringing up children bilingually. The first is well-meaning relatives who are uncomfortable with the idea of bilingualism, believing it will do the child more harm than good. The suggested solution for unwanted interference is gentle education: 'Point out the benefits you see for the child (being able to speak to certain relatives, for instance), introduce them to bilingual families you know, or encourage them to read books you have found useful.' The second problem is the 'authorities' – teachers, doctors, health visitors – who sometimes offer unhelpful advice. Here the suggested solution is either gentle education or simply to ignore them: 'Remember that no matter how much the pediatrician, for instance, may know about your child's sniffles and scratches, he or she is not an expert on language.[40]

Linguistic balance sheets

Potentially bilingual families in the inner-circle countries are involved in a cost-benefit analysis. The costs are huge. The omnipresence of English in the media, in school and in society at large drowns out the use of other languages. The main concern of children is to fit in and fight shy of anything that marks them out as different from their peers. Widespread misunderstanding about language acquisition undermines the confidence of parents, whose prime concern will always be the welfare of their children.

The benefits for many families, however, are far greater. Children who speak the minority language are able to communicate with the wider family and community. They have a deeper understanding of the cultural values of their community and a firmer sense of their own identity. As researchers have debunked the myths associated with bilingualism, they have also started to identify the cognitive and intellectual benefits of speaking other languages. And, as society has started to recognize minority rights, the competitive edge of bilinguals in the employment market has became increasingly apparent to all concerned.

Bringing up children bilingually is not an easy option, and without the support of a wider group of family and friends, the likelihood of success is greatly reduced. Community activities that create opportunities for using other languages are an indispensable support. So, too, are the attitudes and responses of the education system, which form the subject of the next chapter.

Notes

1   Clyne (1991).
2   Goodz (1994).
3   Baron (2001).
4   Ortiz (2003).
5   Nicolau and Valdivieso (1992).
6   Wong Fillmore (1991).
7   Euromosaic Project (1996).
8   Tentative analysis of 2001 census details, Welsh Language Board, October 2003.
9   Kublu and Mallon (1999).
10   Pye (1992).
11   Hinton (1999).
12   Samson et al. (1999: 21).
13   Hall (2003).
14   Shebala (1999).
15   Pease-Alvarez (2003: 13).
16   Euromosaic Project (1996).
17   Davies (1993).
18   Bélanger (2000).
19   Baker (2001: 136–40).
20   Cummins (2001: 173–4); Baker (2001: 163–6).
21   Bourdieu (1986).
22   Ozolins (1998).
23   Fradd and Lee (1998).
24   Dion (1991).
25   Döpke (1992).
26   Zentella (1997).
27   Poplack (1980).
28   Mitchell and Karchmer (2004).
29   Sacks (1989).
30   For further discussion, see, for instance, Cenoz and Genesee (2001); Baker (2000).
31   Leanne Hinton, cited in McBroom (1995).
32   Greymorning (1999).
33   Ignace (1998: ch. 6).

34   Edwards (2000); more up-to-date details of Welsh-language initiatives can be found on the website of the Welsh Language Board: www.bwrdd-yr-iaith.org.uk

35   www.comhluadar.ie/english.htm

36   www.glornangael.ie

37   www.hie.co.uk/welcome.asp.LocID-hiestrpriculgaepro.htm

38   Chang and Pulido (1994).

39   www.multilingual-matters.com/multi/journals_bfn.asp

40   www.nethelp.no/cindy/biling-fam.html

5

Language and education: a history

Schools play a central role in the socialization of children and embody the values of the dominant group. It is therefore not surprising that this is a setting where tensions between English and minority-language speakers are very obvious. The education of minorities is the subject of fierce debate. Some see diversity as an invaluable cultural resource; others perceive the presence of other languages as a potential threat. The balance between these perspectives has oscillated in recent decades, in response to various economic and political developments. Contemporary views on language in education do not, of course, exist in an historical vacuum. This chapter looks at the ways in which responses to other languages in the public domain, described in chapter 2, have been mirrored in the schools of the inner-circle countries. From early colonial days to modern times, language policy has veered between tolerance and oppression; this perspective on the past is very useful in interpreting the present.

Linguistic tolerance

In the early years of colonization, attitudes to other languages were generally tolerant. It was the normal practice of the church, for instance, to use the mother tongue as the medium of education. Missionaries, it would seem, were more concerned with saving souls than building earthly kingdoms and therefore tended to take a utilitarian stance on language. In eighteenth-century Wales, the circulating schools set up by Griffith Jones to produce 'Christians and heirs to eternal life'[1] taught both children and adults to read in their mother tongue. By 1770, Wales was one of the few countries with a literate majority. In nineteenth-century Hawai'i, missionaries taught first adults and then children to read in

Hawai'ian in a network of folk schools. By 1830, half of the population was literate.[2]

The church not only taught the colonized to read the Bible in the mother tongues; it also helped preserve other languages. In the USA, parochial schools organized German-medium education in many communities in the nineteenth century.[3] Lutherans played a similar role in the education of rural German-speaking communities in Australia.[4] In Quebec, the Catholic church provided French-medium schooling for the Francophone majority until the 1960s.[5]

The church was also instrumental in the founding of schools for the Deaf where sign languages were the universal medium of instruction. The educational accomplishments of Deaf students in the nineteenth century were impressive: many went on to become teachers, artists, and professionals of various kinds.[6] Prominent Deaf figures included Douglas Tilden, one of California's finest sculptors, and Thomas Widd, the first Deaf teacher at the Protestant Montreal Deaf institution.

In the pioneer days, language policy in US education was pragmatic. Schools came under the control of towns or districts and the language of instruction was usually the language of the community. The use of German was particularly widespread and, as late as 1900, some 600,000 elementary-school children were still receiving part or all of their instruction through the language.[7] Spanish was often the language of education in California and the southwest, while all European languages were permitted in Wisconsin. Bilingual schools were officially authorized in 12 states and operated unofficially in many areas with high concentrations of other languages.

Australians were equally pragmatic and bilingual education was offered in many schools, private and secular, from the 1850s onwards. Although initially targeted at children from particular ethnic communities, they were also open to children from other language backgrounds. An advertisement in an 1865 newspaper explained that: 'Instruction is given in German and English, so that German and English people can learn one another's language.'[8]

Linguistic oppression

Pragmatism, whether driven by religion, politics or harsh conditions, helps to shape liberal attitudes to other languages. However, tolerance tends to falter at times when the majority is intent on extending or consolidating its power base. The swing from liberalism to oppression has often been swift and thorough: physical removal, corporal punishment and legislation have all been used to considerable effect to persuade linguistic minorities of the error of their ways.

Removal

The dominant English-speaking group has imposed the use of English in many different ways, the most radical and oppressive being the actual removal of children from their families. In seventeenth-century Scotland, the Statutes of Iona, a set of laws designed to Anglicize Gaelic society, required the wealthy to send their oldest sons to the Lowlands to be educated in English in Protestant schools. A document published by the Scottish Society for the Propagation of Christian Knowledge in 1696 explains the logic of the policy thus:

> Nothing can be more effectual for reducing these countries to order, and making them usefull to the Commonwealth than teaching them their duty to God, their King and countrey and rooting out their Irish language, and this has been the case of the Society so far as they could, ffor all the Schollars are taught in English.[9]

The move towards the sole use of English has been justified on various grounds. From one perspective, the minority threatens the wellbeing of the dominant group and can only be tolerated if they are prepared to become 'like us'. A central part of being like us is talking like us. From a more benign but no less flawed perspective, the minority needs to be given the opportunity to be 'like us' so that they can compete on more equal terms. But whereas Europeans were sufficiently like the Anglo-Celtic majority to constitute invisible minorities, Indigenous people were physically distinct and therefore more difficult to assimilate. Their separate treatment was justified on the grounds that they were not fully human beings and, as time went by, the desire to make them more 'like us' became particularly pressing.

The first off-reservation school for American Indians was established at Carlisle, Pennsylvania, in 1879, in an attempt to accelerate assimilation; others followed in rapid succession. White styles of dress, the Christian religion and the use of English were all rigorously imposed. Residential schools were also established across Canada for First Nations children and, by the early decades of the twentieth century, attendance was compulsory and jail sentences and fines were imposed on parents who did not comply.[10]

In the conflicts between settlers and Aboriginal peoples in nineteenth-century Australia, there was more interest in the kidnap and exploitation of Indigenous children than in their education, though some merit was seen in inculcating European values and work habits to prepare them for a life of service to colonial settlers. The first of many schools for Aboriginal children was set up at Parramatta in 1814, but boycotted by their families, who failed to see the relevance of a settled agricultural lifestyle and study of the Bible.[11] This school closed within six years; other attempts were also short-lived.

By the end of the century, European control over the lives of Aboriginal peoples was almost total. They were forced to live on reserves, and the rights to marriage and employment were closely regulated. Children were housed in same-sex dormitories and given very limited access to their families. The expressed aim was to accelerate conversion to Christianity and distance them from their traditional lifestyles. The school population often came from different language backgrounds; English quickly became the lingua franca and was the only language tolerated in both classrooms and dormitories. In the atmosphere of social Darwinism of the day, it was assumed that the full-descent population would continue to decline until it became extinct. In contrast, the mixed-descent population was clearly growing. 'Stolen generations' of mixed-race children were forcibly removed from their parents to special homes and foster families and stripped of all vestiges of their linguistic and cultural heritage.[12]

In marked contrast, the placing of Deaf children in residential schools ensured their social and linguistic development. The life-long friendships forged in residential schools also had important cultural consequences. Many students maintained an interest in their schools when their formal education was complete, choosing to make their homes and to take part in Deaf clubs in the vicinity. These Deaf clubs, in turn, form the hub of national networks for marriage and other social partnerships: an estimated 90 per cent of the Deaf, for instance, marry other Deaf people.[13]

Corporal punishment and ridicule

Another effective tool in the imposition of English was the use of corporal punishment. There are many variations on the theme. In Scotland the 'hanging stick' was placed around the neck of any child caught speaking Gaelic and, at the end of the day, the teacher beat all the children who had worn it. Corporal punishment was also commonplace in Cape Breton in Canada, which at one time had an estimated 100,000 speakers of Gaelic.[14] In Ireland, children were forced to wear tally sticks and slates on cords around their necks. Each time they used an Irish word, the teacher would make a notch on the stick or write the word on the slate. The number of notches or words was counted and punishment administered accordingly. In Wales, the Welsh Not – a wooden block – was hung round the neck of any child heard speaking Welsh in class. It was passed from one child to the next, and whoever was wearing it at the end of the day was beaten.[15]

In the USA, J. D. C. Atkins, a commissioner of Indian affairs, banned the use of Indian languages in schools, arguing that: 'The instruction of the Indians in the vernacular is not only of no use to them, but is detrimental to the cause of their education and civilization.'[16] Soap was used to wash out children's mouths when they were caught speaking their own languages. Other punishments included being forced to stand still in the schoolyard or to lie in a row across tables and be spanked.

The pattern in Canada was similar. Children in residential schools were put in solitary confinement, made to do physical labour, and humiliated by their teachers for speaking their language. Ojibway author Basil Johnston recalls the horrors of this appalling regime in particularly graphic terms:

> A kick with a police riding boot administered by a 175-pound man upon the person of an eight-year-old boy for uttering the language of a savage left its pain for days and its bruise upon the spirit for life . . . And if a boot or a fist were not administered, then a lash or a yardstick was plied until the 'Indian' language was beaten out. To boot and fist and lash was added ridicule. Both speaker and his language were assailed. 'What's the use of that language? It isn't polite to speak another language in the presence of other people. Learn English! That's the only way you're going to get ahead. How can you learn two languages at the same time? No wonder kids can't learn anything else. It's a primitive language; hasn't the vocabulary to express abstract ideas, poor. Say "ugh". Say something in your language! . . . How can you get your tongue around those sounds?' On and on the comments were made, disparaging, until in too many the language was shamed into silence and disuse.[17]

A similar regime has been applied to Spanish speakers in more recent times. Victims speak movingly of the 'deathly fear' of being 'paddled or swatted on the butt' or having their mouth washed out with soap for speaking the language during Americanization classes in Arizona, a scheme that lasted from 1919 to 1967.[18] This practice appears to be widespread. Nuns used a strap to hit children caught speaking French in public schools in the northeast USA as recently as the 1950s. A teachers' handbook for the school district in question issued the following stern warning: 'Any teacher violates her trust when she encourages children to speak anything but English at recess, around the playground, before or after school or even away from school.'[19]

Corporal punishment was, of course, just one weapon in the armoury of the powerful; verbal attacks on the moral fibre of minority speakers have been equally effective. An 1847 government inquiry into the state of education in Wales concluded that speaking Welsh was holding the people back, both materially and morally. The report was prepared by three commissioners who, by today's standards, would be considered ill-qualified for the job: they spoke no Welsh, had little understanding of working-class life and, unlike the non-conformist majority in Wales, professed the Anglican faith. One of the more outrageous claims was that Welsh women were nearly all unchaste and that non-conformist religious meetings were occasions for illicit sex.[20]

An equally demeaning practice was the use of numbers for names. Annie Meekitjuk, for instance, is an Inuit woman known as Lutaaq, Pilitaq, Palluq or Inusiq to her parents and elders. In school, however, she was known as Annie E7–121. 'Annie' was chosen because her personal name was considered too hard to pronounce. The number – her unique identifier – was engraved on a metal disc, which she wore around her neck.[21] Children attending residential schools for the Deaf in the UK have also been called by numbers within living memory.

In an age where the rights of the child are protected by both national and international laws, it is easy to assume that such outrages have been relegated to the pages of history books. But while corporal punishment is indeed a thing of the past, there is no shortage of evidence of more subtle pressure. An Irish Deaf woman tells the story of how her former principal told the manager of the large department store where she had started work that she was not allowed to sign. The manager, in turn, circulated a letter to the staff instructing them neither to sign to her, nor to accept signs. When another Deaf school leaver found a job in the same store the following year, the manager gave instructions that they were not to meet during break times.[22]

There are still occasional cases of teachers reprimanding children for using their home languages. A Spanish-speaking child about to enter a US kindergarten recently asked: 'Do you know if I can speak Spanish in school? Marcy told me that if you use Spanish words in school . . . the teacher punishes you. She said three "Mejicanos" could not go out to play . . . because they kept forgetting. Can you find out if I will be punished too?'[23]

Legislation

The introduction of compulsory education in the nineteenth century was an important turning point. When schooling was the responsibility of the family, attitudes towards the language of instruction were flexible. As control was more centralized, formal schooling became another instrument in the imposition of English.

The Celtic languages were greatly weakened by legislation requiring English to be the sole medium of instruction.[24] When the 1870 Education Act brought Welsh elementary schools in line with provision in England, Welsh speakers represented over 70 per cent of the population. By the turn of the century, they made up slightly under half. Compulsory education was by no means the only factor in this dramatic decline but, none the less, it played a significant role. So, too, did the system of payment by results introduced in 1861, which assessed performance in arithmetic and reading and writing in English, but not in Welsh. From this point onwards there was no incentive to teach the language.

The introduction of a non-sectarian education system, paid for by taxes, was an important landmark in the USA, too. The impact was minimal at first and parents remained unconvinced of the merits of the new system for some time. During this period, immigrants were viewed as potential consumers who needed to be accommodated, particularly in areas where children were attending private academies that offered education in other languages. With the passage of time, however, religious schools declined and public schools grew, both in numbers and in influence. As quotas for filling classrooms were reached, the needs of immigrants were placed lower on the political agenda, a trend encouraged by increasing xenophobia and concern about the need to curb immigration. Laws mandating English as the sole language of instruction began appearing on the statute books in the late 1880s and by 1920 some 37 states had passed legislation of this kind.[25]

Sectarian and language issues overlapped to some extent, since many Germans were also Catholic. Groups such as the Know-Nothing Party and the American Protective Association campaigned against the parochial schools and contributed to the demise of German instruction in a number of cities. The efforts of the Americanization movement, which stressed the links between speaking English and citizenship, together with the onset of World War I, sealed the fate of other languages in education.[26] By the 1930s bilingual instruction of any kind had virtually disappeared.

Court actions at the time give useful insights into the complexity of the situation. In the 1924 case of *Meyer v. Nebraska*, Robert Meyer, a teacher in a parochial school in Nebraska, was convicted of violating a 1919 statute mandating English-only instruction when he taught a Bible story in German.[27] In a seemingly contradictory ruling, the Supreme Court overturned the conviction of the lower court as a violation of Meyer's civil liberties but, at the same time, upheld the power of the state to specify the language of instruction. Objections to foreign-language teaching were by no means limited to German. Attempts – albeit unsuccessful – were made to ban Chinese, Japanese and Korean private language schools in Hawai'i and California on the grounds that efforts to promote heritage languages and cultures would produce untrustworthy Americans.

Events unfolded in Australia in a very similar way. Between 1872 and 1880, state education was established as free, compulsory, secular and in English in most of the colonies, and religious and private schools thus became the last bastion of bilingual education. Although the educational balance was moving unmistakably towards English-only, by the turn of the century there were still almost a hundred bilingual schools, mainly in South Australia and Victoria. The same xenophobic impulses that marked US public policy at this time were also very much in evidence in Australia. During World War I, education acts in various Australian states banned the use of languages other than English as the medium of instruction. In 1919, Frank Tate, the director of education for Victoria, expressed his opposition to the teaching of religion in German on the grounds that impressionable young children might develop a 'respect and devotion to a foreign language which will alienate them from English'.[28] Other languages survived only in Saturday schools.

It is no accident that the first significant challenge to the use of sign languages in education came at the same time as attempts to control other minority languages. Unfortunately, the implications for the Deaf were even further reaching: the imposition of a purely oral education almost led to the total disintegration of the Deaf community. The death knell for sign languages was first sounded at the Second International Congress on Education of the Deaf in Milan in 1880. By this time there was a growing body of opinion that deafness was a pathological con-dition that must be cured. The president of the Royal Institute for the Deaf in Milan set the tone for the congress with the assertion that 'the manual alphabet and the use of signs will be no more . . . the word will conquer; it is a privilege of man, the sole and certain vehicle of thought, the gift of God'.[29] Oralist policies, which focused exclusively on the need to teach speech, were implemented with varying degrees of speed and enthusiasm. Most Deaf schools in southern England, Australia and the

USA, for instance, were using an Oralist approach by 1900, though Catholic institutions in the Irish Republic continued to teach in sign until the 1960s.

Challenges to the status quo

By the early decades of the twentieth century, legislative efforts had ensured that English-only policies were firmly in place. There were, however, important exceptions to this general trend. In Ireland, bilingual education was introduced into primary schools in Irish-speaking areas in 1906 and, when the Irish Free State was established in 1921, Irish language teaching was, predictably, a key policy.[30] By the mid-1930s, between 25 and 30 per cent of children were attending Irish-immersion schools and a further quarter was being taught more than two subjects through the medium of Irish. The state was not responsible for secondary education at this time, but the Irish-language requirement for entry to the National University and Public Service was a powerful incentive for continued study. The fate of Irish in the Republic stands in marked contrast to that in Northern Ireland. Here an internal memo from the minister of education in 1928 expressed the view that 'we should avoid carefully the impression that we desire to encourage the teaching of [Irish]'.[31]

Elsewhere, too, there was evidence of unease with English-only policies. The first challenge to the status quo in the USA came with the recommendations of the Meriam Report in 1928 that the language of the Indian child should be 'taken into account'.[32] The Indian Service Summer School in 1936 offered classes in Sioux and Navajo; there were also demonstration classes in bilingual education. These gains were short-lived and by 1944 the House Indian Affairs Committee was advising a return to earlier policies.

The Deaf community also offered some resistance. The British Deaf and Dumb Association protested indignantly 'against the imputation . . . that the finger and signed language is barbarous' and presented to King Edward VII a petition with over 1,000 signatures calling for the restoration of signing to Deaf education.[33] Their protests were ignored. Some schools banned sign language only in the classroom; in others, sign was outlawed even in student dormitories. Among the first casualties of Oralism were the born-Deaf teachers who had played a prominent role in Deaf education prior to the Congress of Milan. In the UK, they were eliminated altogether; in the USA, they fared a little better but, even at the zenith of Oralism in 1920s, as few as 15 per cent of teachers were Deaf.

Within half a century, Oralism was the unchallenged orthodoxy; successful Deaf professionals disappeared into history.

The dawn of a new age

In chapter 2, we saw how attitudes to the use of languages in public life were determined in the main by pragmatic concerns. At times when the English-speaking majority needed new sources of labour to fuel expansion, attitudes were a great deal more accommodating than when the economy was in recession or in response to unwelcome developments of the world political stage. The same patterns are easily discernible in educational policies for minority-language students. Despite differences in local conditions, there are striking similarities between the responses of all the inner-circle countries.

Although opposition to English-only education policies was widespread in the first half of the twentieth century, it was poorly organized and ineffective. In the second half of the century, various developments – the post-colonial independence of new nations, the civil rights movement in the United States, United Nations work on human rights, and mass communication which made the reporting of events almost instantaneous – were helping to make the world a very different place. Speakers of languages that had effectively been cleansed from schools and classrooms began asserting their rights to express their cultural identity in ways they felt appropriate. Ethnic revival in Indigenous and established communities in turn affected attitudes to the languages spoken by the large numbers of migrants arriving to bolster the economies of inner-circle countries. This new world order had an enormous impact on language and education, and it is to this that we turn next.

Notes

1   Davies (1993: 307).
2   www.ahapunanaleo.org/OL.htm
3   Kloss (1998); Rippley (1976).
4   Clyne (1991).
5   Bélanger (2000).
6   Carbin (1996).
7   Crawford (2000: 100).
8   Example translated by Clyne (1991: 8).

 9   Cited in Withers (1988: 122).
10   Buti (2001).
11   Fletcher (1989).
12   HREOC (1997).
13   Paddy Ladd (personal communication).
14   Cummins and Danesi (1990: 11).
15   Smith (1999: 182–3).
16   Atkins (1887: xxi–xxiii).
17   Johnston (1990).
18   Cited in Monaghan (2003).
19   Education Alliance at Brown University (2003b).
20   Davies (1993: 391–3); Peate et al. (1998: 92).
21   Hanson (undated).
22   Ladd (2003).
23   Díaz Soto et al. (1999).
24   Smith (1999).
25   Crawford (1999).
26   Higham (1988: ch. 9).
27   Del Valle (2003).
28   Clyne (1991: 13).
29   Istituto di Scienze e Tecnologie della Cognizione (undated).
30   Ó Dochartaigh (2000).
31   Andrews (1991).
32   Meriam (1928).
33   British Sign Language Info-Web (undated).

6

Language and education in the modern world

Educational policies on minority languages today vary a great deal not only from one country to another but according to the language. It is ironic that, as Indigenous and established languages struggle for survival, the very education systems that engineered their decline are now helping to repair the damage. When parents have limited fluency, 'immersion' schooling in the early years is the only way to ensure that children acquire the language. New minorities face different realities. For many teachers, the most urgent need is to ensure that children acquire a sound knowledge of English as quickly as possible. Parents share this aim but, in many cases, also want their children to continue speaking the languages of the home. Speakers of marginalized languages form another important group. The distinctive language of African Caribbeans in the UK and Canada and of African Americans in the USA has long been dismissed as inferior to standard English. So, too, have Hawai'ian Creole English and Australian Aboriginal English. Sign languages have traditionally enjoyed even lower status and it is only in very recent times that they have been recognized as languages at all.

Schools in inner-circle countries in the modern world serve multilingual populations. This chapter, then, looks at the ways they have responded to the needs of diverse groups of children.

Indigenous languages

As issues of social equity made their way up the political agenda, Indigenous languages appeared increasingly on the curriculum as part of second-language programmes. However, with the dramatic shift to English in recent generations, children who speak an Indigenous language when they arrive in school are very much the exception to the rule. Second-language instruction is simply not enough to ensure that children become fluent speakers; nor is it sensitive to demands that Indigenous peoples should be responsible for the education of their children.

Political activism played a major part in establishing Māori as a language of education in Aotearoa/New Zealand.[1] In 1972, Nga Tamatoa, a Māori lobby group, presented a petition to parliament calling for Māori language courses in schools. Continued pressure led to the establishment of the first bilingual school at Ruatoki in 1977, followed by similar developments in other tribal areas. Further government responses included the setting up of bilingual units; Taha Māori (Māori-enriched) programmes where students learn Māori songs, greetings and simple words; and the teaching of Māori as a subject. All options are open to both Māori and Pakeha (or non-Māori) children.[2]

The most significant developments, however, have come from within the Māori community. The leaders' priority was to reattach the language to the people at community level. Te kohanga reo, or language nests, where pre-school children are immersed in the language, were established by parents in the early 1980s and are staffed by Māori-speaking parents, grandparents and caregivers. They follow a curriculum that validates Māori knowledge, learning styles and administrative practices. It is no accident that Māori enrolments in pre-school education have greatly increased since the introduction of the language nests. The levels of fluency achieved are impressive, with 5-year-olds in language nests outperforming 15-year-old students in state oral exams.[3]

Parents anxious to maintain the gains made by their children in the language nests pressed for the setting up of kura kaupapa Māori – Māori-medium primary schools. The first kura kaupapa opened in Auckland in the late 1980s and by 1999 they numbered 60.[4] The demand, however, still far outstrips the places available, and there is no legislative requirement to provide Māori-medium education at the secondary level. The success of Māori communities working independently of government to identify the needs of Māori learners is leading many activists to argue for an independent Māori education authority.

In Australia, the return of a Labor government in 1972 marked the start of a willingness to engage with Aboriginal languages in education. On a visit to schools in the Northern Territory, Kim Beasley Senior, the minister for education at the time, was impressed by the fact that students taught in their own language in a mission school were far more responsive than students taught in English in government schools.[5] A convert to bilingual education, the minister proposed legislation allowing students in the Northern Territory to be taught in their own languages when this accorded with their parents' wishes. Within two years, programmes had been established in 22 different Aboriginal languages.

The original bilingual education programmes were intended to help children acquire English rather than maintain their own languages and cultures. Over time, however, the emphasis began to change.[6] In the early days, schools had adopted a team-teaching approach, with non-Aboriginal teachers responsible for the delivery of the curriculum in English and Aboriginal teachers for delivery in Aboriginal languages. As more Aboriginal people qualified as teachers, the team-teaching approach came under more careful scrutiny, partly because it was cheaper to employ one teacher than two and partly because Aboriginal teachers were now able to deliver the curriculum in both English and their own language. Differences in opinion emerged about the goals of bilingual education, with Aboriginal teachers tending to favour the cultural maintenance model, which promoted both English and the Aboriginal language, and non-Aboriginal teachers tending to attach more importance to using the Aboriginal language simply to help children make a successful transition to English. As was the case for the Māori in Aotearoa/New Zealand, control of education became an important issue, with growing numbers of Aboriginal head teachers and parent bodies.

Political support for bilingual education became increasingly uncertain following the election of a conservative government in 1996. The decision to replace bilingual programs for Aboriginal students in the Northern Territory in 1998 with classes in English as a Second Language (ESL) gave rise to particular consternation.[7] The reason for the closure of these programmes was alleged poor standards in English literacy in bilingual schools, in comparison with English-only schools. However, no statistical data was offered to support this claim. There would also seem to be a fundamental misunderstanding about the nature of existing provision, since bilingual programmes have always included the teaching of ESL. Although Northern Territory education minister Peter Adamson claimed that the cuts had overwhelming support from the Aboriginal communities, responses from the communities themselves would suggest that this was not the case. Protestors delivered the largest petition in the history of the Northern Territory parliament. The 20 communities most directly affected marshalled arguments appealing to their human and linguistic rights. Significantly, the review panel that made the recommendations for closure consisted of four government appointees from outside those communities. Things would appear to have changed little in this respect since three Anglican, middle-class, English-speaking commissioners presented their report on education in non-conformist, working-class, Welsh-speaking Wales in the nineteenth century.[8]

It is interesting to speculate on the reasons for the about-face.[9] The axing of bilingual curricula in public schools has much to recommend itself as a cost-cutting measure that would save the government $A3.7 million. The relative success of bilingual programmes also threatens European hegemony. They have, for instance, encouraged greater participation of Aboriginal peoples through the training and hiring of teachers and assistants, providing them with a stable economic base. Land-ownership issues have also been raised as a possible reason for resistance. It is arguably in the interests of non-Aboriginal peoples in the Northern Territory to extinguish knowledge of Aboriginal languages, since many land claims have failed when there has been insufficient linguistic evidence of ownership.

The First Nations of Canada have similar concerns about community control. A 1972 policy document issued by the National Indian Brotherhood[10] set out the need to recognize parents' responsibility for their children's education and the importance of a good grounding in ancestral languages. A wide range of immersion programmes in Indigenous languages is now available. Most provision, however, is in the form of second-language programmes, which are unlikely to be effective in reversing language shift. In recognition of the seriousness of the situation, the Assembly of First Nations (AFN) passed a resolution in 1998 declaring a state of emergency. A Languages Secretariat has now been set up for the protection, promotion and enhancement of First Nations languages.

American Indians first took control of their children's education in 1966. As part of the federal War on Poverty programme, the Rough Rock Demonstration School was set up under local management on the Navajo reservation in Arizona. Parents and community leaders were responsible for a programme that offered initial literacy in Navajo, a medicine-man training project and various community initiatives.[11] Several legislative developments, and in particular the 1975 Indian Self-Determination and Educational Assistance Act, paved the way for other communities to set up similar programmes. Although beset with financial problems, the Rough Rock project was a beacon for the future development of local control, and many other communities have followed the example. Progress, however, has been disappointingly slow. Although it has been government policy to promote and protect American Indian languages since the passage of the 1990 Native American Language Act (NALA), implementation has been hampered by the lack of funding.[12] In the first year, a mere $US5 million was allocated to language projects and the training of teachers, translators and interpreters. In the second year, the budget was reduced to $US2 million. In addition, grants awarded under the NALA cannot exceed 80 per cent of the cost of the project and, in very many cases, the community cannot raise the remaining 20 per cent. Government commitment, it would seem, is more rhetorical than real.

Most initiatives rely heavily on the involvement of elders. In Montana, the state can certify elders as language specialists, allowing them to teach in public schools without a four-year degree; the Oregon legislature has approved a similar law. The Tribal Colleges movement has also made an important contribution to language revitalization. The movement started with the Navajo Community College in 1969 and now includes 31 colleges in the USA and one in Canada.

Community involvement is also central in Hawai'i.[13] In the early 1980s, fewer than 50 children under the age of 18 were fluent in Hawai'ian and most of the estimated 2,000 native speakers were over the age of 50. A small group of parents banded together to set up the first Hawai'ian-medium pre-schools in private homes. Participants in the Aha Pünana Leo movement show a very high level of commitment. In order to produce bilingual, biliterate children, the school day extends over 10 hours, and only Hawai'ian is spoken. Parents attend weekly classes so that they can reinforce the use of the language at home. They are also required to offer eight hours a month of service in kind to the school.

The state response to these developments was slow. A ban on the use of Hawai'ian was still on the statute books, and it took a boycott of the public school system in 1986 to overturn the law. Parental efforts finally prevailed and the State Department of Education now offers 10 pre-schools and 14 schools with immersion classes. The first students in over a hundred years to be educated entirely in Hawai'ian graduated in 1999, at which point there were approximately 2,000 students enrolled in programs taught through Hawai'ian, at all levels from pre-school to high school. In spite of these achievements, parents and language activists feel the need to exert continuing pressure to ensure that provision meets their needs.

Established languages

Established minorities have much in common with Indigenous peoples. Urbanization has resulted in the fragmentation of the traditional heartlands of the language and the numbers of speakers have rapidly declined. For children whose parents now speak only English, school is the main point of contact with the language. Wales is an interesting case in point.[14] Campaigns for bilingual schooling have received support from all sections of the community: Welsh-speaking parents are concerned about their ability to transmit the language to their children in the face of growing pressure from English; English-speaking parents want their children to benefit from access to two languages and cultures. Both groups of parents believe their children will have better employment prospects in a country where increasing numbers of jobs in both the public and private sectors require bilingual and biliterate skills.

Demand for Welsh-medium education has gained considerable momentum since the first school was opened in 1947. Early successes gave growing numbers of families the confidence to make this the preferred option for their children. One in five primary school children is now taught in Welsh, and over 50 secondary schools teach a substantial number of subjects through the medium of Welsh. The 1988 Education Reform Act has further strengthened the position of the language by stipulating that all children in English-medium schools between the ages of 5 and 16 must study Welsh, with a compulsory public exam in the language at age 16. Census figures leave little doubt as to the effectiveness of these developments, and much of the increase in both the numbers and proportion of Welsh speakers reported in the 2001 census can be attributed to bilingual education. At the tertiary level, teacher training is available through the medium of Welsh; so, too, are degree courses in Welsh language and literature and several other subjects. A range of options is also available to adults, from learning experiences modelled on the Israeli 'ulpan', or intensive courses, to evening classes.

Pre-school provision has been a very important focus for those involved in Welsh-medium education. Mudiad Ysgolion Meithrin (the Nursery Education Movement) plays a crucial role in preparing children from families where English is the first language for immersion schooling.[15] There are currently almost 600 playgroups with places for about 14,000 children between the ages of 2 and 5. The playgroups are fed, in turn, by a growing network of parents, carers and children, who meet in Cylchoedd Ti a Fi to socialize in an informal Welsh atmosphere. Welsh nursery education has been an important model for parallel developments in Gaelic pre-school provision in Scotland and for the naíonraí or Irish-language nursery school movement in Ireland.[16]

Evaluation of Welsh-medium education is problematic. The Department for Education and Skills does not currently publish comparative data for bilingual and English-medium schools and access to government-owned data by independent researchers is difficult. The public perception is, however, that the outcomes of Welsh-medium education are good. It has been suggested that central government inaction on this issue is due to concern that any analysis which shows bilingual education in a favourable light would create pressure for resources to be moved from English-medium, a development that would probably be resisted by the mono-lingual majority.[17]

Gaelic-medium primary education was first introduced in the tradi-tional heartlands of the language in Scotland in the mid-1970s, and soon followed in the wake of Gaels who had migrated to urban and Lowland areas. There is a clear mandate from parents for Gaelic-medium education: most believe that children can become bilingual without any disadvantage to their achievement in English and about half would be prepared to enrol their children in Gaelic-medium units if they were available.[18] The Parents' Charter introduced by the federal conservative government in 1994 made it increasingly difficult to resist consumer pressure and, by 2003–4, there were 60 Gaelic units – schools or special classes attached to English-medium schools – throughout Scotland, with Gaelic-medium classes increasingly continuing through to secondary education. At the tertiary level, it is possible to study for a degree in Gaelic and in Celtic studies; courses in teacher training, business, management, the arts, broad-casting and information technology are also available through Gaelic. In addition, there is an extensive network of adult courses.

In Ireland, early gains in establishing Irish as a language of education proved ephemeral and by 1980 only 3 per cent of secondary students were receiving Irish-medium education. Arguably, the government had too much confidence in the ability of schools to Gaelicize the country and overlooked the importance of creating opportunities to use the language in daily life. While there has been a rapid rise in the number of Irish-medium primary schools, provision at post-primary level remains limited.[19]

Yet Irish remains a badge of identity in spite of its decline. The situ-ation is particularly interesting in Northern Ireland. Here Irish was taught as a subject in only a small number of Catholic schools, and the sole Irish-medium school in Ulster was organized by parents in Belfast. Ironic-ally, the main informal learning of the language took place in H-Block of the Maze Prison, where Republicans protested at their classification as criminal rather than political prisoners.[20] Bobby Sands, who later died following a hunger strike, taught others Irish by shouting the lessons up and down the wing: 'students' wrote on toilet paper and walls, or tried to commit the lesson to memory. Since most officials spoke only English, the study of Irish became a vital part of resistance to the prison regime. Such was the success of their efforts that, when the protests ended, prisoners set up a formal education programme, which they organized themselves.

The main breakthrough for Irish in the wider Northern Ireland community, however, came with the Good Friday Agreement of 1998 between the governments of the UK and Ireland. The legislation which followed now places a duty on the Department for Education and Skills to promote Irish medium education; and the UK government recognizes both 'the importance of the Irish language to many people in Northern Ireland' and its contribution to 'the cultural identity and heritage of Northern Ireland's children'.[21] There are currently 18 Irish-medium schools (15 primary and three secondary) with 2,598 pupils, and 10 Irish-medium primary units within larger schools, with plans for others to follow. At the tertiary level, two universities offer courses in Irish language and literature and one teacher-training college provides for the teaching of Irish.

Francophones in Canada

The position of Francophones in Canada is rather different. Here the French language has not only held its ground over several centuries but has greatly strengthened its position. The traditional focus for Francophone identity in Canada was religion rather than language. This focus shifted to language when a Ministry of Education was established in Quebec in 1963 with responsibility for both French-speaking Catholic and English-speaking Protestant schools. Much public debate around this time centred on the need to maintain Quebec as a bulwark against the all-engulfing tide of English, and language lay at the centre of a fierce political battle.

The spark for one of the most explosive debacles of recent times was the growing number of so-called Allophones – speakers of languages other than French and English – arriving in the province, most of whom were choosing English-medium instruction for their children.[22] Many Francophones wanted to extend French-medium education to the Allophones, a suggestion which was resisted by Anglophones and Allophones alike, and which led ultimately to a violent confrontation in a suburb of Montreal. A series of new laws succeeded only in inflaming the situation further. When the Quebec government passed Bill 63, which reaffirmed parents' right to choose the language of instruction, Francophones showed their dissatisfaction by bringing down the government in the provincial elections of 1970. The bill also acted as a trigger for the kidnapping of a diplomat and the assassination of a Quebec cabinet minister by separatists. In 1974, Quebec passed Bill 22, the Official Language Act: parents no longer had the right to choose the language of instruction and English-language tests were introduced for Allophone children who wanted to attend English-medium schools. Predictably, this development met resistance from many Allophones *and* Anglophones. In 1978 the Charter of the French Language (Bill 101) threw the ball back into the Francophone court, stipulating that only children whose parents or older siblings had attended school in English in Quebec had the right to attend English-medium public schools. Subsequently, this stipulation was deemed unconstitutional and the courts ruled that parents educated in English in other provinces should have the same rights as parents in Quebec.

While much of the debate has taken place in Quebec, other provinces have also needed to address the language issue. A specific requirement of the 1982 Canadian Charter of Rights and Freedoms is that children of families with an official minority-language background should have the right to schooling in their home language. This means that Francophone children have the right to French-medium schooling in provinces such as Ontario or British Columbia, while Anglophone families in Quebec or regions of New Brunswick have the right to English-medium schooling.[23]

Canadian Francophones, then, are the only minority in the inner-circle countries not only to have maintained their right to educate their children in the language of the home, but also to have influenced the language education of the English-speaking majority. Their success is due in part to their numerical strength and their territorial base in Quebec. It can also be attributed to the Quiet Revolution, which established Francophones for the first time in their history as a serious economic force, able to exert political pressure.

New minority languages

For Indigenous and established minorities, the priority has been to maintain minority languages. The focus for the new minorities has been rather different. Here the assumption is that children should acquire English as quickly as possible and the main issue has been how this can best be achieved.

Policy and practice in the 1950s and 1960s was laissez-faire; the unquestioned assumption was that children would 'pick up English in the playground' and that the language of the home had no place in schools. The report of a 1960 inquiry into the 'progress and assimilation of

In the 1960s and 1970s, the assumption was that newly arrived children would pick up English in the playground; they were allowed to sink or swim. Photograph by Dave Andrews.

migrant children in Australia' is typical of the thinking of the day. Parents were encouraged to speak English at home, irrespective of their own levels of fluency.[24] No information was gathered by schools on birthplace or home language, a policy that was justified on the grounds that 'once they are enrolled in school, they are, from our point of view, Australian children'.[25]

It was some time before the consequences of inaction were finally acknowledged: far too many children exposed to 'submersion English' were sinking rather than swimming. In the UK, funding to address the language-learning needs of New Commonwealth children first became available in 1966. Teaching took place in special reception centres or 'withdrawal' classes in the same school, and the sole emphasis was on learning English. In Australia, the Child Migrant Education Program was finally set up in 1971. No attention was paid in either country to the linguistic and cultural capital which children brought with them to the classroom.

New arrivals in the USA at this time included large numbers of Spanish speakers. 'Pull-out' classes were introduced, where students were given ESL instruction away from regular classrooms, but this provision was very uneven and, even in the late 1960s, only a very small proportion of children were in programmes of this kind.[26] Even where pull-out classes were available, there was little evidence of their effectiveness and dropout rates were high. The role of other languages in education was first recognized in the wake of the 1964 Civil Rights Act. Title VI of the act made it illegal to exclude any person from participation in federal programmes on the grounds of race, colour or national origin. Within a short space of time, Hispanic groups in the southwest had begun to file lawsuits requiring schools to address the language needs of children who had been left to sink or swim in English-only classrooms.

The role of federal government in US language policy is to defend individual civil rights. In Canada, in contrast, the federal role is to arbitrate between the two largest language groups, Francophones and Anglophones, and speakers of other languages have tended to be overlooked. The first official recognition of the needs of Allophones came with the 1971 Multiculturalism Act, which pledged to promote respect for all languages and cultures across the country and was clearly intended to minimize the backlash from other groups to the declaration of French and English as official languages.[27]

Similar developments were already under way in the UK. The 1975 Bullock Report, *A Language for Life*, made an impassioned plea for schools to respect the cultural and linguistic diversity of their students: 'No child should be expected to cast off the language and culture of the home as he crosses the school threshold and the curriculum should reflect those aspects of his life.' Bilingualism was presented as an asset to be nurtured and schools were encouraged to 'help maintain and deepen . . . knowledge of the mother tongues'.[28] Other developments added weight to the recommendations of the Bullock Report. A directive from the Council of Europe required member states to promote the teaching of the mother tongue of the children of migrant workers 'in accordance with national circumstances and legal systems'.[29] The UK response was sluggish, and in 1984 only 2.2 per cent of primary-aged children from other language backgrounds were receiving home-language teaching in school.[30] None the less, a growing emphasis was placed on developing children's full linguistic repertoire, and language teaching was expanded to include the teaching of non-traditional languages. These developments were intended to speed children's acquisition of English rather than as a worthwhile exercise in their own right.

UK attitudes towards bilingualism are inconsistent. Official support is given to education through the medium of Welsh in Wales, Gaelic in

Scotland and Irish in Ireland, where the aim is balanced bilingualism and full biliteracy. The possibility of extending bilingual education to other languages, however, received a body blow with the publication in 1985 of the Swann Report, *Education for All*, which recommended that there should be no separate provision for language-maintenance programmes.[31] In the belief that any attempt to promote minority languages in the mainstream was potentially divisive, the main responsibility was placed on ethnic minority communities themselves. There were two exceptions to this policy. The first was that, where practicable, children should be provided with 'bilingual support' – classroom assistants or teachers able to speak to them in their own language and help them make the transition from home to school; the second was the inclusion of non-traditional languages in the curriculum of secondary schools where there was suffi-cient demand. Official policy deviated little in the next twenty years.[32] At a grassroots level, there was a great deal of experimentation into ways in which other languages might be used in the classroom, and, a growing emphasis on anti-racist teaching initiatives. However, new requirements for funding ensured that the sole emphasis was on English-language teaching once more.[33]

In Australia, events took a rather different course.[34] Concern for social equity was reinforced by the quest for a new national identity. As ties with Britain were gradually loosened, a new policy of 'unity in diversity' challenged traditional notions of nationality. The debate was broadened from the language-learning needs of individuals to multicultural educa-tion for all. The 1976 report of the Committee on the Teaching of Migrant Languages in School, for instance, recommended not only that schools should meet the continuing needs of migrant children to learn their own languages but that all children should have the opportunity to learn other languages from the earliest years of primary school. Ongoing activism on the part of ethnic minority communities, linguists and other intellectuals led ultimately to the groundbreaking National Policy on Languages in 1987.[35] The policy was based on four main principles: availability of English and English literacy for all; support for Aboriginal and Torres Strait Island (ATSI) languages; a language other than English for all; and access for all to equitable language services. One of its more notable achievements was the way in which other languages were presented as complementary – and not subordinated – to English. Subsequent fine-tuning reduced the impact of the original manifesto. The subtitle of the 1991 White Paper, *The Australian Language and Literacy Policy*, gives important clues about new priorities, with the change from *languages* to *language* and the addition of *literacy*.[36] Although many of the original commitments remained, the notion of the nation's languages as an important cultural resource was considerably underplayed.[37]

Work on a national languages policy, following similar principles to those of the Australian document, also took place in Aotearoa/New Zealand. When *Aoteareo: Speaking for Ourselves*[38] was published in 1992, it identified several priority areas: revitalization of the Māori language; adult literacy; ESL and language maintenance for children; adult ESL; national capabilities in international languages; and the provision of services in other languages, as a temporary measure for new settlers and a permanent arrangement for Deaf people. The Ministry of Education, however, distanced itself from the report by publishing it under the author's name rather than as a government paper, and no official languages policy was ever adopted. None the less, various education policies, including the Ten Point Plan for Māori education and the Aotearoa/New Zealand Curriculum Framework, were essentially in harmony with the proposals contained in *Aoteareo*.[39]

Bilingual education in the USA

One development in the USA deserves particular attention. From the early 1960s, teachers were actively exploring alternative solutions to the problems faced by non-English-speaking children, including bilingual education. Middle-class Cuban refugees in Florida were among the earliest to demand changes in their children's education.[40] The first experimental bilingual programme was opened to Spanish- and English-speaking students at the Coral Way Elementary School in 1963. Cuban children were taught in Spanish in the morning and English in the afternoon; English-speaking children spent the morning in English and the afternoon in Spanish. The two groups were mixed for art, music, recess and lunch. Significantly, both groups achieved the same level as or higher than their counterparts in mainstream schools. The success of Coral Way led to similar programmes across the country.

The enthusiasm of educators soon attracted political support and in 1967 some 37 bills dealing with bilingual education were introduced in Congress. In particular, the Bilingual Education Act (BEA) was passed by a large margin and became law in January 1968. As more money became available for the implementation of the act, the Department of Health, Education and Welfare began developing guidelines, and in 1970 a memorandum was issued requiring school districts with at least a 5 per cent minority student population to comply with the law. While some districts took the necessary steps, others did nothing. It rapidly became clear that something stronger than a memorandum would be necessary to ensure compliance with the law.

The first significant legal challenge grew out of the frustrations of the Chinese community in San Francisco. There was growing anger that children were being offered little or no support in school; large numbers of young people were dropping out and becoming involved in street gangs.[41] Edward Steinman, a poverty lawyer, first learned about the problems faced by Chinese children in the city's schools in 1969 from Kam Wai Lau, whose 6-year old son Kinney was one of at least 1,800 Chinese-speaking children who were receiving no language support in school. Steinman began legal action, and Kinney Kinmon Lau was the head plaintiff in a class-action suit on behalf of Chinese-heritage students against the San Francisco Unified School District, which argued that the students were disadvantaged because they could not understand the language of instruction. After a series of defeats in lower courts, the Supreme Court finally sided with Lau in 1974.

Procedures to be followed by school boards for the implementation of this judgement were first outlined in the so-called Lau Remedies and later spelled out in official regulations published by the Office of Civil Rights. Students dominant in a language other than English were to be placed in bilingual programmes; English-dominant students could be placed in English-only programmes; students with equal proficiency in two languages could choose either an English-only or a bilingual programme. Compliance with the Lau decision, however, was patchy.

Shortages of trained teachers and teaching materials meant that bilingual education programmes remained an option for a relatively small proportion of students. Only a third to a half of these students were receiving any instruction in their native language in two main kinds of programme: early-exit and late-exit. Early-exit – or transitional – bilingual programmes provide initial instruction in the children's first language, in the early stages of learning to read and also for purposes of clarification. First-language instruction is phased out rapidly, so that most students are in mainstream classes by the end of first or second grade. In late-exit programmes, which continue throughout elementary school, students receive part of their instruction in their first language, even when they have achieved fluency in English. Early-exit programmes tend to view children's home languages as a problem to be solved; late-exit models consider home languages a resource.

While the public was relatively content to support transitional bilingual programmes, there was considerable opposition to the use of federal funds for maintenance programmes. Proponents of bilingual education received a body blow when Ronald Reagan, a firm advocate of English submersion, became president in 1981. The reauthorizations of the BEA in the 1980s began to give greater prominence to English-language programmes, as political pressure against bilingual education grew. Faced with the erosion of support, senators in favour of bilingual education ordered a study by the General Accounting Office, which reported in 1987 that bilingual education programmes *were* effective.[42] In a compromise move, Congress stopped short of bringing bilingual education programmes to an end but agreed that English-only programmes would qualify for the same federal funds.

Bilingual education has become a political football in a highly volatile and ideologically driven debate. Critics argue that this approach creates a cycle of dependency on the first language that slows student progress in English. They also contend that bilingual education accentuates divisions within American society. Advocates of bilingual education highlight the social, cognitive and academic benefits. They argue, for instance, that the maintenance of the first language in no way impedes the acquisition of other languages and that content taught in the native language can be transferred to the second language. In contrast, children in English-only classrooms are often unable to access either the content or the language.[43]

Attempts to evaluate studies of bilingual and immersion education have done little to clarify the situation. Some critics argue that the great majority of studies are so fundamentally flawed that their findings are useless.[44] Take, for instance, the review of research undertaken by Rossell and Baker, which is frequently cited by opponents of bilingual education.[45] Programmes in El Paso, which they labelled as 'English immersion' and found superior to bilingual education, were in fact taught through the medium of the children's home language for a substantial part of the day. Similarly, many of the studies described as examples of transitional bilingual programmes were in fact Canadian French immersion programmes, typically targeted at English speakers. Two large-scale longitudinal studies, in contrast, offer strong support for language-maintenance programmes. The first examined the progress of 2,000 children over four years in three kinds of programme – English immersion, and early-exit and late-exit bilingual education – and found that late-exit programmes were most beneficial.[46] The second study, based on the records of 700,000 minority-language students between 1982 and 1990, also found that late-exit programmes delivered the best results.[47]

The bilingual debate is clearly more influenced by political concerns than by the findings of researchers. Leading figures such as Ron Unz, who funds English-only campaigns with his personal fortune, accuse pro-bilingual researchers of 'making things up', a position which has clearly gained credence with many sections of the media. Between 1984 and 1994, 87 per cent of academic publications had conclusions favourable to bilingual education, compared with only 45 per cent of media reports in the same period.[48] A large proportion of the American public has been persuaded by the arguments of the media. In 1998, California voters approved Proposition 227, an initiative that largely eliminated bilingual education from the state's public schools. Arizona followed in 2000 with a measure similar to the California initiative, Proposition 203. Unz also funded the unsuccessful campaign for Amendment 31 to the Colorado constitution, which would, among other things, have invited lawsuits against educators and public officials who failed to observe the English-only mandate, holding them personally liable for financial damages and removing them from their jobs for at least five years.[49]

After 34 years of controversy, the BEA was finally replaced in 2002 by Title III of No Child Left Behind, in which the sole emphasis is on the rapid acquisition of English. The National Clearinghouse for Bilingual Education became the National Clearinghouse for English Language Acquisition and Language Instruction Educational Programs, with the memorable acronym NCELALIEP. The intention is to establish 'measur-able achievement objectives', and to punish failure to show progress in annual English assessments. There is a real danger, then, that the new law could be used as a weapon by those who wish to dismantle native-language programmes. It is no accident that opposition to bilingual education has coincided with the highest levels of immigration since the early twentieth century and with rapid growth in the Latino population. Significantly, the English-only movement has no objection to bilingual programmes for Native Americans and their endangered languages: unlike Hispanics, these groups represent no threat to the dominance of English.

Bilingual education in the US is notable both for the accompanying political furore and for its preoccupation with providing only transitional support for learning English. Bilingual education in Australia, in contrast, emphasizes bilingualism as a personal and national resource, rather than as an anti-poverty measure. Canada also favours the cultural maintenance model. Alberta, Manitoba and Saskatchewan all offer Ukrainian and German bilingual programmes. Hebrew, Yiddish, Polish, Chinese and Arabic bilingual programmes have also been pioneered in Alberta and, in particular, the Edmonton Public School System. In Quebec, bilingual provision outside French immersion programmes, which will be discussed later, has been concentrated in the private sector, and in the region of 30 schools – mainly Jewish, Armenian and Greek – receive a substantial proportion of their operating budgets from the provincial government. In contrast, Ontario refuses to allow instruction through any language except French and English other than for short-term transitional purposes.[50]

Community efforts to maintain minority languages

Differences in terminology add to the complexities of cross-national discussions. Languages taught as subjects in school are usually referred to as foreign languages; languages spoken by new minority communities are known as community languages in the UK, Ireland, Australia and Aotearoa/New Zealand and as heritage languages in the USA and Canada. Some North American writers extend the use of the term 'heritage languages' to Indigenous languages. A further complication arises when languages such as German and Spanish are both community or heritage languages and foreign languages. In very many cases, the same language has higher status when taught as a foreign language than when used by minority communities.

Two broad generalizations can be made about the education of new minority students. The first is that, with some notable exceptions, the priority of the education system is the teaching of English; other languages are used mainly as a transitional support. The second is that, while mainstream education is much more responsive to community or heritage languages today than in the past, a great deal of responsibility for this area remains with minority-language communities themselves.

The relationship between voluntary and public schooling is complex. While mainstream schooling was studiously ignoring the fact that large numbers of children spoke other languages, minority communities were more proactive. US Chinese-language schools, for instance, date back to 1848, when classes in Cantonese were organized for the residents of Chinatown in a number of large US cities.[51] Documentation on the development of heritage language teaching is relatively sparse. Joshua Fishman, a leading figure in the field, wryly comments that the only reason for reference to heritage language schools in official documents is when they have been cited for lack of bathrooms, windows or fire escapes. His own survey of heritage languages in the USA between 1960 and 1963 located 1,885 community schools operating in dozens of different, mainly European languages.[52] He suspects that he failed to uncover many other schools because of fear of government interference in the McCarthyite Cold War years. Such concerns are almost certainly well founded. Fishman was questioned on one occasion by the FBI as to whether these ethnic schools were communist dominated. A second survey nearly 20 years later identified some 6,553 schools involving 145 different languages, though, again, this figure is likely to have been a considerable underestimate.[53]

Religious institutions – the church, the mosque, the temple – have frequently played a vital role in the organization of classes. Overseas governments have also taken a lead. For many decades, the Tsarist government assisted Orthodox schools for Russians in Alaska. In 1905, the Chinese secretary of justice recommended that the Chinese government fund US Chinese-language schools. For much of the first half of the twentieth century, the French government funded French instruction in public and private elementary and high schools in various cities and states. Italian, Spanish and Greek governments have also provided a high level of support for language teaching in inner-circle countries.

Traditionally, new arrivals were faced with two stark options: assimilate to the English-speaking majority; or maintain heritage languages quietly at home and within the immediate ethnic community. The increasing demographic and economic strength of minorities has cleared the way for alternative courses of action. Developments in the Italian community in Toronto offer a good example of the political clout of ethnic minority taxpayers and voters. In the early 1970s, the public school system made no provision for heritage languages. When the Catholic-run Metropolitan Separate School Board offered an Italian programme funded by the Italian government, growing numbers of families transferred their children from the public school system. In an attempt to curb this flow – and what some perceived to be interference by a foreign power – the government of Ontario finally adopted its own Heritage Language Program.[54]

Heritage-language teaching has been debated in Canada at federal, provincial and local school-board level since the mid-1970s. The 1967 report of the Royal Commission on Bilingualism and Biculturalism declared linguistic diversity an unquestionable advantage, but, at the same time, recommended that heritage languages should not be promoted at the expense of French and English. In order to test the political temperature, the federal government commissioned two national surveys. *The Non-Official Languages* study[55] of 10 different ethnic groups showed that the large majority was in favour of including heritage-language instruction in public schools, particularly at the elementary level. In contrast, the *Multiculturalism and Ethnic Attitudes* study[56] showed much less enthusiasm for teaching heritage languages as part of the regular school programme. There was in fact considerable opposition at first to heritage-language teaching. At one point, teachers in the Toronto Board of Education worked to rule for a period of six months in protest against plans to integrate the programme into an extended school day. However, since 1976, a succession of reports has reiterated official support for heritage-language teaching.[57] About half of the provinces of Canada now have heritage-language programmes in their official school curricula, although course offerings and programme types differ greatly from board to board and from school to school. Most are delivered either on Saturdays or in the late afternoon in schools and in the community.

Migrant groups also played a role in achieving official support for other languages in Australia, where both federal and state governments offer support for language teaching. A Saturday school gives students the opportunity to study the languages they speak at home, when no classes are available at their own school or college. Arrangements vary from state to state. The New South Wales Department of Education and Training, for instance, administers a programme which gives schools a payment for each student enrolled. It also provides free access to government school premises and supports the professional development of teachers. At the time of writing, New South Wales offers 47 languages in 454 schools to approximately 31,000 students. In South Australia, more than 100 affiliated school authorities teach almost 50 languages to over 9,000 students.[58]

Levels of official support for community-based language teaching are more impressive in Canada and Australia than in the UK and USA, where the main responsibility falls on the communities themselves. The patterns of the past, together with record levels of immigration in the late twentieth century, suggest that the demand for minority-language teaching in the USA is greater than ever. To take just one example, in the mid-1990s some 83,000 students were enrolled in more than 600 Chinese-language schools.[59] Options for Chinese include childcare centres; weekend, after-school and summer programmes; and tutorial programmes for secondary school students. A small number of classes run by religious organizations are offered free of charge, but most are funded from tuition fees and fundraising. Against a backdrop of growing interest in this area, the National Foreign Language Center and the Center for Applied Linguistics are currently collaborating in the Heritage Language Initiative. The aim is to make the education system more responsive to heritage communities and national language needs and to produce a cadre of people who can function professionally in both English and another language.[60]

In the UK, the bulk of language teaching, takes place in weekend classes organized by minority communities.[61] A thousand groups are involved in London alone. Official support comes mainly in the form of free accommodation in state schools, though some charitable foundations also offer limited financial support. Minority languages are now commonly taught as subjects in the secondary curriculum in areas with a high proportion of minority-language speakers. At the primary level, they are sometimes taught informally in lunchtime and after-school clubs; they are also promoted through 'language-awareness' activities.

Ongoing concerns

Several issues affect minority-language teaching irrespective of whether this takes place in the community or in mainstream education. Of these, the most widely discussed include the need for professional development and accreditation, and the availability of appropriate pedagogies and resources.

Recognition of the professional development needs of minority-language teachers has been slow. As is the case elsewhere, most minority-language teachers in the UK are volunteers and few have adequate levels of training. There was, until recently, no initial teacher training in community languages, thus perpetuating the underdog status of this group of teachers and, by extension, their languages. Many are on part-time, temporary contracts, which affect their status within schools. Similar status issues are found in Canada. When the Heritage Language Program was introduced in Ontario, it was funded under the Continuing Education Program. Instructors did not require Ontario teaching certification and were therefore paid at much lower rates. The main impetus for training often comes from the communities themselves. Religious and cultural organizations, such as the Korean Schools Association in the USA and the Chinese Scholars' Association in the UK, provide support in the form of materials, training and advice. On other occasions, broader umbrella organisations fulfil this role. The British Columbian Heritage Language Association, for instance, provides support for 150 other organizations in the province.

Accreditation is a useful indicator of the status of other languages. In the UK, the only opportunity to gain formal recognition of heritage language skills is through public examinations in the last three years of school. Although there has been a steady increase in the numbers of students entered for these examinations, some minority-language groups have had to fight to prevent the disappearance of courses. There are also very few degree programmes in non-traditional languages. The British approach to accreditation stands in marked contrast to developments in Australia.[62] From 1972, various Australian states gave languages such as Greek, Indonesian and Italian 'first-language' status with French. Victoria was the first Australian state to offer accreditation of heritage languages as matriculation subjects, in 1973, and other states rapidly followed this lead. School-leaving examinations are now available in 43 different languages.

In North America, where accreditation focuses more on ongoing school-based assessment than on fixed-point public examinations, the response has also been more flexible. Small but growing numbers of public high schools now grant credit to students for classes taken in the community, and provision for languages with larger numbers of speakers is constantly improving. The San Francisco City Bureau of Education and the American College Board, for instance, both offer standardized tests for Chinese children.[63] Similar developments are taking place in Canada, where, in some provinces, formal curricula and academic credits for languages such as German, Japanese, Mandarin, Panjabi and Spanish were developed in the mid-1990s.[64]

Another recurring problem is the shortage of suitable teaching materials and pedagogies. It is now widely recognized that minority-language teaching is not simply an extension of foreign-language teaching; the needs of the two groups of students are quite distinct. Very often books and courses produced in the home country fail to speak to the experience of locally born children and the linguistic level for any given age range is too advanced. As a result teachers have to spend a great deal of time in lesson preparation and the production of resources.

In short, while heritage-language teaching is not a new development, great progress has been made in recent decades, partly as a result of political pressure from minority communities and partly because of growing awareness of the importance of multilingualism. The extent to which minority languages are incorporated into mainstream curricula varies greatly from one country to another, as do opportunities for accreditation. National language policies ensure a high level of support in Canada and Australia; traditional antipathy and indifference in the UK and USA have resulted in a much lower level of support. In all settings, however, the communities themselves assume a leading role in language teaching. There is a broad consensus that while externally supported programmes and top-down policies are important, they do not remove the need for bottom-up efforts in the home and community.

Marginalized languages

Non-standard languages and sign languages have much in common with other minority languages. They, too, have been excluded from formal schooling, often with unfortunate consequences. Children who speak non-standard forms of English are sometimes dismissed as stupid or lazy, although such judgements are often couched in more politically correct terms such as 'disadvantaged' or 'language deficient'. It is only since the 1960s that linguists and educators have acknowledged that the varieties spoken by minorities such as African Caribbeans in the UK, African Americans in the USA and Aboriginals in Australia are valid, rule-governed language systems. The recognition of the sign languages of the inner-circle countries, such as BSL, ASL, Auslan and langue des signes de Québec (LSQ), came even later. Here the issue was not so much whether these varieties were substandard as whether they were languages at all.

Black English

As we saw in chapter 2, attitudes towards Black speakers and their distinctive forms of speech have been highly prejudicial. In the UK, recognition of the important differences between British English and the language of settlers from the former British West Indies was slow. By the time that awareness had been raised in educational circles, the ability to code-switch between the local British dialect and Black British English was widespread; the distinctively Black British variety which was emerging among second-generation children was essentially a marker of identity. Canadian educators adopted a more proactive course, developing materials and pedagogies that highlighted the differences between Caribbean varieties and the standard.[65]

The situation in the USA was rather different. Historically, African Americans constitute a much larger proportion of the population than do African Caribbeans in Canada and the UK. The continuing social distance between Black and White America is reflected in ongoing differences between standard English and the Black speech known at various times as Black English Vernacular, African American Vernacular English and Ebonics. A substantial body of sociolinguistic research undertaken from the 1970s describes the features that differentiate it from other varieties of English. There is a very high unanimity among linguists on both the rule-governed and systematic nature of Black varieties of English and the potentially negative effects of teacher insensitivity on students.

The issue of Black language in education has in fact been the subject of a legal challenge. The rather unlikely setting for the 1979 case of *Martin Luther King Jr Elementary School v. Ann Arbor School District Board* was an affluent college town in the mid-west.[66] Here African Americans were over-represented in the number of suspensions and under-represented in honours classes. Two-thirds of the plaintiff children in the class action had been classified as having special educational needs.

The court accepted expert testimony that, by looking at Black English Vernacular as a series of mistakes, teachers were failing to understand its logic and its structures. Although Black English is not an obstacle in itself, it was judged that teacher insensitivity could pose a barrier to learning to read and use standard English. The ruling did not require the school board to teach children in or through Black English, but simply to help its teachers to recognize the home language of the students and to use that knowledge in teaching reading skills in standard English. The principle established in the case of *Lau v. Nichols*, that each district 'take appropriate action to overcome language barriers that impede equal participation by its students in its instructional programs', had now been extended to minority dialects.

Nearly 20 years later, the circumstances surrounding the resolution passed by the Oakland Unified School District Board of Education in California bore a striking resemblance to the Ann Arbor case.[67] The Oakland African-American Task Force was faced with alarming discrepancies between the attainment of African American and other students: the grade point average for African American students was 1.8, compared with 2.7 for White students and 2.4 for Asian American students. Other indicators were also cause for alarm: African Americans, who made up 53 per cent of the student population, represented 80 per cent of suspensions and 71 per cent of students with special educational needs.

Members of the task force were, however, struck by the above-average performance of African American students at Prescott Elementary School, the only school in Oakland where most teachers were participating in the Standard English Proficiency programme (SEP), a state-wide initiative which used Black English to help children learn to read and write in standard English. In December 1996, the board unanimously passed the Ebonics Resolution, which required all schools in the district to take part in the SEP programme as part of a broad strategy aimed at improving the school performance of African American students.

The intensity of response to the resolution was unprecedented. The media, in the form of editorial writers, columnists and talk-show hosts, were almost universally hostile. Many African American leaders also attacked the board for its decision. The invective piled upon the School Board included 'lunatics' and 'Afro-centrist'; accusations were made that they were 'giving up' on Black students. The most common distortion was the assumption that Oakland students would be taught Ebonics instead of standard English. Sentences and phrases in the original resolution were taken out of context; rebuttals from spokespeople for the board were ignored.

Linguists and educators united in an attempt to provide an informed perspective on the confused public debate. The 13 members of the Coalition on Language Diversity in Education included the American Association for Applied Linguistics, the Linguistic Society of America, and the Office of Educational Research and Improvement. The efforts of professionals, sadly, were to limited effect: the furore over the Oakland resolution goes well beyond linguistics. Like bilingual education, it is a debate about culture, power, identity and control. The bottom line is that minority students are only too well aware that, even if they use the majority dialect, they will not automatically be accepted into the mainstream.

Hawai'ian Creole English

The Black English debate has resonances with educational controversies in other parts of the world. The linguistic situation in Hawai'i, for instance, is complex. Large numbers of immigrants from many different countries came in the late nineteenth century to work on sugar and pineapple plantations and soon outnumbered the Indigenous population.[68] At first, basic communication between these diverse groups relied on Hawai'ian Pidgin English (HPE). In the course of the next generation, children developed HPE into Hawai'ian Creole English (HCE), a language capable of fulfilling all their communication needs, although 'Pidgin' remains the popular name for the language. By 1920, pressure from a small but influential group of White Anglophones, concerned about exposing their children to the 'corrupting influences' of HPE and HCE, had produced a two-tier education system, where students were allocated to schools on the basis of their proficiency in English. This practice, which continued until the early 1960s, reinforced Pidgin as a marker of both class and ethnic differences.

Throughout this period, the message about the social desirability of speaking standard English was very clear. Teachers were urged to tell children 'that the Pidgin English which they speak is not good English; that it is not spoken by good Americans'.[69] Pidgin was compared with the frogs, toads and snakes that came from the mouth of the wicked sister in fairy tales; 'good speech' was like the roses, pearls and diamonds that dropped from the lips of the beautiful, good sister who helped people. As was also the case in continental USA, language differences were pathologized. In 1939–40, for instance, newly trained speech specialists found defects in 675 of the 800 children they tested in schools. A new category of defect, Pidgin dialectalisms, was listed alongside language handicaps, reading handicaps, mental deficiency and cleft-palate speech.[70]

In the 1970s, the work of sociolinguists in challenging theories of language deficit helped to influence the attitudes of educators in Hawai'i, as in many parts of the world. There was greater tolerance of Pidgin in classroom talk and two official initiatives, Project Holopono and Project Akamai, included activities to help Pidgin-speaking students recognize differences between their language and standard English; some use was also made of locally produced literature in Pidgin. Attitudes have none the less remained ambivalent. In 1987, for instance, a proposal was made to ban Pidgin from classrooms. In 1998, disappointing results in national writing tests ignited the debate once again. The chair of the Board of Education attempted to implicate Pidgin in the poor results, arguing that: 'We ought to have classrooms where standard English is the norm rather than teachers having to use Pidgin English to get points across.'[71]

Da Pidgin Coup, a group of linguists and educators at the University of Hawai'i, made a valuable contribution to the debate by challenging the myths associated with Pidgin.[72] They suggested a programme of language awareness seminars, classes or in-services for teachers, consistent with the judgement in the Ann Arbor case, which examine strategies for building on the home language, and for understanding language systems. They also pointed to the usefulness of language-awareness programmes for helping students to learn about the history and social functions of both Pidgin and English, and to discover ways in which Pidgin and English are different.

Aboriginal English

Responses to Aboriginal English in Australia follow a very similar pattern. Aboriginal English is spoken as either a first or second language by the great majority of Aboriginal people. Since the 1960s, linguists have described a number of varieties, including Koori English, Alice Springs Aboriginal English and Western Australian Aboriginal English. Although certain features are found only in some dialects, many are widespread. Examples which differ systematically from standard Australian English and serve as important markers of Aboriginal identity include 'Him finish' to mean 'He is dead'; 'dust' as a verb, meaning to overtake a car on a dusty road; and the lack of the possessive -s (*Ann book*) and initial *h* (*'appy*).

Most non-Aboriginal Australians have little understanding of the nature of Aboriginal English. Misconceptions about language in the wider community are harmful, but when stereotypes extend to teachers in the classroom, the damage is much greater. Traditionally, Aboriginal English was seen by schools as something aberrant, which needed to be suppressed. However, attempts at eradication have been singularly unsuccessful in equipping speakers with skills in standard Australian English. Most children who feel that they are being asked to choose between loyalty to family, friends and their way of life, on the one hand, and school, on the other, reject the school.

The *Report of the Inquiry into Aboriginal and Torres Strait Islander Language Maintenance* identifies the failure by schools and teachers to identify, accept and take into account the differences between Aboriginal English and standard Australian English as a major factor in Aboriginal children's poor performance in school. The report sums up the situation in the following terms: 'It is now a well-known fact that such "weeding" programmes were mostly unsuccessful: the "precious plant" of standard English did not often grow "naturally" on the silenced lips of non-standard speakers.' However, some progress has been made and several states now have literacy programmes for Aboriginal English speakers that build on the students' home language.[73]

The public debate on Aboriginal English in education has avoided the excesses of polemic and hostility witnessed in the USA. Teacher attitudes have become more accepting over time, though even those who view Aboriginal English positively vary considerably in how they see its role in education. Approaches fall into two main categories: language awareness and teaching standard English as a second dialect (TSESD). The most common approach is language awareness and most states have Aboriginal studies courses for Aboriginal and non-Aboriginal students. The TSESD approach, in contrast, is aimed at Aboriginal students and makes explicit the differences from standard English in the same way as the SEP program in the Oakland School Board.[74] Curriculum material to support the teaching of English as a second dialect is developing apace with courses, resources, kits and programmes. Western Australia has been particularly proactive in educating teachers about the systematic differences between Aboriginal English and standard Australian English.[75] Resources are now available to support their Two-Way programme, which sees the acquisition of standard English as a process requiring understanding on the part of both dialect and standard speakers.

Sign languages

While dialects are often grudgingly considered to be inferior versions of the standard language, sign languages have been treated with even greater contempt. Oralist policies for the education of the Deaf fail to recognize ASL, BSL, LSQ or Auslan as languages at all and have placed a high premium on eliminating them from the classroom.

The devastating effects of Oralism remained concealed for decades, during which the historical accomplishments of Deaf professionals were long forgotten. This complacency was dented in 1979 with the publication of a survey of all UK Deaf school leavers.[76] The findings were stark and sobering: Deaf 16-year-old had an average reading age of less than 9 years and much of their spoken English was unintelligible. Equally shocking was the fact that their lip-reading skills were no better than those of hearing people trying to lip-read for the first time. This is not altogether surprising. Many sounds use similar lip patterns: it is impossible to distinguish, on the basis of lip shapes alone, between *m*, *p* and *b*, or *n*, *t* and *d*. Lip-reading involves a great deal of guesswork, even when the speaker articulates clearly.

These appalling levels of achievement were by no means limited to the UK. American researchers have also commented that Deaf children seem to reach a plateau at third-grade reading comprehension levels, and that Deaf speech is difficult to understand.[77] In one study of over 2,000 Deaf children and young people, even teachers of the Deaf found that the speech of a little over half was unintelligible.[78] Despite the claims of Oralists, Deaf children in the twentieth century were clearly achieving far less than children educated through sign in the previous century.

The mid-1970s saw the introduction of a compromise measure, an approach known as Total Communication, which involves the simultaneous use of sign and speech. The sign in question, however, was not ASL, BSL or Auslan but an artificial system, specially devised to follow English grammar. The results were disappointing. Although the intention was to help children acquire spoken English, differences in modality – sound versus vision – mean that Signed English is often difficult to follow for children accustomed to natural sign languages. Things are complicated still further by the tendency in actual usage to drop some of the signs accompanying the spoken language: the result is essentially visual gibberish.[79] The use of Signed English to teach spoken English to Deaf children is thus akin to using French to teach German to Spanish students. Hearing teachers who fail to appreciate that sign language has its own visual grammar are likely to have very limited success in communicating complex concepts and explanations; they will also be seriously hampered in their ability to understand what Deaf children are saying to them or to each other.

As recognition of the various natural sign languages has grown, so, too, have calls for bilingual education. In the USA schools such as the Indiana and the California Schools for the Deaf have been developing bilingual, bicultural programmes since the 1980s. The Ontario Ministry of Education and Training has had a bilingual, bicultural policy in its three provincial schools for Deaf students since 1993.[80] Alberta and Manitoba also recognize ASL as a sociocultural and socioeducational language. In Australia, the Victorian College for the Deaf is committed to providing an environment which promotes clear and effective communication using two languages, Auslan as the visual language and English as the language for reading, writing and speaking.[81] Such developments, however, are the exception rather than the rule. It is sobering to remember that even in the USA, the country where Oralism has arguably had least influence, many severely and profoundly Deaf students still attend Oral education programmes.

Another serious challenge for Deaf education came with the decision to class Deaf with disabled children as part of the move to include all children in mainstream schooling. The Deaf community has none the less grown in political awareness and self-confidence. While most hearing people continue to perceive deafness as a disability, many Deaf people argue that they are in fact members of a cultural and linguistic minority. In Canada, the Deaf community reacted angrily to the decision to award the Order of Canada to Oralist Dr Daniel Ling for his work with Deaf children. Particular exception was taken to the comment attributed to Dr Ling that his method would 'put an end to the Deaf community'.[82] The Deaf are also resolute in their opposition to cochlear implants in young children, partly because this untried technology destroys any residual hearing; partly because children cannot be involved in decisions which will affect their entire lives; but mainly because this technological advance is a denial of Deaf people's cultural identity and has led to a resurgence of Oralism.

Languages for learning

Writers such as Joshua Fishman insist that it is unrealistic to treat the school as the main agent of language reproduction; the family and the wider community must also take responsibility. The evidence of history supports this position. The Irish Republic, for instance, achieved disappointing results by making education the main plank of its policy for reversing language shift. That said, education clearly has a role to play, and it is a wonderful irony that the very institutions that helped bring about the decline of minority languages are now contributing to their revitalization. Particularly in Indigenous and established communities, where parents are no longer able to transmit languages in the traditional way, the only hope of survival lies in immersion schooling. The success of this approach is impressive, with children achieving high levels of proficiency in minority languages at no cost to their attainment in English. Indigenous peoples are also gaining growing control over their children's education, ensuring that form and content are consistent with their cultural values.

The teaching of the new minority languages raises different issues. While the main focus continues to be the teaching of English, there is a much better understanding that this need not involve abandoning the languages of the home. There is also greater recognition of the importance of language competency, and curricula have been expanded to include a much wider range of languages, particularly in areas of high immigrant settlement. The political power of minority taxpayers and voters has ensured growing levels of support for initiatives both in and outside school. Non-standard and sign languages have also made considerable advances and are now widely recognized as valid linguistic systems in their own right.

These gains have not, however, won universal approval. Changing political priorities have had devastating effects on a wide range of programmes, and inadequate funding continues to be a major obstacle to progress. Most new minority children depend on community support for their language learning; mainstream educators tend either to ignore their languages or to regard them as a temporary crutch as children acquire English. Only in a relatively small proportion of cases do other languages play a meaningful role in content-based instruction. Popular prejudice is also a threat to the progress of non-standard languages.

In much the same way as education policy oscillated in earlier times in response to increased immigration and world events, the social equity agenda of the 1960s and 1970s came under increasing threat in the closing decades of the twentieth century. Future developments, however, are very difficult to predict. In an age of globalization, growing awareness of the importance of language competence – the subject of the next chapter – may yet provide a powerful counterbalance to the growing tide of xenophobia and patriotism.

Notes

1   Jackson (1993: 215).
2   May (2001: 285–306).
3   Benton (1996).
4   Ministry of Education (2000).
5   Beasley (1999: 5); Malcolm (2002).
6   House of Representatives Standing Committee on Aboriginal and Torres Strait Islander Affairs (1992).
7   Nicholls (2001); Gaglioti (1999).
8   See chapter 5, p. 99.
9   Nicholls (2001).
10   Later the Assembly of First Nations.
11   Reyhner (1990); McCarty (2002).
12   Francis and Reyhner (2002).
13   Stiles (1997).
14   Baker (1997); Peate et al. (1998).
15   www.mym.co.uk
16   Hickey (1997).
17   Baker (1997).
18   Baker (1997).
19   In 2003, there were 149 primary and 33 post-primary schools serving 30,000 children; www.gaelscoileanna.ie
20   Dana and McMonagle (1994).
21   DENI (1998).
22   Burnaby (1996).
23   Cumming (2000).
24   Department of Immigration (1960).
25   Ozolins (1993).
26   Crawford (1999).
27   Burnaby (1996).
28   Bullock (1975: 543).
29   Council of Europe (1977).
30   EC (1984).
31   The only notable exception was the Bradford Mother Tongue and English Teaching Project (Fitzpatrick 1987), which had in fact begun before the publication of the Swann Report.

32 See, for instance, Bourne (1989); Edwards (1998).
33 More recent funding arrangements are discussed in Eversley (2000).
34 See, for instance, Ozolins (1993); Herriman (1996).
35 Lo Bianco (1987).
36 Australia (1991).
37 Herriman (1996); Malcolm (2002).
38 Waite (1992). The first word of the title is a pun playing on the Māori words for Aotearoa/New Zealand (Aoteoroa) and language (reo).
39 Benton (1996: 75–6).
40 Crawford (1999).
41 Del Valle (2003).
42 US General Accounting Office (1987).
43 Krashen (1992); Cummins (2001).
44 Cummins (1998).
45 Rossell and Baker (1996).
46 Ramirez et al. (1991).
47 Thomas and Collier (2002).
48 McQuillan and Tse (1996).
49 ourworld.compuserve.com/homepages/JWCRAWFORD/co-unz01.htm
50 Cummins and Danesi (1990).
51 Chao (1997).
52 Fishman (1966).
53 Fishman (2001).
54 Cummins and Danesi (1990: 36).
55 O'Bryan et al. (1976).
56 Berry et al. (1977).
57 Burnaby (1996); Cumming (2000).
58 www.det.nsw.edu.au/eas/commlang/about/about.html
59 Chao (1997).
60 www.nflc.org/activities/projects/hli.htm
61 Edwards (2001).
62 Clyne (1991); Ozolins (1993: 132).
63 Brecht and Ingold (1998).
64 Cumming (2000).
65 Coelho (1988).
66 Labov (1982).
67 Perry and Delpit (1997).
68 Sato (1985).
69 Da Pidgin Coup (1999).
70 Da Pidgin Coup (1999).
71 Anon. (1999).
72 Da Pidgin Coup (1999).
73 House of Representatives Standing Committee on Aboriginal and Torres Strait Islander Affairs (1992).

74 Goodwin (1998).
75 Malcolm (1995).
76 Conrad (1979).
77 Bowe (1991).
78 Wolk and Schildroth (1986).
79 Ladd (2003).
80 Gibson et al. (1997).
81 www.vcd.vic.edu.au
82 OAD (1999).

7

Minority languages and majority speakers

English speakers have a reputation as unenthusiastic language learners. There is more than an element of truth in this broad generalization. In the UK, for instance, modern languages are not as widely available as in other European countries and are not a popular option, especially with boys. In a recent multinational survey of language use, almost half the British respondents said they spoke only English.[1] In the Irish Republic, where 59 per cent reported that they could not speak another language, it would seem that things are even worse. Canada fares somewhat better. Bilingualism in French and English is commonplace in cities such as Montreal, Moncton or Ottawa, as is bilingualism in English and another language in cities of high immigrant settlement, such as Vancouver or Toronto. Elsewhere, most people who have studied languages in school are likely to be able to read simple texts but would probably have difficulty in conducting a conversation or following a TV programme in the language. Historically, Australians and Americans also have an unimpressive record of achievement as language learners. In Australia, foreign-language teaching in the 1970s was described as in 'an alarming state of decline', and the national policy on languages bemoaned a deep and pervasive malaise in language teaching;[2] the situation in the USA, for its part, has been described as 'scandalous'.[3]

There have, however, been important changes in perceptions and the value of language teaching is now widely recognized, at least on a rhetorical level. This chapter looks at three areas of activity specifically targeted at English speakers: immersion schooling, dual-language immersion and foreign-language teaching.

Immersion schooling

The most striking example of the new openness of English speakers can be traced to the efforts of a small group of parents in St Lambert, a suburb of Montreal, who realized in the mid-1960s that proficiency in French would soon be essential for economic survival. In their view, the regime of grammar, translation and drills experienced by previous generations had been a poor preparation either for work or for socialization in French, and so the group started to explore possible alternatives in discussion with scholars in bilingualism at McGill University.[4] In the model they proposed, English-speaking children would be immersed in French for the first years of schooling; English would then be introduced gradually until half the curriculum was in English and half in French. Pressure from parents and the local press finally persuaded the school board to provide the necessary support. Ironically, then, the teaching model which has worked so well for Indigenous and established languages was initially developed for the benefit of English speakers.

Throughout this period, the Royal Commission on Bilingualism and Biculturalism and the 1969 Official Languages Act were helping to promote the value of a knowledge of French. Interest across the country was fanned by media stories about immersion education in Quebec, and assisted by financial support from the 1970 Official Languages in Education Program. Another factor was the intense interest of researchers in the achievements of immersion schooling, and the widespread dissemination of their results. The findings from research in Canada (and subsequently in many other countries) show consistently that immersion students acquire normal English proficiency as well as a high level in the second language.[5] Current enrolment stands at about 300,000 students or 7 per cent of the total school population.[6]

As immersion education spread to other settings, it gradually mutated. Although there is considerable variation, in most total-immersion programmes all the subjects in the lower grades (from kindergarten to grade 2) are taught in the second language, and instruction in English increases in the upper grades (3–6) to between 20 and 50 per cent. In partial-immersion programmes, up to half the subjects are taught in the second language; sometimes the material taught in the second language is reinforced in English. There is also variation in the stage at which the second language is introduced. Mid-immersion programmes start in grades 4 or 5 and late-immersion programmes in grades 6 or 7. Immersion programmes have also gained ground in the USA, though their impact has been much more limited than in Canada.

In Australia, the policy of support for multiculturalism and 'unity in diversity' in the 1970s led to a renewal of interest in languages other than English (LOTEs). Content-based teaching – where one or more areas of the curriculum are taught through the medium of the second language – can be traced to Bayswater South Primary School in Victoria in the 1980s.[7] The success of these programmes served as a catalyst for other developments across Australia at both primary and secondary levels. Sometimes all the children in the school take part in the programme; more often, one class is involved and participation is on a voluntary basis. Early initiatives centred on 'safe languages' such as French and German, but gradually spread to include Indonesian, Hebrew, Arabic, Chinese, Japanese, Vietnamese, Auslan, Greek and Italian. There are currently well over 40 programmes, almost two-thirds of which are offered at the primary level. A small number of programmes in Japanese, Chinese and French have also been developed at university level.

The UK has shown far less enthusiasm for content teaching. CLIP (Content and Language Integration Project), the first initiative of this kind, was launched only in 2002. Eight schools have been selected to look at the potential of this approach for raising standards.[8]

Dual-language immersion

An interesting development in the USA concerns dual or 'two-way' immersion programmes, involving a balance of minority-language and majority-language students, where each group makes up between one-third and two-thirds of the student population.[9] Instruction takes place in both languages, but the non-English language is used at least half of the time. The aim is to promote high academic achievement, first- and second-language development, and cross-cultural understanding. As was the case in Canada, many English-speaking parents have been receptive to arguments that 'bilingual is beautiful', though the overall numbers remain relatively small. In the region of 20,000 English-background students are involved in two-way programmes, compared with the 300,000 students in French-immersion programmes in Canada, a country with one-tenth the population of the USA. Parents see two-way immersion as a means of developing the social as well as the linguistic skills required for a multicultural future.

There are many variations on the theme even within the same school. In the Amigos Program[10] at Robert F. Kennedy School in Cambridge, Massachusetts, for instance, students spend approximately half their instruction time in Spanish and the other half in English, but precise arrangements differ according to the age of the children. Kindergarten students receive instruction in Spanish for two days and then in English for two days. Grades 1–6 spend one week in Spanish and one week in English, covering all subjects in each language.

How does two-way immersion operate in practice? Take the case of a second-grade Amigos class working on a lesson about fables. The teacher always spoke in Spanish; children were free to respond to questions in either language, but were encouraged to speak in Spanish. A student who had been absent the previous day asked, 'What is fábulas (fables)?' The teacher reviewed the previous day's lesson, asking the class about the characteristics of fables. When one of the students offered that they were 'not true', the teacher asked '¿Cómo se dice "not true" en español?' ('How do you say "not true" in Spanish?'). Another student supplied the answer in Spanish.

Foreign-language teaching

Attitudes towards language teaching have undergone considerable change in inner-circle countries in recent times. In the UK, membership of the European Union has undoubtedly helped to bring about a more favourable climate and recent surveys of public opinion put support for multilingualism at between 74 and 86 per cent.[11] The creation of specialist 'language colleges' in England and Wales in the late 1990s signalled a new commitment to foreign-language teaching, and by 2002, 141 specialist colleges had been established with the aim of raising standards of achievement. In the same year the government published a strategy for language with three overarching objectives: to improve teaching and learning of languages; to introduce a recognition system to give people credit for their language skills; and to increase the number of people studying languages in further and higher education.[12]

Australia has responded with particular enthusiasm to geographical and economic realities and, since the late 1980s, has used economic, diplomatic and cultural criteria for deciding which languages should be included in the curriculum.[13] Debate in Aotearoa/New Zealand has proceeded along similar lines.[14] American politicians are also expressing support for strengthening foreign-language instruction. Richard Riley,

Native speakers of modern foreign languages from around the world are
recruited through the British Council to work as language assistants, helping to
improve student fluency and confidence.
Reproduced with permission from the British Council.

the secretary of education, went on record in 2000 with a statement that
this course of action would build a better workforce, ensure national
security, and improve other areas of education.[15] Since the events of 11
September 2001, interest in the teaching and learning of Arabic, Pashto
and Farsi has increased dramatically.[16]

Recent times have witnessed a marked shift in the choice of foreign
languages. Australia and Aotearoa/New Zealand have both experienced
a decline in the number of students studying traditional languages, such
as French and German, and an increase in the numbers learning languages
of regional and international importance, such as Chinese, Japanese and
Spanish. The presence of a large and growing Hispanic population in
the USA makes Spanish a more attractive proposition than the more
traditional French and German; there has also been a steady increase in
programmes for less commonly taught languages such as Japanese, Russian
and Italian. In Canada, too, traditional-language teaching has expanded
to take on board many of the languages of recently arrived groups, though

in most cases these form part of specific heritage language programmes. In the UK, language colleges are committed to teaching a much wider range of languages than has traditionally been the case.

Renewed interest in language learning at both ends of the age spectrum has in fact been evident since the late 1980s. In the UK, the large numbers of adults who enrol on language courses spend an estimated £14 million a year on learning materials.[17] Welsh is a particularly popular option, with a dramatic increase in the number of learners since the *Welsh for Adults Strategy* was published in 1999.[18] Welsh is, however, by no means the only language attracting new learners. Over 100,000 hearing people have studied BSL since it first began appearing in television and film in the 1980s, and there is a shortage of trained teachers for adult classes. The BBC's languages website records nearly one million hits a day, and there are plans to expand from its present core of European and Celtic languages to Japanese, Mandarin, Greek and Portuguese.[19] Spanish, however, is particularly popular at the time of writing. The Open University reported a surge in registrations for its Spanish courses following the transfer of English soccer captain David Beckham to Real Madrid.

Adult education is not the only growth area for language learning; increasing numbers of programmes are also being developed for younger learners. The arguments in favour of an early start are well rehearsed: language-learning ability is at its peak in childhood, and students who learn at least one other language at an early age often find it easier to learn other languages as adults.[20] The UK has enjoyed notable successes with the early learning of Welsh and Gaelic, but attitudes towards other languages remained guarded following the failure of a pilot experiment in French teaching in primary schools in the 1960s.[21] The rapid growth of French classes for young learners, often on a voluntary basis and staffed by parents, has, however, helped to bring about a major change in policy. In 2002, the government announced that all children would be entitled within 10 years to learn a new language from the age of 7. In Scotland, most primary schools already offer children the opportunity to learn French, German, Italian or Spanish. There has also been a growth in elementary school foreign-language programmes in the USA, where nearly a third of schools now offer foreign-language classes,[22] although most children still do not begin study until the age of 14. In Aotearoa/ New Zealand, one of the aims of the Second Language Learning Project, announced in 1995, was to lower the starting age for language study, and there have been modest increases in the numbers of primary school children learning languages other than te reo Māori.[23] In Canada, most early language learners are catered for in immersion programmes. The starting age for language study in the rest of the school population varies by province. In Ontario, for example, core French is taught as a school subject for several hours a week to students between the ages of 10 and 14.[24]

Although there have been many encouraging developments, the overall decline in the teaching of languages is an ongoing cause for concern. In Aotearoa/New Zealand, the dramatic increase in the numbers of students learning Māori has not been matched by similar growth in the study of other languages.[25] In the USA, while foreign-language teaching at the elementary level has increased, the overall proportion of schools offering language programmes remains at less than one in three. And although nine out of ten secondary schools offer foreign languages, not all students in these schools actually study foreign languages.[26] In the UK, plans to relax the requirement that all students study a modern foreign language to the age of 16 are likely to reduce to crisis proportions the numbers of students wishing to continue with languages in higher education, and university language departments are expressing concern about their viability.[27]

Another issue is the high rate of attrition. For instance, only 17 per cent of Aotearoa/New Zealand children who began to study French in the first year of high school in the period between 1989 and 1991 were still studying the language four years later.[28] In the UK, 90 per cent study languages for five years, a marked improvement on the situation 30 years ago when only a minority studied languages. The fact remains, however, that only a tenth of students continue the study of a language beyond the age of 16.

A third and no less pressing concern is the disappointing level of proficiency which students achieve. According to the American Council on the Teaching of Foreign Languages, only 3 per cent of high school graduates and 5 per cent of college graduates reach 'meaningful proficiency in a second language'.[29]

Continuity is another ongoing problem. Students who have studied a foreign language in elementary school are often placed in classes at the secondary level alongside students who have had no prior exposure to the language. Children who have studied one language at the elementary level may find that, when they transfer to secondary education, there is no provision for that language. In short, in spite of considerable progress on a number of fronts, much work remains to be done.

Talking to God

Language teaching is full of paradoxes. The foreign languages taught in school enjoy high status with the dominant English-speaking group; the heritage languages associated with minority groups are regularly marginalized. The problem comes when the same language is both a foreign language and a heritage language. It is especially difficult to understand why Spanish, the language of a poor and marginalized community in the USA, is the most popular choice for foreign-language study.

The traditional arrogance and complacency of English speakers is neatly encapsulated in a comment in 1935 from Clarence Shepard Day, the American essayist: 'Imagine the Lord talking French! Aside from a few odd words in Hebrew, I took it completely for granted that God had never spoken anything but the most dignified English.'[30] The events of the last half-century have, however, helped to shape a rather different worldview. Initiatives such as immersion schooling and dual-language immersion are responses to the perception that English is no longer enough, a theme that will be developed later in this book. International events have helped to persuade English speakers in the inner-circle countries of the usefulness of competence in other languages. UK and Irish membership of the European Union, the new identities of Australia and Aotearoa/New Zealand as Pacific nations, the official recognition of French language rights in Canada, and the increasing globalization of trade are just some of the developments which have helped to change perceptions. Growing numbers of adults are involved in language learning and many parents are eager for their children to gain experience of other languages at the earliest opportunity. The much larger range of languages now on offer at all phases of education is also a reflection of this broader vision.

The least enthusiastic parties are, in fact, the secondary age students who have traditionally been the main targets for language teaching. It is certainly the case that the lack of 'joined-up' thinking in language policy has made young people's experiences of language learning less than satisfactory. Issues such as lack of continuity, teacher shortages and inflexible approaches to the accreditation of learning do little to enhance the status of other languages. This is, however, an area where practice in inner-circle countries has diverged. Dual-language immersion, for instance, is limited to the USA, while Australia has accumulated a great deal of experience of content-based learning. There is thus no shortage of opportunities to learn from the experience of others. At a time of heightened interest in language learning, we may just be moving a little closer to the multilingual aspirations of Charles V, the sixteenth-century Holy Roman Emperor: 'I speak Spanish to God, Italian to women, French to men, and German to my horse.'

Notes

1   BBC (2002).
2   Ozolins (1993: 14); Lo Bianco (1987).
3   Panetta (undated).
4   Baker and Prys Jones (1998).
5   Baker (2001).
6   Cumming (2000).
7   Truckenbrodt and de Courcy (2002).
8   www.cilt.org.uk/clip
9   Freeman (1998).
10   Education Alliance at Brown University (2003a).
11   EC (2001).
12   www.cilt.org.uk/languagecolleges
13   Herriman (1996); Ozolins (1993).
14   Benton (1996: 89–91).
15   Pufahl et al. (2000).
16   Morrison (2003).
17   Nuffield Language Inquiry (2000).
18   Welsh Language Board (1999).
19   Connell (2002).
20   Baker (2001).
21   Burstall et al. (1974).
22   Baldauf (1997).
23   Peddie (2003).
24   Cumming (2000).
25   Benton (1996: 70).
26   Panetta (undated).
27   Beckett (2002).
28   Benton (1996).
29   ACTFL Public Awareness Newsletter, May 1987, cited in Crawford (1997).
30   Day (1935).

Part III

Language in the
wider community

8

Language and the economy

Although language is part of our cultural capital, its market value is variable. Members of minorities often find themselves at a disadvantage in relation to the dominant English-speaking group. Thus, while middle-class Cuban Americans dominate the economic life of Miami, Hispanics in other parts of the USA fare less well. Typical jobs for Spanish in El Paso, Texas, for instance, include construction, assembly line, janitorial services, yard work, house cleaning and farm work;[1] only a tiny proportion of businesses are owned by Hispanics. Until quite recently, Francophones in Canada earned significantly less than Anglophones. Income in four out of five Pakistani and Bangladeshi households in the UK is below the national average.[2] As Colin Williams points out, minority groups fight to promote their language not only for reasons of cultural attachment, but often in 'a rational and instrumental attempt to reduce socio-economic inequality'.[3]

In growing numbers of cases, however, perceptions of the economic value of other languages are changing. To take just a few examples, the emergence of Japan as a major trading partner has produced an unprecedented demand for the study of Japanese. The greater economic power of Quebec has given birth to French-immersion education in English-speaking Canada. Official status for Welsh and Māori is generating a range of employment prospects for minority-language speakers in education, the media and government. While English remains the language of big business and power, there is far greater awareness of the economic advantages of multilingualism, both for minority communities and for the wider society. This chapter looks at the complex inter-relationships between language and the economy.

Minority economies

In the traditional heartlands of Indigenous and established languages, people not only live together but work together and, in many cases, the workplace provides a natural context for using the minority language. When migrants settle in a new country, they inevitably gravitate towards family and friends who have already made the journey. Soon they find themselves a part of larger communities, which seek to re-create important elements of the lives they have left behind – shops that sell the kinds of food they enjoy eating, travel agents to help arrange the trips back home, newspapers which report on events in the home country. In all these situations and many more, minority economies – and minority languages – play a central role.

Indigenous economies

Indigenous communities have a long history of trade with incomers. Business relations with European settlers have, in the main, been highly exploitative, although there are occasional examples of Indigenous peoples selectively adapting the economic agenda of mainstream society to their advantage. In the late nineteenth and early twentieth centuries, the Menominees of Wisconsin ran a successful lumber business. In the same period, the Metlakatlans in the northwest operated a salmon cannery. In both cases, these communities used selected elements of North American capitalism as a means of maintaining their independence; significantly, they did so with far greater success than those who became wage earners in the White man's world.[4]

Increasingly, Indigenous communities are trying to steer a course between the unchecked individualism associated with the Western world and traditional communal values. Aboriginal Canadian companies, for instance, are active in all business sectors, including manufacturing, forestry, traditional crafts and software development. They already sustain thousands of jobs and have the potential to create many more in the future. In Australia, the Central Australian Aboriginal Media Association (CAAMA) is responsible for a thriving retail, wholesale and distribution business selling Aboriginal videos, artefacts, music, literature and craft. Their record label produces Indigenous music for the world.

In the USA, an unexpected – and dramatic – development came with the burgeoning of the gaming industry on American Indian reservations. Most American states prohibit gambling, thus creating business opportunities for Indian communities. Indian governments, as independent sovereign nations, have been able since 1997 to conduct gaming on tribal homelands, free from state interference or consent. One-third of the 557 federally recognized reservations now have some form of commercial gaming; almost as many more hope to be able to follow.[5] Casinos are most beneficial to very small communities, located close to major urban areas or areas with a well-developed tourist industry. Mystic Lake Casino, for instance, is operated by the Shakopee Mdewakanton Dakota of Prior Lake in Minnesota and is one of the most profitable Indian casinos in the USA. It operates shuttle buses from the nearby metropolitan area, and is a magnet for thousands of tour groups. Gaming income offers many communities a significant economic base: it creates jobs for tribal members, and pays for food and medical care for elders, and housing for on-reservation tribal members. In many cases, it offers the only practical solution while other sources of income, usually related to tourism, are developed.

The importance of Indigenous economies is clear. Local initiatives slow the flow of population from traditional homelands to the city. They offer communities the possibility of independence, the power to conduct their affairs in accordance with their own values and traditions. In communities where language loss is not too far advanced, they also offer the freedom to use Indigenous languages in the workplace.

Established economies

Although established minorities have not been treated with the same levels of contempt as Indigenous peoples, they have none the less been systematically disadvantaged. In Canada, the Catholic church historically discouraged Francophones from involvement in business and the economy was dominated by an English-speaking elite. The 1967 Laurendeau-Dunton Commission found that monolingual Anglophone males were the most economically privileged group in Canada, while Francophone males earned 35 per cent less. One of the main features of the Quiet Revolution of the 1960s was the Francophone reclamation of the economy. By 1980, the income gap between English-speaking and French-speaking Quebeckers had decreased by more than half and, by 1990, bilingual Francophones were earning more than either bilingual or monolingual Anglophones. There has also been an increase in the number of Francophone-owned businesses and of Francophones in higher-level positions.[6]

In Ireland, English colonial policies affected not only the economic health of Irish speakers, but also their very survival. Forced to retreat to the poor and underdeveloped areas of the west and later subjected to the potato starvation, vast numbers departed for the New World.[7] Ireland's economic recovery finally took off only in the 1990s, mainly as a result of membership of the European Union. Although Irish had been recognized as a co-official language since the establishment of the Free State in 1921, short-sighted policies placed too much dependence on education as the main tool for language revitalization and did very little to curb the tide of language loss. Arguably, it is only since the redefinition of Irish as a minority language within the broader European context that more realistic policies have been pursued.

The fate of the Gaels was very similar. The greater profitability of renting land to Lowland sheep farmers led to the Highland clearances of the nineteenth century. Many of those evicted to poor coastal plots were unable to make a living and, like the Irish, Gaels migrated in very large numbers. The discovery of offshore oil in the 1970s helped to fuel nationalist demands for separation. While independence remains the goal of relatively few, the aspirations of the majority for greater autonomy were recognized following a 1997 referendum with the setting up of a separate Scottish Parliament. The importance for language of this development lies in the willingness of the Scottish Executive to allocate more generous budgets to Gaelic-medium education, Gaelic television and radio and Gaelic arts.[8] These developments, in turn, have spin-offs in terms of job creation in the civil service, the media, education, translation and tourism. Most initiatives designed to preserve minority languages in fact have economic benefits. The aim of Gaelic Energy Centres, for instance, is to provide a 'space' where everyday activities are conducted in the language. However, this scheme has also created jobs for administrators and local builders and offers a base for local small businesses.[9]

Historically, the situation in Wales is different.[10] The discovery of the south Wales coal fields that fuelled the Industrial Revolution meant that internal migration was an alternative for the rural poor. The larger numbers of Welsh speakers remaining in Wales thus ensured a stronger political base. The emergence of separate Welsh institutions from the 1950s onwards laid the foundations for various acts of parliament which gave increasing recognition of the language. Most notably, the 1993 Welsh Language Act has created more favourable conditions for the language in most aspects of life in Wales. The implications for business of these developments are even more far-reaching in Wales than in Scotland.

The gradual recognition of the Deaf as linguistic minorities also has economic spin-offs. The development of programmes for the accreditation of teachers of sign language and sign-language interpreters has helped

Deaf people break through the glass ceiling, and there is now a growing cadre of Deaf professionals.[11]

New minority economies

New minorities have always played an important role in the economy. Flemish weavers were asked to help upgrade the English textile industry in the fourteenth century. The Jews provided financial services from the eleventh century and the Lombards brought foreign banking to England from northern Italy in the Middle Ages. The Huguenots, escaping from persecution in France, were also active in the world of finance, as witnessed by the fact that seven out of the 24 founder directors of the Bank of England in 1694 had Huguenot or Walloon names.[12] London street names such as Old Jewry and Lombard Street are an ongoing reminder of historic links with these groups.

From the late nineteenth century, newcomers to the USA hired themselves out as groups with their own interpreter for work in foundries, stockyards and construction projects. Being part of a group allowed them to learn about labour laws and union practices and also about practical issues such as transportation.

From the beginning, new arrivals have established themselves in a particular market niche. Chin-Yee's, the first Chinese laundry in the UK, opened in Merseyside in 1887. Laundries spread rapidly and by 1911 over a quarter of the Chinese in London were employed in laundry and washing-service occupations.[13] With the advent of the launderette and the widespread ownership of washing machines, laundries disappeared and many Chinese workers transferred to the catering industry. Other languages also have strong associations with business, and particularly with the food industry. A walk along the main streets of many cities reveals a wide range of restaurants, from Indian to Chinese, from Italian to Thai.

The progress of each immigrant group depends to a large extent on the support structures that are put in place as members of the same family, village, region or country recognize common bonds and mutual obligations. Sometimes whole areas of cities are settled by a particular group. In the years following World War II, Toronto became the largest and most ethnically diverse city in Canada. As part of this process, waves of new immigrants re-created many aspects of the lives that they had left behind. Portuguese businesses, for instance, are concentrated in an area known as 'Little Portugal'. They serve a largely Portuguese clientele and tend to rely heavily on family members and Portuguese employees. The main language of communication is Portuguese. Entrepreneurs explain that having employees who speak the same language gives clients 'a sense of trust and confidence' and makes them 'comfortable and happy'.[14] Knowledge of the clients' needs and preferences is also important. As one businessman explained, 'In my field you must understand the Portuguese culture to really be successful in the market.' Until the mid-1970s, the Portuguese economy was distinctly food-oriented, with large numbers of grocery, fruit, meat and fish stores. Subsequently there has been greater diversification. For instance, as the community has gradually dispersed, real-estate businesses which particularly target Portuguese clients have grown up along the corridor from the inner city to the suburbs.

Similar patterns can be observed in other inner-circle countries. Brick Lane in the London Borough of Tower Hamlets is another example of a thriving ethnic economy. Its proximity to the docks has meant that it has long been a popular area of settlement for immigrants and, in the early twentieth century, it was home to a large Jewish community. Jews have gradually been replaced over the years by Bangladeshis, and the main legacy of former times is two Jewish baker's shops. In contrast, the Bangladeshi presence is seen in the form of sweet shops, clothes shops, shops carrying Asian music, video and books, a halal butcher, a night club dedicated to Bhangra music, fabric shops and large numbers of restaurants and takeaways. Ethnic economies of this kind not only provide employment for large numbers of workers; they also create an environment where it is more natural to use the minority language than English.

Individual benefits

The financial benefits of bilingualism for the individual are clear. The use of Indigenous and established languages in education, the law, the media, politics and public services is creating an ever-increasing number of jobs that require bilingual skills. This, in turn, continues to drive the demand for bilingual education, as young people and their parents recognize the economic value of other languages.

Quite often there is a bilingual premium. In the 1960s, secretaries in Canadian federal government service were given a 10 per cent bonus if they used both languages 10 per cent of the time.[15] The Public Service Board in Australia used a similar strategy in the 1970s when federal officers in public contact work were given a Linguistic Availability Performance Allowance (LAPA) as an incentive to use their bilingual skills in their official duties.[16] More recently, the Los Angeles Police Department offered a 2.75 per cent salary increase to officers who speak Spanish or one of a number of Asian languages, rising to 5 per cent if they can demonstrate proficiency in reading and writing the language.[17] In the private sector, the shortage of bilingual skills in e-commerce has led some Internet companies to raise salaries for bilingual staff by as much as half.

The usefulness of bilingual and bicultural skills is recognized in other ways, too, including access to training and higher education in shortage professions. The *Los Angeles Times* recently called on Spanish speakers to apply to medical schools, arguing that admissions committees should place a higher premium on language competence and cultural sensitivity than on the highest possible MCAT (Medical College Admission Tests) scores.[18]

Global markets

Other languages play a role not only in ethnic economies but also in global markets. Knowledge of other languages is now widely recognized as offering businesses a competitive edge. While English may be the language of wider communication for the educated elite, the great bulk of the world's population only understand the local language. The implications are clear to see. To take just one example, North America has dominated e-commerce, but its share of the market is forecast to reduce to less than 50 per cent by 2004, because of very rapid growth in demand from Europe and Asia, where knowledge of other languages is essential to successful competition.[19]

Wendy Cai, the winner of the US Asian Women in Business award of 2000, is clear about the advantages of speaking Chinese in meetings in China: 'People in the room loosen up, and it makes negotiations much easier.'[20] Susan Au Allen, the president of the US Pan-Asian American Chamber of Commerce, makes a similar point when she argues for the potential of minority-owned businesses in developing products for new markets.

The City of London has the highest concentration of foreign banks in the world and its foreign exchange market accounts for over 30 per cent of world turnover. It is also the largest international insurance market. The focus on global trade and services has helped create a multilingual working environment. One of the reasons offered by international firms such as Delta Air Lines and Air France for maintaining London as a pan-European base for their customer call centres is the availability of staff with native-speaker skills in a very wide range of languages. Company headquarters coordinating geographically dispersed operations find London an attractive location for the same reasons.[21]

There is, of course, nothing novel about the cosmopolitan nature of the capital. Joseph Addison, writing in the early eighteenth century, talks of his personal pleasure and excitement at the multilingual nature of the Royal Exchange, which he describes as 'a kind of emporium for the whole earth'.[22] At the end of the nineteenth century, over a third of leading City firms employed foreigners. These companies were particularly popular with German clerks, who were prepared to work for a lower salary to gain experience, which would be valued on return to the home country.

Most multinational firms today employ people whose language skills are already in place. There is, however, no shortage of evidence that employees without these skills are eager to acquire them. In the insurance industry in London, Lloyds and the International Underwriting Association, for instance, have developed clubs in a range of languages. Teachers are provided for classes at beginner and lower intermediate levels but members also learn informally from each other, and web-support is targeted at members whose work requires them to travel, often at short notice.[23]

Although awareness of the need for foreign-language skills in business appears to be growing, positive strategies for responding to this need are not always evident. A 1992 survey commissioned by the London City Corporation and the Bank of England showed that an overwhelming majority of firms expected to conduct 'significant business' with the non-English-speaking world; of these, more than three-quarters considered that language skills would make a significant contribution to their competitiveness. Yet only half of the companies included in the survey had a policy on language skills and training.[24]

Australia, in contrast, has been more proactive and has started dealing with the training issue from the bottom up. When the entry of the UK into the European Community forced Australian exporters to reconsider their traditional markets, the inevitable conclusion was that the future lay in Asian markets.[25] The Productive Diversity Program encourages business to harness language skills and cultural knowledge of the workforce through resources such as case studies and training kits.[26] Australia is a country where one in five jobs are export-related, and over 40 per cent of the workforce were either born overseas themselves or have a parent born overseas. This means that Australian companies are well placed to exploit networks and knowledge of business practices in overseas markets, as well as of consumer tastes and preferences. The introduction of Chinese, Japanese, Indonesian and Korean into the secondary curriculum is another measure intended to allow Australians to compete more successfully. Aotearoa/New Zealand, too, has also broadened its outlook in response to trading realities.[27]

Minority markets

Minority communities not only have a part to play in reaching wider markets; they also form a niche market for mainstream businesses and corporations. This is certainly the case, for instance, with the Hispanic home market in the USA.[28] *Selecciones*, the Spanish-language version of *Reader's Digest*, has made a deliberate attempt to make its content more relevant to the target population; and Home Box Office has launched a Latino channel. Several corporations produce magazines targeted specifically at Hispanics. Procter and Gamble delivered *Avanzando con tu familia* (*Moving On with Your Family*) to 4.5 million households in a marketing initiative designed to gain consumer trust; *Nuestra gente* (*Our People*), a quarterly magazine with articles on Hispanic celebrities and fashion produced by Sears, has a circulation of 700,000.

Many companies have increased their efforts to reach ethnic consumers through telemarketing and advertising, and these, in turn, are generating specialist businesses to meet their needs. Asian American Telemarketing (AAT) offers services in six Asian languages and English to a wide range of clients, including telecommunications corporations such as MCI and Sprint, and express and logistics company DHL. A workforce of 1,200 interpreters at AT&T's LanguageLine offers telephone interpreting and document translation in 140 languages. Some businesses also maximize their potential client base by advertising their language skills. Deafweb Washington, for instance, contains listings of real-estate agents who know sign language.

Things are developing in a similar way in the UK. The organization Race for Opportunity (RfO) offers support to over 170 leading private- and public-sector organizations in marketing to ethnic minorities and provides support for ethnic minority businesses as part of the supplier chain. Allan Leighton, the chairman of RfO, is quick to point out that 'successful business people are neither colour-blind nor prejudiced, but ones that are able to see all people, regardless of ethnic background, as people with bank accounts, degrees, families and lifestyles'.[29] HSBC, one of its supporters, is currently offering a banking service specifically tailored to the needs of the South Asian business community. Significantly, almost half of the staff involved in this initiative are from South Asian backgrounds.

Australian business has identified similar concerns.[30] The overall ethnic market in Australia consists of approximately 4 million potential buyers, a significant market segment, particularly in cities like Sydney and Melbourne where in the region of half the residents (or one of their parents) were born overseas.

Tourism

Other languages are important for the cultural tourism industry, a growing source of income for many established and Indigenous communities. It gives visitors access to the lifestyles, heritages, languages and peoples that help to make the destination distinctive. Surveys undertaken by the industry show consistently that a significant and increasing proportion of visitors look for cultural experiences as a major component of their holidays.[31] Other languages play an essential role in this process.

In the British Isles, there is a growing recognition that the use of Welsh, Irish and Gaelic helps to win new customers. Within the hospitality industry, many tourist operators seek out establishments that provide their customers with an experience unique to the country they are visiting. Seeing and hearing another language adds a sense of difference. The Welsh Tourist Board, for instance, offers financial support for bilingual signs and particularly favours 'cluster schemes', where all the businesses in a particular neighbourhood apply for funding in order to make a stronger visual impact. Bilingual signs contribute to 'a sense of place', a clear selling point for visitors.

Port Meirion, a private village and holiday centre in North Wales, is an interesting case study of new attitudes towards Welsh in the service industries. The 85 per cent of employees who are already Welsh speakers are encouraged to use Welsh as well as English in all aspects of their work and customer relations; English-speaking staff wishing to learn the language are offered active support. Portmeirion's managing director, Robin Llywelyn, sums up the success of this policy: 'Our extensive use of Welsh creates a sense of local goodwill and enriches our visitors' experience. It also ensures that we attract significant numbers of Welsh people to stay and visit. Guests realise they have come to a place which plays a part in the history and culture of the surrounding area, rather than merely being in a "tourist trap".'[32]

In Ireland, the value of the Irish language was estimated in 2000 at about £IR50 million a year in Galway City alone.[33] Proposals to establish the city as the world centre of living, traditional Irish and Celtic culture

The bilingual 'Working Welsh' promotional materials help to market Wales and Welsh products and services by creating a sense of place.
Reproduced with permission from the Welsh Language Board.

are confidently expected to attract growing numbers of tourists and also to stimulate economic and social development. The Irish language is central to plans for special events and festivals involving music, dance and theatre.

In recent years, the enormous growth of interest in Gaelic language and culture has affected all areas of life in Scotland. In the early 1990s, the 'Gaelic Economy' was sustaining an estimated 1,000 full-time equivalent jobs and contributing £UK42.5 million to the Scottish gross domestic product.[34] The Failte project, based on four bilingual communities in the Western Isles, is a good example of attempts to realize the commercial potential of bilingualism. Visitors experience at first hand the language, culture and traditions of the region at the same time as providing year-round employment.

Indigenous languages and cultures are also attracting attention. In Aotearoa/New Zealand, Māori culture is now widely accepted as a key factor in Aotearoa/New Zealand identity, and many visitors are at least as interested in Indigenous culture as in the landscape.[35] In material directed at potential sponsors, it was claimed that the campaign to use 'kia ora' (Māori for 'be well') as a national greeting and farewell would help businesses expand into an international market worth $NZ1.7 billion annually. The promotion of the language in this way raises some uncomfortable questions as to who precisely owns the language. The Māori Language Commission supported the campaign, but with the proviso that it hoped it would lead to a deeper knowledge of the Māori language in the tourist industry.

One of the main issues for those involved in cultural tourism in Australian Aboriginal communities is the amount of knowledge that should be shared with those outside; another is the placing of monetary value on a living, ancient culture. The interpretation of Aboriginal culture by non-Aboriginal guides is also a matter of concern.[36] In this respect, the growth of Aboriginal-owned companies such as Anangu Tours is to be welcomed. Anangu offer first-hand experience of Aboriginal life, including living off the land and learning the many stories connected to the land, in Uluru Kata Tjuta National Park. Cultural tourism and ecotourism are also thriving in Canada, where Aboriginal Business Canada helps individuals and communities develop commercially viable tourism products sensitive to Aboriginal traditions and values. Language is a central element in this process. As is the case in other locations, it helps enhance the sense of place essential to the tourist experience and, at the same time, offers ideal conditions for the use of Indigenous languages in the workplace.

Cultural difference is now receiving recognition for its contribution to the economy not only in established and Indigenous communities but also among new minorities. The United Colours of London pages of the BBC website, for instance, draw attention to: '33 boroughs, seven million people, 300 languages and enough bars and restaurants to experience a different part of the world everyday. Welcome to London, the multicultural epicentre of Europe.'[37] Information on some 30 different communities includes links to food and shopping.

Cultural tourism is, of course, just one aspect of a much larger growth industry. Since the early 1980s, the number of overseas tourists to Australia each year has more than tripled and export earnings have grown by more than 500 per cent.[38] Tourism is similarly a growth industry in the UK, with an estimated 38 million visitors each year by 2010.[39] Although English is very widely used as a lingua franca, it cannot be assumed that tourists will be willing or able to communicate in English. Both Aotearoa/New Zealand and Australia, for instance, receive large numbers of Japanese and Chinese visitors whose level of competence in English is often low. The ability to offer services in other languages thus gives businesses a keen competitive edge.

Language and the workplace

There is, of course, a tension between the policies which have helped to weaken the multilingual capacity of inner-circle countries over the years and the current rhetoric surrounding the usefulness of other languages in tourism and other areas of the economy. One obvious inconsistency concerns status. While the bilingualism of upper-class speakers is valued, the language skills of lower-class employees are often overlooked, even when there are obvious applications in the workplace. A consequence of this ambivalence is the serious shortage of people with bilingual skills.[40]

When a business employs people from the same language background, it is only natural that they should use this language in the workplace. But when the management of the business in question is English speaking, the situation is sometimes less clear-cut. In Canada, the language of the workplace has become a highly charged political issue. The federal government responded to pressure from Quebec by establishing a Royal Commission on Bilingualism and Biculturalism (1963–71). The impact of the commission was first seen in changes in public service at the federal level. The Treasury Board announced objectives for providing all correspondence with the public in both languages and for increasing the numbers of bilingual employees. A resolution was passed giving French and English equal status as the language of work in the federal civil service, in order to ensure the full participation of members of both language communities. Public servants were offered language training and language was identified as a criterion for appointment.[41]

As the political power of Francophones increased, so, too, did the measures designed to protect language rights in the workplace.[42] With the passing of the Charter of the French Language in 1977, all businesses with over 50 employees had to undertake 'francization' programmes to make it possible to work in French in both the public and the private sectors. This legislation was so successful in opening up a range of higher-status occupations that much of the machinery for its enforcement was abolished in 1993. Monitoring, however, has remained an important issue and questions on language use in the workplace were included for the first time in the 2001 census. The data they produce will be used in forecasting language-training requirements and planning the services required by the Official Languages Act.

The position of Welsh in the workplace has also undergone important change. The requirement to provide public services through the medium of Welsh is a core element of the 1993 Welsh Language Act. Bilingual skills are now required in an ever-widening range of situations: interpreters and officials in courts of law where Welsh is the medium of communication; translators of official documents; receptionists handling calls from Welsh speakers; secretaries and executive officers needing to process written inquiries in Welsh. The 1993 legislation places an obligation on public bodies to prepare Welsh-language schemes, setting out the practical steps required to ensure that Welsh and English are dealt with on the basis of equality.[43]

The principle is now extending from public to commercial bodies and partnership agreements have been established between the Welsh Language Board and a wide range of companies, including several banks and a large supermarket chain. The board is also spearheading a number of initiatives to promote the language in business settings. Bilingualism gives a clear advantage when dealing with Welsh-speaking customers, and 'Iaith gwaith/Working Welsh' badges, signs and stickers help customers recognize members of staff who speak the language. The use of Welsh in marketing activities such as advertisements, brochures and leaflets also sends a very positive message, particularly to Welsh speakers, while bilingual packaging and labelling of goods made in Wales gives manufacturers a chance to add to their exclusivity. Another significant development concerns the mentrau iaith, a network of community-based local language initiatives, which offer businesses advice and practical assistance on how Welsh might be used more.

Gains for Welsh in the workplace have, however, been contested. The BBC recently reported that the owner of the Celtic Royal hotel had admitted that staff working as porters in the restaurant or in the reception area were forbidden to speak Welsh if non-Welsh-speaking visitors were present. Examples of this kind are, however, rare.[44]

The language of the workplace is also emerging as an issue in the US.[45] Here the Equal Employment Opportunity Commission (EEOC) has written guidelines designed to ensure that no individual is subject to discrimination on the basis of 'the linguistic characteristics of a national group'. The EEOC recognizes that there are situations where employees may need to use English in conducting business, but deems that attempts to prohibit the use of other languages during personal time create an atmosphere of intimidation, inferiority and isolation, and therefore constitute national origin discrimination.

The number of English-only charges filed with the EEOC and with state and local Fair Employment Practices Agencies increased from 91 in 1996 to 443 in 2000. Hispanic employees are often the subject of discrimination. In Texas, Premier Operator Services, Inc., a long-distance operator service, banned the use of other languages at all times, including lunch and other breaks. The company's language policy was posted on a sign at the entrance of the building, alongside a warning that 'absolutely no guns, knives or weapons of any kind' were allowed on the premises.[46] Thirteen Hispanic employees, who, ironically, had been hired because they could speak Spanish, were fired after refusing to sign the company language policy, and filed discrimination charges with the EEOC. In finding in favour of the plaintiffs, magistrate judge Paul D. Stickney was persuaded by expert testimony from Susan Berk-Seligson, a linguist from the University of Pittsburgh, that the unconscious habit of code-switching between languages makes it very difficult for bilinguals to speak English all the time. He also rejected the idea that English-only policies promote harmony: 'Quite the opposite . . . the policy served to create a disruption in the workplace and feelings of alienation and inadequacy by . . . proven performers.'

Another case involving Hispanic employees was a class-action lawsuit brought against the University of the Incarnate Word (UIW), a private university in San Antonio, Texas, on behalf of 18 housekeepers.[47] The director of housekeeping had required the housekeepers to speak only English at all times, and those who failed to comply were subjected to repeated verbal and physical abuse, as well as ethnic slurs. Meanwhile in Illinois, Watlow Batavia, Inc., disciplined employees for speaking Spanish to co-workers and friends. One assembly-line worker, Marcelina Navar, was fired after greeting a co-worker with 'Buenas dias'.

Other groups have also exercised their legal rights. In Page, Arizona, a policy was posted at RD's Drive-In, a diner where the vast majority of employees spoke Navajo, stating: 'The owner of this business can speak and understand only English. While the owner is paying you as an employee, you are required to use English at all times. The only exception is when the customer can not understand English. If you feel unable to comply with this requirement, you may find another job.'[48] Two employees, Roxanne Cahoon and Freda Douglas, who refused to agree to the policy and were asked to leave their employment, won compensatory and punitive damages.

Working languages

Inter-relationships between language and the economy are both complex and productive. Ethnic economies provide important opportunities to use minority languages. It is more natural and efficient to communicate with co-workers in the other language; customers also feel more comfortable. The workplace provides an additional context for using minority languages, helping ensure their vitality. The use of other languages can also be an attraction for outsiders. Tourists, for instance, are interested not only in the scenery but in new cultural experiences: other languages help create a sense of place and mark the destination out as different.

English may be the language of global trading, but the ability to speak other languages none the less ensures a competitive edge. The multilingual populations of inner-circle countries are a valuable resource, which we overlook at our peril. Their contribution to international business is becoming increasingly evident in areas such as China and the Middle East. Until the recent migrations, the capacity of English-speaking countries to use the languages of these regions was exceptionally weak. The growing bilingual, bicultural population has the confidence of both parties in negotiations; they are invaluable assets in any business setting.

Language is also an important tool in reaching minority markets. Business has only recently awoken to the fact that minority communities make up a significant market segment and that the most effective way of reaching these communities is through the minority-language media. Initiatives that target minorities rely heavily on the knowledge and experience of minority-language speakers. So, too, do the public and private agencies which provide services for minority communities. Bilinguals are a marketable commodity; the ability to speak other languages opens up a far wider range of better-paid employment opportunities than might otherwise be the case.

As is the case in other areas of activity, minority languages are sometimes the subject of suspicion and the right to use them is contested. While legislation protects members of minority communities from the worst excesses of prejudice, the desire to curb the use of other languages in the workplace is a reminder of the fragility of minority rights.

Notes

1   Teschner (1995).
2   Modood et al. (1997).
3   Williams (1984).
4   Hosmer (1999).
5   MHA (1992).
6   Dion (1991).
7   Guinnane (1997).
8   Taskforce on Public Funding of Gaelic (2000).
9   For further discussion of the Gaelic economy, see Sproull (1996).
10 Davies (1993).
11 Ladd (2003).
12 Connell (2000: 73–9).
13 Holmes (1988: 53).
14 Teixeira (2001).
15 Burnaby (1996: 164).
16 Ozolins (1998).
17 Carreira and Armengol (2001: 112).
18 Carreira and Armengol (2001. 122).
19 Crystal (2001).
20 Carreira and Armengol (2001: 115).
21 Land (2000).
22 *Spectator*, no. 69, 1711, cited in Connell (2000: 74).
23 Land (2000: 76).
24 Land (2000: 77).
25 Herriman (1996).
26 www.immi.gov.au/facts/07productive.htm
27 Waite (1992); Peddie (2003: 16–17).
28 Carreira and Armengol (2001: 113–14).
29 Business in the Community (2003).
30 LEBA Ethnic Media (undated).
31 See, for instance, Australia (1994); van Aalst and Daly (2002).
32 Welsh Language Board (2002).
33 www.gleg.ie/gaeilge_saghno4.html
34 Sproull (1996).
35 Benton (1996: 77).
36 Lester (2002).
37 www.bbc.co.uk/london/yourlondon/unitedcolours/index.shtml
38 Australia (1994).

39   Nuffield Languages Inquiry (2000: 25).
40   Mears (1997).
41   Burnaby (1996).
42   Levine (1991).
43   www.bwrdd-yr-iaith.org.uk
44   BBC (2000).
45   EEOC (2000).
46   Del Valle (2003).
47   EEOC (2001).
48   EEOC (2002).

9

Language and the media

In the early days of migration, the only means of mass communication was print – newspapers, pamphlets and books. The twentieth century, in contrast, saw a dramatic proliferation of the media, starting with radio and television and progressing to transnational broadcasts via satellite and the Internet. In most inner-circle countries, the state played a leading role in the development of the new media and exercised considerable influence over content. With the notable exception of Ireland, minority languages were effectively excluded. Recent technological advances, however, have created a range of opportunities for other languages. The easy availability of personal computers and desktop publishing software has reduced the cost of producing print media and made it possible to publish on the Internet. Digitization and satellite technology, in turn, have increased the range of options for low-cost broadcasting to remote locations. In the same way as the dominance of American films and TV played a key role in the development of English as a global language, programming in other languages influences the health and vitality of minority languages.

Because the media are such an integral part of daily life, the languages associated with them have a profound influence. As one commentator has pointed out: 'Language denied access to media is discriminated against, accorded inferior status and is unlikely to survive.'[1] This chapter looks at the impact of the efforts of minority communities in this area.

The minority press

The minority press, the longest established of the media, is vibrant in the inner-circle countries. It takes a wide variety of forms and serves many different functions. There is inevitably a shift from minority languages to English over time. However, the use of other languages remains widespread, making information more accessible to many readers at the same time as reinforcing group identity.

The Indigenous press

Indigenous peoples in many parts of the world were disenfranchised until the 1960s and lacked even symbolic access to mainstream media. Their voices have remained largely silent in mainstream newspapers, even in coverage of events that centrally concern them. Case studies of the Australian press in the late 1990s, for instance, showed Aboriginal people were used as sources as little as 20 per cent of the time in articles on Indigenous issues.[2] The minority press has thus provided an outlet for reporting matters important to the target audience.

Although graphic representations, such as symbols in sand writing and body painting, have been widely used by Indigenous peoples for thousands of years, their languages were unwritten before the advent of European settlers. Literacy, at first in Indigenous languages and later in English, was introduced either by missionaries or through contact with the newcomers. The Cherokee silversmith Sequoyah, for instance, became convinced of the value of literacy for his people after being shown how to write his name by a White farmer.[3] The Talking Leaves syllabary, which he developed for writing his language, was used in the *Cherokee Phoenix*, a bilingual newspaper, first published in 1828. The power of print in giving voice to Indigenous aspirations was quickly recognized by the US government, which responded by smashing the printing presses and evicting the Cherokee from their tribal lands.

The first regular Indigenous publication in Australia, the *Aboriginal* or *Flinders Island Chronicle*, appeared in 1836, but lasted only a year.[4] Subsequently the only written sources of Aboriginal news were small, community-based publications, some of which used local languages. It was not until the 1960s and 1970s that the number of these publications dramatically increased. Often produced in collaboration with the local school to support a bilingual literacy programme, these magazines and newsletters usually consisted of traditional stories, together with community notices and health messages.[5] More recently, local provision has expanded into national reporting on Aboriginal matters in the *Koori News*, a weekly publication with subscriptions from large numbers of ATSI organizations all over the country.

Indigenous language publishing in Aotearoa/New Zealand was more widespread than in Australia and has been preserved in a remarkable digital collection – the Niupepa – which consists of over 17,000 pages taken from 34 separate periodicals between 1842 and 1943.[6] Only 2 per cent of this collection is written solely in English; well over half is in Māori, and the rest is bilingual. Some of the niupepa were government sponsored; others were initiated by Māoris or religious organizations.

In Canada, the Aboriginal press underwent a renaissance in the 1960s following modest funding from the federal government through the Native Communication Program, and by the mid-1980s, the combined circulation of Aboriginal newspapers had reached 46,000.[7] The *Wawatay News* achieved the status of the most widely read literature written in Oji-Cree syllabics after the Bible. The sudden withdrawal of government support in 1990 meant that fewer than half of the publications established in this period have survived. None the less, some publications continue to thrive. *Tusagaksait*, for instance, is published in three different languages – English, French and Inuktitut – and two different scripts – syllabics for readers in the eastern Arctic region and Roman orthography for readers elsewhere in Nunavut.[8] The vast majority of Indigenous publications today, however, are written in English.

The established language press

Provision for established languages varies a great deal from community to community. Given its size and political strength, the Francophone community in Canada is, predictably, by far the best served of the established language groups. Quebec has a wide range of dailies, such as the Montreal-based *La Presse*, *La Tribune* in Sherbrooke and *Le Nouvelliste* in Trois Rivières. There is also a plethora of weekly, monthly and periodical publications. Outside Quebec, the Manitoba-based *La Liberté* is one of a number of daily newspapers serving provincial audiences. Local community-based publications are also widespread. *L'Informel*, a newsletter produced by the Franco-Ontarian community in Kingston, is typical of such local publications. Fifteen hundred copies are distributed to Francophone schools, the university, the military college, offices and libraries. A small team of volunteers is responsible for all aspects of production, from page layout to distribution. Nicole Bérubé, the editor, describes the main function of *L'Informel* as: 'informing Francophones and Francophiles about what's happening in French in Kingston and in the wider French-speaking community'.[9]

tusagaksait ⊃ᖅᐅᒃᓴᐃᑦ

Vol.2 No.1 Winter 2001/2002

ᐃᓄᐃᑦ ᑕᐱᕇᒃᓴᑦ ᑲᓇᑕᒥ ᐊᑎᒥᖕᓂᒃ
ᐊᓯᔾᔨᖅᓯᓚᐅᕐᒪᑕ ᐃᓄᐃᑦ ᑕᐱᕇᑦ ᑲᓇᑕᒥᒧᑦ

inuit tapiriiksat kanatami atimingnik asijjiqsilaurmata inuit tapiriit kanatamimut

INUIT TAPIRISAT OF CANADA CHANGES NAME TO INUIT TAPIRIIT KANATAMI
INUIT TAPIRISAT DU CANADA DEVIENT INUIT TAPIRIIT KANATAMI

The Inuit Tapirisat of Canada (ITC) has changed its name to Inuit Tapiriit Kanatami (ITK). The new name celebrates the achievement of the previous ITC mandate, now that land claims settlements are complete in three regions, the Inuvialuit region, Nunavut and Nunavik, and an agreement-in-principle with Labrador just this past year.

When ITC was founded in 1971, the term 'Tapirisat' indicated that Inuit were 'going to be united' within Canada. 'Tapiriit' signifies that Inuit are united within Canada.

The name change is also significant because it includes the Inuktitut language within a multicultural and multilingual society. "Kanatami" is Inuktitut for "in Canada". Another minor but significant advantage stemming from the change is the acronym. With the change, ITK is less likely to be confused with ICC (Inuit Circumpolar Conference).

Although the new name is already verbally in use, the name change process won't be complete until this spring. Until then, ITK will use the remaining stock of ITC letterhead, business cards and other stationary. ITK is also in the midst of selecting a new logo. The new visual identity will be unveiled on April 1 2002.

inuit tapiriiksat kanatami atimingnik asijjiqsilaurmata inuit tapiriit kanatamimut. atiqtaasaarijangat nakunaiqsiniuvuq inuit tapiriiksakkut piliriaksarilauqtanginnik pijariiqsisimalirnirminik, nunataarasugutaujut pingasuujunit nunanit inuvialuit nunangat, nunavut ammalu nunavik angirutausimaanilirmata ammaluttauq laapatuarimiut angirutimik arraanisaaq atiliulaurillutik.

inuit tapiriiksat pigiaqtitautillugu 1971mi, uqausinga 'tapiriiksat' tukiqalaurmat inuit tapiriililaarninginnik kanatami. 'tapiriit' tukiqaapuq inuit tapiriiraanilirmata kanatami.

atingata asijjiqtauninga piuniqarivuq inuit uqausingannik aturmat inungnut ajjiigiinngittunut nunagijaujumiitilluta. 'kanatami' inuktitut titiraqsimangmat. ammattauq pimmariulunanngittuuqaluarli, asijjiqtauninga qallunaatitut ITK nalulirutauqattajjaanngilirmat ICCmut (inuit silarjuami katujjiqatigiikkunnut).

atitaasaarijanga atuqtauliuniktuq uqausiinnakkut, titiqqatigut asingitigullu pianitainnamiaqtuq kisiani upirngaaq. upirngalaunginningani ITKkkut ITC titirarviksaqutivininginnik turaaqtautinginnik asinginniglu titirarviksanginnik aturniaqtut. inuit tapiriikkut maanna niruarasukpallialiqtut titiraujagariniaqtamingnik. titiraujagaq niruarijaujuq saqqitaulaaqtuq April 1, 2002mi.

Inuit Tapirisat du Canada (ITC) s'appellera désormais Inuit Tapiriit Kanatami (ITK). Ce nouveau nom traduit les réalisations enregistrées pendant le mandat précédent d'ITC alors que les revendications territoriales sont terminées dans trois régions, celles d'Inuvialuit, de Nunavut et de Nunavik, et qu'un accord de principe a été conclu l'a dernier avec le Labrador.

Lors de la création d'ITC en 1971, le terme « Tapirisat » indiquait que les Inuit (allaient être unis) au sein du Canada. « Tapiriit veut que les Inuit soient unis au sein du Canada.

L'adoption du nouveau nom est également significative parce qu'elle fait appel à la langue inuktitut au sein d'une société multiculturelle et multilingue. « Kanatami » est le terme inuktitut pour « Au Canada ». Un autre avantage mineur, sans être pour autant négligeable, du nouveau sigle est que ITK sera moins facile à confondre avec ICC (Conférence circumpolaire inuit).

Si la nouvelle appellation est déjà utilisée oralement, le processus de changement de nom ne sera pas terminé avant ce printemps. D'ici là, ITK utilisera les stocks qui lui restent de papier à en-tête, de cartes d'affaires et d'autre papeterie d'ITC. ITK va également se choisir un nouveau local. La nouvelle identité visuelle sera dévoilée le 1er avril 2002.

Tusagaksait, the publication of Inuit Tapiriit Kanatami – the organization which speaks out on behalf of the Inuit of Canada (www.itk.ca) – is published in English, French and Inuktitut. The eastern Arctic region uses syllabics; the rest of Nunavut uses Roman orthography.

The Celtic languages are rather less well served, with no daily papers but a wide range of periodicals. There is also a network of Welsh-language community newspapers in Wales. Scots now appears regularly in two major daily newspapers, and *Ullans*, the annual magazine of the Ulster-Scots Language Society, serves as a forum for new writing in Ulster-Scots.

The press in new minority communities

The minority press has a long history of catering for the needs of people who are literate in other languages. The first German-language newspaper in the USA, *Die Philadelphische Zeitung*, dates back to 1732.[10] Its editor, Benjamin Franklin, who was at times critical of the growing influence of German, was none the less able to recognize a commercial opportunity. In the most comprehensive survey of the minority press ever undertaken, Joshua Fishman shows the decline in the US minority press between 1910 and 1960, a period during which the scale of immigration had reduced to a trickle. Yet even in the 1960s, the non-English press boasted a readership of approximately five and a half million. Predictably, the relaxation of immigration restrictions in North America from the 1960s onwards has had the effect of revitalizing the minority press. The tiny Korean community of Toronto is a case in point.[11] Until the 1970s, it depended on newspapers received by mail either from Korea, or from US cities where there were older and larger Korean settlements. As the numbers of Koreans in Toronto increased, small grocery stores throughout the city began distributing the *Korea Times* from Seoul. The first local newspaper in Korean appeared in 1971; in the next 10 years, another seven titles followed.

The German-language press in Australia dates from 1848, and was soon joined by newspapers in Chinese, French, Gaelic, Scandinavian languages and Welsh. As was the case in the USA, English-speaking politicians used the German-language press to reach electors in Victoria and South Australia. Official announcements also appeared in newspapers in the languages of all the larger immigrant groups. Only seven newspapers survived government restrictions dating from World War I on the foreign-language press. However, many of the community bulletins serving displaced persons after World War II developed into newspaper format, and mass-circulation newspapers from the home countries were also widely available.[12]

The minority press is currently flourishing in the inner-circle countries. In the UK, 40 or so newspapers and periodicals serve 11 different language communities. In Australia, more than 150 publications meet the needs of some 38 language communities.[13] In Canada, there are in excess of 100 daily, weekly, monthly or quarterly ethnic-language publications in Toronto alone. New York is also experiencing a boom: in 2000, almost 200 magazines and newspapers representing over 50 ethnic and national groups were publishing in 36 languages.[14] Nationally, the combined circulation of the Chinese-language US dailies grew from about 170,000 in 1990 to half a million at the end of the century. The large Hispanic communities are particularly well served, with four Spanish-language dailies and 13 weekly or monthly newspapers that focus on a specific country of origin.

The minority press usually starts as a small-scale operation, with the same person often serving as journalist, editor, distributor and printer. Many publications are family-owned and invest whatever they earn back into their enterprise. Although most titles remain in the hands of independent owners, there are exceptions. Media companies in Taiwan or Hong Kong own the major US Chinese papers, while the *Korea Central Daily News* is the US edition of a Samsung-owned paper in Korea. In the UK, *Parikiaki*, the London Greek Cypriot newspaper, is affiliated to *Haravgi*, a newspaper in Cyprus.

In the newer communities, the minority press usually focuses on national and international news, and news and sports from the home country. In older, more established communities, the assumption is that most readers will be able to access news in English and so the focus is on the home country. Newspapers try, of course, to address as wide an audience as possible and use language accordingly. Thus *Parikiaki* uses Greek for news that is likely to be mainly of interest to the migrant generation and English for information likely to appeal to younger people.[15] On other occasions, bilingual publications are designed to reach diverse audiences rather than bridge the generation gap. In London, the Tower Hamlets Council established *East End Life* in the early 1990s to make public information more easily available.[16] The balance has gradually shifted over the years from information to news, and now it has the feel of a local newspaper. Free copies are delivered to every home in the borough – 72,000 a week. The council funds the paper to provide public information, while other aspects of its work are covered by advertising revenue. Although English is the dominant language, two pages of each issue are dedicated to the other main languages of Tower Hamlets: Bengali and Somali. An opinion poll commissioned by the paper showed that it was the main source of information about news in the area for non-English speakers. In New York, neighbourhood newspapers sometimes serve a similar purpose, carrying local news in Spanish and in English.

Radio and TV

The minority press has a number of functions. On the one hand, it is an effective tool for the preservation of minority languages and cultures; on the other hand, it provides an effective means of communication both within the communities in question and with mainstream society. Radio and TV fulfil these functions, too. However, they are also an important medium of entertainment, with the potential to reach a much wider audience, including those who are illiterate in the minority language, in English or in both.

During the first half of the twentieth century, state control of radio and television in Europe and Australia was strong. The reasons for state involvement were partly financial, since the infrastructure for broadcasting required massive investment and few organizations had the resources to take on a project of this size.[17] But governments were also quick to see the potential of media that would ultimately reach into every home, not simply as tools for entertainment but also to reinforce the core values of those in power. The monopoly of state-owned companies such as the BBC and Radio Telefís Éireann (RTÉ) gave way to market pressure for a wider range of programming only in the late twentieth century. Today, state companies in these countries coexist with local, national, foreign and international services on cable, satellite and digital networks.

Broadcasting in Indigenous languages

Radio and, later, television were limited in the early years to densely populated areas on the grounds of cost. Despite the growing urbanization of Indigenous peoples, many remain in remote and scattered homelands. It was only in the mid-1970s that new technologies using video-tape, microwave and, in due course, satellite made the delivery of services to even for the most distant communities economically viable. Significantly, these technical advances coincided with the growing politicization of Indigenous peoples, who were only too aware of the threat of mainstream media to traditional languages and cultures. Rosemarie Kuptana, a former president of the Inuit Broadcasting Corporation, once likened 'southern' television to a neutron bomb, while Australian Aboriginal linguist Eve Fesl described English satellite TV as 'cultural nerve gas'.[18] The challenges posed by Western media are neatly illustrated by an Inuit woman's description of her first viewing of *All in the Family* (the US version of the British sitcom *'Til Death Us Do Part*):

There was the father, obviously a stupid man, shouting at his children and his wife. He seemed to hate them. They were lying to him, they were treating him with contempt, they were screaming back at him and then in the last five minutes everyone kissed and made up. We were always taught to treat our elders with respect. I was embarrassed for those people on TV. I know I always thought white people were weird. I wondered if that was really what people were like in the South.[19]

Indigenous peoples have pressed for local control of telecommunications as a means of resisting the destructive potential of mainstream media. Yet, unlike disputes over land claims, native-language broadcasting has been a relatively uncontentious issue. Developments in this area have allowed governments to appear to be listening to Aboriginal peoples, at the same time as providing a showcase for their technological capabilities. Telecommunications is thus one of those rare areas where there has been a convergence of interests with mainstream society.

In Canada, native broadcasting has been receiving federal support since the Northern Native Broadcast Access Program (NNBAP) was established in 1983 with a specific remit to protect and enhance native languages and cultures in the north. It was, however, almost a decade later that Indigenous broadcasting came of age with the launch of Television Northern Canada (TVNC), a dedicated native satellite television network, broadcasting to an estimated audience of 100,000. Building on the success of TVNC, the Aboriginal Peoples Television Network (APTN) was launched in 1999 as a cable service available throughout Canada.[20] Seen by many as a major step in building bridges of understanding between the Aboriginal and non-aboriginal peoples of Canada, APTN broadcasts approximately 120 hours per week of programming in English, French and Aboriginal languages.

Advances in technology have also contributed to new developments in radio. In a very recent development, the Aboriginal peoples of Canada are finally able to listen to programmes provided by a national network, Aboriginal Voices Radio (AVR), distributed through over-the-air broadcasting on AVR stations in major urban centres and direct transmission by cable, satellite and the Internet.[21] AVR aims to provide an everyday connection between the growing urban Indigenous populations and more rural communities. News and spoken-word programmes are broadcast in at least six of Canada's most commonly used Aboriginal languages.

Local control has often led to highly innovative uses of new technologies. Most mainstream communities look to radio for entertainment and news. Yet when a network of high-frequency radios was introduced in the early 1970s, the Nishnawbe-Aski Nation were much more excited at their potential for point-to-point communication for people who were lonely or lost out on the trap line, and who needed to reach their home base.[22] The Wawatay Communications Society has been particularly successful in adapting the technology to meet local needs. Originally established to produce native-language newspapers, they diversified to become local experts in a wide range of media. They won government funding in 1974 to set up an FM radio system, but rapidly branched out into AM radio stations, developing a 'package' which any community could buy, with all the equipment necessary for a one-watt radio station broadcasting within a radius of a mile. In the late 1970s, a communications satellite was used to connect four communities, allowing a regular exchange of news and information.

In order to qualify for federal funding, Canadian communications societies had to be managed by people of native ancestry, serve a designated native audience and demonstrate popular support for their efforts. Local control is also a feature of Australian Indigenous broadcasting. Some communities effectively invented their own television service, using domestic video and audio equipment to produce videos for hire as an alternative to film nights organized by Europeans.[23] It was not until the mid-1980s that the Broadcasting in Remote Aboriginal Communities Service (BRACS) provided the technology for communities to over-ride satellite TV and radio services, and broadcast their own locally produced programmes.

Indigenous broadcasting is beset with problems: coverage is required in a large numbers of languages for small numbers of people on very low budgets. Attempts to find solutions include spot programming in individual languages and the sharing of programme material between broadcasters. However, even small changes in personnel or levels of funding can have the effect of reducing or even eliminating Indigenous-language programmes.[24]

Indigenous broadcasting is highly distinctive: the contrast with mainstream programming is clearly illustrated by looking at different treatments of the same theme. European films of traditional ceremonies, for instance, tend to be tightly edited with an ongoing narrative. Aboriginal programmes are made in real time, with conversations between the songs and dances assuming as much importance as the action. Sometimes one kinship group is responsible for production while the other actually appears in the film, thus mirroring traditional practice where one clan conducts the ceremony and the other clan takes a supporting role. Similar patterns were in evidence when 27 Warlpiri were required to vouch for the legitimacy of a story, even though only a small number appeared on camera.[25] Style is also highly distinctive. A hallmark of many Aboriginal productions is the long, uninterrupted shots of landscape, often accompanied by traditional music. The Inuit also tend to favour long takes and natural sound.

The convergence of various telecommunications technologies has opened up a range of possibilities of particular interest for Aboriginal communities.[26] Small television networks allow speakers in separate communities to share experiences in their common language. Video-conferencing is used for many different purposes – family and ceremonial links, negotiations for the sale of arts and crafts, education and medical consultations. It is even used to verify the presence of people who have committed minor offences as part of community detention programmes.

The clear focus on commercial imperatives in US broadcasting has meant that Indigenous media have developed in rather different ways. Indigenous radio has a relatively long history, though coverage was for many years extremely patchy. Until the 1970s, for instance, broadcasting in the Navajo language was confined to small programme blocks on border-town stations.[27] The first native-owned, native-language station, KTDB, went live in 1972 to serve the Ramah Navajo Reservation. Today there are several Navajo-language radio stations, public and private, as well as regular programmes on local Christian radio. The launch of KTNN Radio in 1986, however, was groundbreaking in that it reached the entire Navajo Nation. Today it claims to be the largest Indigenous-language commercial radio in the world.

Although there is no support for US Indigenous broadcasting comparable to that in Canada and Australia, the Federal Communications Commission requires cable companies to make their airwaves available to the public. The Intertribal Wordpath Society (IWS) is one of many Indigenous groups to make use of this public access, in this case to produce *Wordpath*, a 30-minute weekly television show about Oklahoma Indian languages.[28] A typical show consists of an interview with one or more guests who talk about their background and why their language is important. They often tell a story or sing a song in their language, which can be used in classes later. A grant from the Endangered Language Fund is allowing IWS to develop two mini-dramas – one in Creek, the other in Choctaw – for the entertainment of fluent speakers and for use in language classes. The programme reaches 20,000 households in the Norman, Oklahoma, area. Copies are also placed in libraries around the state, so that people outside Norman or without cable can view them.

In Aotearoa/New Zealand, developments in the media have been slow. Māori was first introduced to the National Programme of Radio

Aotearoa/New Zealand in 1970, and then only in the form of two five-minutes news bulletins each day. A short daily newscast in Māori was introduced on one of the two television channels as part of Māori Language Week in 1982 and subsequently became a regular feature. After years of procrastination, a separate Māori television channel was launched in 2002. Activists, however, were angry at the decision that only half the programmes were to be in Māori and threatened a boycott of the station.[29]

Broadcasting in established languages

As is the case for newspapers, the very large numbers and the territorial base of Francophones in Canada ensure that they are by far the best provided of the established language minorities in broadcasting. The French-medium television and radio networks of Radio Canada are broadcast nationwide. In Ontario, Télévision Franco-Ontarienne (TFO) broadcasts continuous French-medium programming, primarily serving Francophone Canadians, but also providing programmes for school-age learners of the language. There are also three French-language cable stations (one for news, one for films and one for regular television programming), as well as the international format of Canal 5 from France.

Radio and television services for the much smaller numbers of speakers of Celtic languages in the British Isles are less extensive. In Ireland, where Irish is the co-official language with English, the climate was for many years more favourable than in the UK. With the establishment of the Irish Free State, broadcasting was seen as an essential element in language revival. Concerned to establish a distinctive Irish identity, early years of broadcasting on Radio Éireann consisted mainly of Irish music, religious programmes, Gaelic Athletics Association matches, Irish-language programmes and programmes for Irish learners.[30]

Government continues to be supportive of Irish-language programming, even though it has done little to promote it actively. Radió na Gaeltachta, for instance, was established as an RTÉ service in 1971 in response to pressure from the Gaeltacht Civil Rights Movement. An estimated 85 per cent of all Irish-speaking adults listen regularly to this station, which permits no English in conversation or songs. With the rapid expansion of commercial broadcasting, English speakers in Ireland have a large choice of stations; Irish speakers outside Dublin have just one. While English-language stations can maximize their audiences by adjusting content and style to particular segments, Raidió na Gaeltachta has to address not only all ages and interests, but varying levels of competence in the language.[31]

As Ireland has embraced full integration into Europe, Irish speakers have been reformulated as a cultural and linguistic minority. One of the clearest indications of this new policy is the setting up in 1996 of Teilifís na Gaeilge (TG4), a separate Irish-language television channel. The culmination of years of political campaigning, TG4 broadcasts approximately 90 hours of Irish a week, in contrast with the four or so a week provided by state broadcasting. TG4 has, in fact, been described as taking up the torch of language revival from 'the tired, arthritic hand of the state'.[32] Although the overall numbers of viewers remain small, this channel has up to 50 per cent penetration of the Irish-speaking population at peak times. Even operating on a tiny budget, it provides a wide range of programmes and is carving itself a niche in the life of Irish-speaking Ireland. In Northern Ireland, the BBC makes a small further contribution to Irish-language programming on radio and TV, though language activists have been frustrated at the limited support for Irish broadcasting and the failure to collaborate more imaginatively with broadcasters in the Republic.[33]

In the rest of the UK, the level of provision in other Celtic languages was, for many years, woefully inadequate in terms of the number of hours broadcast each week and the range and quality of programming. Political activism and, in particular, the threat of Gwynfor Evans, a Welsh Nationalist Member of Parliament, to go on hunger strike finally led to the setting up of Sianel Pedwar Cymru, or S4C, in 1982. S4C currently broadcasts some 34 hours a week in Welsh and is playing a crucial part in the revitalization of the language. More recently S4C has been joined by two digital channels. The first broadcasts some 80 hours per week in Welsh, including all the output of the analogue channel. The second broadcasts coverage from the National Assembly and the Wales Digital College. A dedicated Welsh-language radio station broadcasts for 20 hours a day.

Provision for Gaelic is distinctly less impressive. There is still no dedicated Gaelic radio station and Gaelic television is treated differently in terms of legislation, funding, regulation and delivery. The Gaelic Television Fund was established as part of the 1990 Broadcasting Act to finance up to 200 hours a year of Gaelic television in addition to the 100 hours already being transmitted. Some 10 years later, the Gaelic Broadcasting Taskforce argued that the arrangements for this expansion of services had proved woefully inadequate and recommended the establishment of a Gaelic Broadcasting Authority to run a new digital Gaelic channel.[34]

Television is also a concern for Deaf people. While subtitles have been used for many years, signing is a more recent development. The first UK broadcast in sign – a prototype Deaf magazine programme – came in 1979 in response to lobbying from Deaf activists and under the wing of the BBC Community Programmes Unit.[35] It paved the way for regular sign-language programmes, achieving long overdue visibility and prestige for the Deaf community. The 1990 Broadcasting Act now requires that terrestrial broadcasters provide BSL interpreting for 5 per cent of programmes.[36] This use of sign in television has undoubtedly been a major factor in the dramatic increase in the numbers of hearing people wishing to learn BSL. In the USA, there was a spate of programmes in sign in the late 1970s, but since the 1990s, despite the proliferation of channels, Deaf programming has been minimal. In other countries, too, there is also growing pressure to increase both the number of programmes targeted at the Deaf community and the use of captioning and sign interpreting.

Broadcasting in the new minority languages

The fate of more recently arrived languages is variable. As early as 1942, over 200 different US radio stations were regularly broadcasting in 26 non-English languages. There was also a small number of TV broadcasts in other languages in the 1950s, including weekly programmes in German in St Louis, Missouri, and in Pennsylvania Dutch in Reading, Pennsylvania.[37] Today, ethnic media reach very large numbers of people. According to a 2002 survey by New California Media, television stations, radio stations and newspapers reach 84 per cent of all Californians who self-identify as Hispanic, African American or Asian American, and a significant proportion of these prefer ethnic media to their English-language counterparts.[38]

In Australia, commercial radio stations were legally bound for many years to devote no more than 2.5 per cent of transmission time to other languages.[39] Television was also limited to English until well into the 1970s. A request to ABC for subtitled films was turned down on technical grounds (subtitles for wide-vision films would not be fully reproduced on television screens) and because of lack of appeal to the broadest possible audience. Only one commercial channel carried community-language programmes at this time – two one-hour programmes a week in Greek and one in Italian.

The first important turning point came in 1975, when two radio stations – 2CH in Sydney and 3XY in Melbourne – were established specifically to broadcast to minority-language communities as part of a three-month experimental service to explain Australia's new health-care system. The experiment was a success and, within three years, the Special

Broadcasting Service (SBS) was formally established to develop provision. Today SBS is a national, public broadcaster with a special mandate to 'to provide multilingual and multicultural radio and television services that inform, educate and entertain all Australians, and, in doing so, reflect Australia's multicultural society'.[40]

Radio programmes are broadcast in English and 67 other languages. Beginning at 6 o'clock every morning, a different-language programme is heard every hour until midnight. Independent audience surveys of the largest language groups show that, for the majority, SBS Radio is the main source of news and information. The size of the community and other factors, such as proficiency in English and the proportion of new arrivals, determine the time allocated to each language. The major-language programs – Arabic, Greek, Italian, Cantonese, Mandarin and Vietnamese – are broadcast twice daily, seven days a week, while some smaller language groups are allocated just one hour a week. In 1980 SBS expanded to include television. Over half its broadcast hours are in the 60 or so languages other than English spoken in the community. By providing English subtitles, SBS makes these programmes accessible to all Australians, allowing cultures to be shared, and the service is watched by more than 50 per cent of Australian households each week.

In Canada, Channel 47, the free, over-the-air, multilingual television system which dates back to 1977, now reaches approximately 90 per cent of viewers in Ontario and is also available via cable to viewers across Canada. It broadcasts in 15 different languages and is responsible for 22 hours of original multilingual programming each week. Most large cities in Canada now have one local multilingual, multicultural station, providing programmes and news in a range of languages. Although targeted in the main at minority-language communities, some programmes also offer opportunities for language learning.

In the UK, the proliferation of radio stations came considerably later than in the US. Growing numbers now carry programmes for minority communities; most cater for speakers of South Asian languages. Sometimes minority media are small, short-lived projects produced by families, groups and associations. Currently well over 100 aspiring community radio groups make use of a 28-day licence once a year, often during religious celebrations, such as Ramadan and Vaisaiki.[41]

Digitization has, of course, created many new possibilities for minority media. In some cases, viewers are able to access international TV networks, such as RaiUno for Italian or Deutsche Welle for German. These networks provide an invaluable source of news and entertainment from the home country. In the UK, every third Cypriot household in one area of north

London has a satellite dish in order to watch the evening news from Greece. In other cases, local networks specifically target overseas communities.[42] Several UK networks, for instance, provide entertainment in English, Urdu and Hindi for viewers from the Indian subcontinent. In Canada, Telelatino offers a variety of domestic and international programming in Italian, Spanish and English to 3.5 million viewers, while Fairchild Television has a prominent presence in the Chinese community. In the US, Univision and Telemundo both reach over 90 per cent of Hispanic viewers.

Last but not least, the Internet has revolutionized communication in minority communities. There has been a proliferation of websites dedicated to minority languages, cultures and political causes. Dozens of new Kurdish websites appear every month, differing considerably in style and content and bringing together large numbers of people dispersed all over the world into virtual communities. The advantages of web publishing are clear to see: it offers a cheap alternative to traditional media, which is not constrained by legislation; it also allows for two-way interaction.[43]

Aims of the media

So what functions do the ethnic media serve? Cultural and linguistic maintenance is clearly high on the agenda. The extent to which this is a conscious goal varies a great deal from one community to the next. The main concern of Spanish media in the USA, for instance, is to provide a wide range of activities and services; the transmission of the language from one generation to the next is not an important priority. In contrast, much greater prominence is given to language in Indigenous and established communities. Thus CAAMA has a clear mandate to promote Aboriginal culture, language, dance and music, while KTNN programming emphasizes Navajo culture and lifestyle.[44] In the UK, a 1978 White Paper highlighted the role of broadcasting 'in the preservation of Gaelic and Welsh as living tongues and in sustaining the distinctive cultures based upon them'.[45]

The media play an active role in the standardization of both spoken and written language in Indigenous and established communities. Those listening to radio and television, after all, form the largest simultaneous audience of the spoken language. The fact that complaints about the Navajo used in KTNN radio broadcasts far outnumber any other listener response attests to the importance of the media in the maintenance and development of the language.

Length of settlement also plays a role. There is a discernible shift in emphasis from language to culture over time, with growing use of English at the expense of the minority languages. But language remains an important focus for more recent arrivals. According to Zeynep, an avid consumer of Turkish satellite TV in the UK: 'I didn't know who I was before this TV thing came along. And I realised, Uh! My music is alright! My people are like this!'[46] In equally enthusiastic terms, a US Chinese student wrote in a language biography: 'Television again came to the rescue. It was the medium that led me to become more fluent and confident with Mandarin since most Chinese television shows on TV were spoken in Mandarin.'[47]

Another important role of the minority media is to provide news and information. Sometimes governments supply this information to help new arrivals understand their rights and responsibilities. This is by no means a recent development. From 1928, the Common Council for American Unity and its successor, the American Council for Nationalities, were responsible not only for a weekly press service in 23 languages to the 850 non-English newspapers, but for a multilanguage news service to the 600 or so radio stations broadcasting in non-English languages.[48] The minority media provide settlement information and services to newly arrived migrants in other countries, too.

On other occasions, the minority communities themselves are the source of news and information. In Australia, CAAMA broadcasts funeral notices to advise family and friends of a death within the community. Public service announcements for ceremonies, chapter meetings and community events are also an important feature of KTNN broadcasts to the Navajo Nation. In Canada, FM radio makes the loneliness and dangers of the trap line more bearable by allowing people to keep in contact with their home base. Video-conferencing and satellite links allow dispersed communities to keep in touch. On a broader front, minority media offer coverage of issues important for local democracy, such as the National Assembly in Wales or the Navajo Nation Tribal Council sessions.

Most important, the minority media represent concerns and opinions of minorities that are overlooked elsewhere. Thus the New York Bangladeshi newspapers *Weekly Thikana* and *New Probashi* have a reputation for quality reporting on the dangers faced by construction and other day workers. In Canada, the Asian Television Network attaches great importance to a range of issues and social problems associated with immigration, including parent–child conflict, family violence, and linguistic and cultural retention. By offering perspectives on life in the new country and the immigrant experience, the minority media help to cement new identities for the groups in question.

As we have already seen in chapter 8, minority media also make an important contribution to the economy. Take the case of S4C in Wales. Because its audience is bilingual, it would have made no sense to broadcast dubbed or subtitled versions of English-language programmes. Instead the channel commissioned new and distinctive programmes, including award-winning drama and animation. S4C has no in-house production facilities and commissions programmes from outside producers. According to one estimate, some 3,000 jobs have been created throughout Wales in small production companies. The development of expertise in broadcasting, film-making, animation and acting means that talented people do not need to move outside the country. Income is also generated by exporting programmes.

S4C is not an isolated example. The objectives of CAAMA include the economic advancement of Aboriginal peoples: its activities generate benefits in the form of training, employment and income. A similar rationale has been used to justify a dedicated new satellite channel for Gaelic: 'It would create significant employment opportunities and therefore contribute towards the government's economic objectives, particularly in the more peripheral parts of Scotland.'[49]

Some issues and challenges

Minority languages are confronted increasingly by commercial concerns. Nowhere is this seen more clearly than at KTNN. Because advertisers wish to reach Navajo parents and grandparents, the listeners with the greatest spending power, more attention is paid to livestock reports and public service announcements that are more attractive to an older audience. These items, however, tend to use more traditional language which younger listeners claim is difficult to understand. Commercial considerations thus stand in the way of community efforts to maintain language and culture, which require the active involvement of the younger generation.[50]

The limited economic appeal of minority languages is often reflected in scheduling. In the early days of ATV in Canada, Indian movies were shown from midnight on Tuesday until 3 o'clock in the morning, and were reputed to have caused a serious social problem in the community because of widespread difficulty in getting up early the next morning. Indigenous broadcasting faced similar challenges.[51] For instance, when Inuit programmes were distributed by the Canadian Broadcasting

Corporation, they could only be transmitted after 11.00 p.m. This situation has been greatly eased by the rapid spread of satellite TV and the development of networks serving widely dispersed communities. TVNC is now broadcast across five time zones, ensuring that programmes in Cree, Ojibway, Inuktitut and a range of Dene languages can be viewed in prime time.

Even countries where radio and television were developed by the state are no longer immune to commercial pressures. In both the Irish Republic and the UK, the growing numbers of commercial broadcasters have made it very clear that Celtic-language broadcasting is an encumbrance for which they have little enthusiasm. Regulatory bodies are required by law to safeguard minority interests but, in practice, have proved ineffective. In Ireland, many of the local stations that included Irish-language programming in their initial licence applications have failed to deliver, and the fact that no sanctions have been imposed means that there is little incentive for any change in practice.[52] Compliance in the UK is grudging. A significant proportion of the Gaelic material reluctantly carried by the Scottish ITV companies is transmitted in the middle of the night.[53]

Government reaction in times of conflict is another area of concern. The efforts of minority communities have sometimes met considerable resistance. During World War I, a US federal law required the non-English press to submit a written translation in English of any articles on foreign policy to the post office at the place of publication.[54] The postmaster general, however, had the power of exemption, which he exercised in large numbers of cases. Congress attempted unsuccessfully to impose a total prohibition of foreign-language newspapers, and a law passed in Oregon in 1920 required non-English newspapers to print a full translation of their entire contents. Similar restrictions were placed on the minority-language press in Australia.[55] The ban on German newspapers remained in place until 1925 and ethnic newspapers were required to publish a section in English until 1956.

Immigrant groups, for their part, have made use of the media to counter mainstream hostility. The Foreign Language Information Service (FLIS), for instance, offered principled opposition to the wave of anti-alien political sentiment that swept the United States in the 1920s. Comprehensive coverage of the experiences and contributions of foreign-born Americans was published in press releases in an attempt to reduce intolerance and discrimination. And ethnic media continue to build bridges with mainstream society. The Asian Television Network is a case in point. Its mandate is to enhance the knowledge of South Asian people and culture among all Canadians. Its director describes the invention of the TV remote control as a great opportunity: 'Many of those viewers who traditionally watched only CBC or CTV now sit in their chairs and flip through the channels. Some will pause at one of our programs and will stay with us'.[56] The impressive achievement of SBS in reaching over half the population of Australia each week with its multilingual and multi-cultural programming also points to the huge potential of the media for promoting mutual understanding.

In an age where anti-immigration sentiments are surfacing once more, we can no doubt expect to see signs of resistance to the ethnic media. Although there is little evidence as yet of mainstream concern in the inner-circle countries, conservative sociologists in Germany are already expressing concern that transnational television is a significant cultural and political threat.[57] Turks, they claim, are choosing to retreat into their own private media world, watching satellite productions from Turkey to the exclusion of German programmes.

Such claims do not stand up to close scrutiny. Satellite TV would appear to serve different purposes for different viewers. In a British study of transnational media, a Turkish woman in her thirties who had come to London 10 years previously describes how she watches Turkish TV for the news, but British programmes for entertainment.[58] Another woman who watched mainly Turkish television explained that she read British newspapers and so was well aware of what was going on around her. Studies of other communities confirm this general observation. A Cypriot fan of television soap describes her patterns for viewing British and Cypriot TV: when her two favourite programmes were broadcast at the same time, she watched one and video-taped the other to view later.[59] Far from retreating into ethnic ghettos, members of minority commun-ities are well placed to move between and evaluate different cultural spaces. They appreciate both positive and negative in the growing media options now available. The ability to speak two languages allows them to maintain a healthy distance from both English and Turkish programming, selecting only those elements that meet their needs. At the same time as some British-born viewers celebrate the role of Turkish television in helping them to discover a distinctive identity, others dismiss the 'flashy stuff, sex films and all that'.[60]

The medium the message

Minority-language media are a vital source of news, information and entertainment for people with limited English. For bilinguals, they extend the range of choice, and individuals are able to steer a rich and complex path through various permutations. For both groups, minority-language media provide coverage of a range of issues consistently ignored by the mainstream media.

The proliferation of technologies is giving far greater control and far more options than has ever been the case: readers, listeners and viewers are able to select from a growing number of local, national and transnational sources. Although minority communities have had to fight for current levels of provision, gains for minority-language media have been far less fiercely contested than is the case, for instance, in education or the workplace. This is due in no small part to a convergence of interests: minority-language speakers are eager to harness the technology; mainstream society is content to have a showcase for its achievements. In addition, the provision of quality multilingual programming with subtitles – with the help of surfing and the remote control – is acting as a bridge between minorities and the English-speaking majority, giving access to entertainment in a range of languages. Last but by no means least, the ease of access to the Internet is revolutionizing communication in minority communities within and beyond national frontiers. Free from the restrictions of legislation and costly set-up and maintenance, the content of web publishing is no longer constrained by the interests of the dominant English-speaking groups, and minorities are free to follow their own agenda.

Notes

1   Thomas (1997).
2   Meadows (1995).
3   Bender (2002).
4   Avison and Meadows (2000).
5   Hale (2001: 280–2).
6   University of Aukland Library (undated).
7   Avison and Meadows (2000).
8   Inuit Tapitiit Kanatami website: www.itk.ca
9   Nicole Bérubé (personal communication).
10   Read (1937).
11   Kim (1982).
12   Ozolins (1993).
13   LEBA Ethnic Media (undated).
14   Scher (2001).
15   Georgiou (2003).
16   Edwards (2000).

17 Ó hIfearnáin (2001).
18 Cited in Meadows (1995).
19 Cited in Buchtmann (1999).
20 Aboriginal Peoples Television Network: www.aptn.ca
21 Aboriginal Voices Radio: www.buffalotracks.com/avr/about.shtml
22 Meadows (1995).
23 Buchtmann (1999).
24 Hale (2001).
25 Meadows (1995).
26 Meadows (1995).
27 Peterson (1997).
28 Anderton (1997).
29 One News (2002).
30 Ó hIfearnáin (2001).
31 Day (2001).
32 Ó hIfearnáin (2001).
33 Mac Póilin (1997).
34 Taskforce on Public Funding of Gaelic (2000).
35 Ladd (2003).
36 Connell (2002).
37 Fishman (1966).
38 Tam (2002).
39 Ozolins (1993).
40 www.sbs.com.au
41 Georgiou (2003).
42 Georgiou (2003).
43 Crystal (2001: 219–21).
44 Peterson (1997).
45 ITC (undated).
46 Robins (2001: 18).
47 Hinton (1999).
48 LexisNexis Academic and Library Solutions (undated).
49 Gaelic Broadcasting Taskforce (2000).
50 Peterson (1997).
51 Chandrasekar (1990).
52 Ó hIfearnáin (2001).
53 Gaelic Broadcasting Taskforce (2000).
54 Fishman (1966).
55 Clyne (1991); Ozolins (1993).
56 Chandrasekar (1990).
57 Robins (2001).
58 Robins (2001).
59 Georgiou (2003).
60 Robins (2001: 16).

10

Language and the arts

Minorities have had an enormous impact on the cultural life in inner-circle countries. Language and culture are dynamic: each generation of actors, storytellers, writers, poets and musicians reinterprets tradition in its own way. The presence of a wide range of art forms reinforces the distinctive identities of minority communities; it also gives English speakers access to a much wider range of experiences and choices, from Qawwali singing in the Sufi tradition to African Caribbean performance poetry, and much more. But creativity is a two-way process: different traditions transcend linguistic and cultural barriers to create hybrid performances with a very broad appeal. This chapter looks at ways in which other languages have both shaped and been shaped by artistic expression in inner-circle countries.

Storytelling

Storytelling is a good place to start a discussion of the arts. From the beginning of verbal communication, story has been the vehicle for moral lessons and the triumphs and tragedies of life. This ancient tradition is currently enjoying a revival in the form of storytelling festivals, which offer audiences a chance to leave their TV sets behind and interact with professionals and amateurs telling their favourite tales in tents, in halls or under the stars. The Yukon Storytelling Festival is a case in point.[1] Storytellers from many different countries join native elders to tell and sing stories in a wide range of languages, with a summary or full translation in English in a celebration under the midnight sun. The ancient art of storytelling is also entering into interesting new relations with digital technology. As part of the Rez02 project, for instance, Native American

Roop Singh captures the attention of his audience in a bilingual storytelling performance in Panjabi and English.
Photograph by Simon Ryder.

and rurally isolated young people have been taught how to use film-making equipment, web design, photography and computer animation in order to record and preserve their heritage in stories.[2]

Storytelling in other languages is also a popular activity with school children. The telling – as opposed to the reading – of a story adds texture. Props, tone of voice, gesture and mime all help the audience understand what is happening, making it quite feasible to shift between two – or more – languages. Growing numbers of professionals now bring a bilingual dimension to storytelling. Roop Singh, for instance, performs in English and Panjabi for children all over the UK.[3] He moulds his tales to the situation, delivering different versions of the same story according to the audience. Roop started his career by telling tales in English, but when asked on one occasion to do 'something different', decided to tell the story of Jack and the beanstalk in Panjabi. He was astonished at its success: the English-speaking members of the audience were able to follow from his gestures and, of course, their prior knowledge of the story. Olga Loya of San José in California is another accomplished bilingual storyteller who performs at festivals, conferences, libraries and schools.

She tells stories from her native Chicano culture that skip seamlessly back and forth between English and Spanish.

Oral poetry

The wealth of oral traditions brought by African slaves to North America and the Caribbean are another rich source for contemporary perform-ance. Sounding, signifying, toasting and playing the dozens are just some of the speech events that have allowed young African Americans and African Caribbeans to hone their verbal skills and establish their place in the pecking order of the peer group.[4] In recent times, the strong underlying rhythms and rhymes have found commercial outlets and a much wider audience.

Rap is an African American development, consisting of improvised rhymes performed to a rhythmic accompaniment. Early raps were boastful tales, and put-downs directed at other rappers. They developed into commentaries on the hardships of ghetto life, with warnings about drugs and teenage love. Today rap has a huge following among people of all ages and from many different backgrounds. Some parent groups and other mainstream organizations have objected to explicit references to sex and drugs, and expressed concern that rap encourages young people to turn to violence and substance abuse. While the performers, for their part, agree that rap deals with harsh topics, they argue that audiences are capable of distinguishing between fantasy and reality, right and wrong.

Dub poetry, in contrast, is an African Caribbean art form, combining Jamaican Patwa lyrics with music in the reggae tradition. Although it is composed for oral performance, its best-known exponent, Linton Kwesi Johnson, has the distinction of being one of only two living poets to have their works published in the Penguin Modern Classics series. The themes of dub poetry are often highly politicized, with performers exploring issues central to their identity in multilingual, multi-ethnic Britain. Take the following extract from Linton Kwesi Johnson's 'It dread inna Inglan', composed for George Lindo, a Jamaican wrongfully accused of armed robbery:[5]

> Maggi Tatcha on di go
> wid a racist show
> but a shi haffi go
> kaw,
> rite now

African
Asian
West Indian
an' Black British
stan firm inna Inglan
inna disya time yah . . .

Other African Caribbean poets perform their work without a musical backing, but make a similar use of underlying rhythm. All are performance poets who place a high premium on interaction with their audience. As Benjamin Zephaniah explains: 'What has always excited me is the fact that there is no expert editor telling you what they think will work, you know how it works immediately, the public tell you. The feedback is automatic and it really is a great feeling to hear hundreds of people chant along with your poem when that poem has never been written down'.[6]

Theatre

The form of theatre varies from one language minority to the next. Indigenous communities have traditionally focused on storytelling and representational performance in song and dance. The 'Ksan Performing Arts Group is typical in this respect. Forming part of a museum and village complex, they perform traditional song and dance for mainstream audiences and view themselves as cultural ambassadors for the Gitxsan people. In communities where the Indigenous language is in decline, bilingual actors tend to be in short supply, although attempts are being made to solve this problem. In Canada, for instance, the Centre for Indigenous Theatre offers introductory training in voice, movement and improvisation, alongside Aboriginal dances, songs and stories from various nations across North America. Another obstacle concerns the choice of language: Indigenous writers may be tempted to write in English to reach the widest possible audiences.

Other-language theatre is also very much part of the cultural tradition of established communities. The large Francophone population of Canada is able to draw not only on the international repertoire, but also on a large pool of home-grown talent, such as Félix Leclerc, Michel Tremblay and Marie Laberge. The rapid development of radio – and, later, television – from the 1940s was a powerful catalyst in the development of writing talent. Unlike its English-language counterpart, dramatic production has always played an important part in the programming of Société Radio

Canada (SRC), the Francophone arm of the Canadian Broadcasting Corporation.[7] Télé-Québec, Quebec's state television, is also supportive of French-language drama and gives high priority to televised productions of stage plays. On the local level, too, there is considerable activity, professional and amateur. Kingston, Ontario, is typical. This predominantly English-speaking city has two theatre companies: the English-language Theatre Kingston and the French-language Les Tréteaux de Kingston.

Although Celtic-language theatre is on a much smaller scale, there is none the less a great deal of activity. In Wales, audiences are served by six professional theatre companies that work only through the medium of Welsh and several others involved in bilingual performance, as well as various amateur groups. Dalier Sylw (Take Note) is generally recognized as the leader in the field, promoting new plays in Welsh by contemporary authors; Sgript Cymru also nurtures work by Welsh playwrights. In Ireland, An Taibhdhearc, the National Theatre of the Irish Language in Galway, produces, on average, six Irish-language productions a year, including dramas, pantomime, traditional and cultural concerts and opera. Scotland has a touring Gaelic company called Tosg and a children's theatre group, Ordag is Sgealbag (Thumb and Forefinger). Amateur Gaelic theatre is widespread and popular.

Support for new writing is a priority. As part of its ongoing quest to discover hidden talent, Sgript Cymru offers a feedback service and a development forum for writers. It also commissions Welsh-language plays as a platform for aspiring actors. Tosg targets emerging writers with appraisals and workshops. SRC's ongoing commitment to made-in-Canada drama provides an outlet for both emerging and established dramatists. Young actors also need to be nurtured.

The situation of the new minority communities is rather different. In an age of cable television and video rental, it is difficult to convey a sense of how important theatre was, and often still is, to the social life of immigrants.[8] Theatre provides a creative outlet, which brings to life values and ideas. The level and kind of activity depend very much on how long communities have been settled. In North America, theatre groups in German and Yiddish can be traced back to the nineteenth century. Chinese theatre also has a long and distinguished history. What initially began as social gatherings of the Chinese community in Toronto, for instance, soon evolved into amateur groups that performed skits in Cantonese that required only minimal acting skills.[9] Later, professionals were brought in from Hong Kong to perform title roles in operas, and by 1935 there were three Chinese opera houses. During the depression and throughout the Sino-Japanese war and World War II, local talent staged regular fundraising events, their ranks swelled by visiting stars escaping to North America from the war.

Toronto has also been home to Bengali theatre, largely through the efforts of Kalyan Banerjee, who first came to Toronto in the late 1960s.[10] Theatre is an important part of cultural life in Calcutta, with drama competitions regularly attracting large numbers of amateur groups. The transplantation of this interest from India to Canada was a very natural development. Banerjee produced and directed the first of many Bengali plays in 1977, drawing on a wide range of amateurs with experience of theatre in Bengal.

While Chinese and South Asian theatre continues to thrive, there has inevitably been a shift from performances in minority languages to English. In contrast, in communities where there is still a regular inflow of new settlers, minority-language theatre is very much alive and well. The Hispanic community is a case in point. One of the showcases for Spanish theatre is the International Hispanic Theatre Festival in Florida, organized by Teatro Avante, the area's most respected and prolific Hispanic theatre company. Over the years, the festival has become the most comprehensive Hispanic theatre event in North America, attracting the best companies in the US, as well as world-class groups from Latin America and Europe.

Bilingual theatre

Bilingual theatre is rapidly emerging as an exciting new genre. On some occasions, the aim is to speak to the experience of bilingual communities. The productions of Sgript Cymru are specifically intended to reflect the bilingual nature of life in Wales; plays such as Fennario's *Balconville*, based on French and English working-class neighbours in Canada, reflect life there. On other occasions, the intention is to bridge the gap between minority and majority communities. One of the objectives of the International Hispanic Theatre Festival, for instance, is to share Hispanic cultural heritage. This commitment to cross over is not simply a feature of the festival; it also informs productions in individual theatres. Most works performed at Teatro Avante are aimed at middle-aged Cuban American audiences. However, non-Spanish speakers are catered for with subtitles on an overhead screen.

The London-based Yellow Earth Theatre has similar aims. Set up in the mid-1990s to considerable critical acclaim, it wanted to produce 'visually exciting, challenging theatre that both explored and celebrated the East Asian experience in Britain'.[11] Bilingualism is an integral part of

Yellow Earth performances and is used to considerable dramatic effect. Take the opening scene of *New Territories*, a rites-of-passage story about a teenager who comes to the UK from Hong Kong. The brother and sister speak Chinese as they play a game together. The brother stops suddenly, looks into the audience, and whispers, 'Speak English!' The sister also looks out and asks 'Deem gai che?' ('Why should I?'), to which her brother replies, 'So they can understand!' – a line which always triggers gentle laughter from the audience, no doubt relieved that the entire performance is not going to be in Chinese! In trying to make productions accessible to a wide a range of audiences, Yellow Earth emphasizes the visual – physical sequences such as Beijing Opera stick fights, shadow fights and ribbon dancing. The ultimate aim is for a young bilingual child and a Chinese-speaking grandfather to enjoy the show together.

Many experiments with bilingualism in mainstream theatre can be traced to theatre-in-education companies.[12] The M6 Theatre Company in northern England is a case in point. It has commissioned a number of new plays that reflect the interests and concerns of young people. One such play, *Two Days as a Tiger* (*Doh din kay shere*), is performed in English and Panjabi and interweaves themes of friendship across cultural boundaries with environmental concerns. Situation determines the use of language. It is only natural, for instance, that the grandmother in this story should use Panjabi, the language of the home, when talking to her granddaughter. The parallel use of Panjabi and English, together with visual language and gesture, allows speakers of both languages to understand what is happening.

The Theatre of the Deaf, based at the University of Reading in the UK, exploits language in a similar way. Its company of Deaf and hearing actors weave sign, mime and language in highly innovative ways. Sign is an integral and creative part of performance, not an adjunct designed to make a hearing production accessible to the Deaf. The resulting fusion is an artistic form in its own right.

Film, video and DVD

Theatre, of course, has an interesting relationship with film, video and DVD, with exciting cross-overs between the arts, on one hand, and the media and technology, on the other. The use of more recent technologies has important implications for many minority communities. Children and young people often view Indigenous and established languages as old-fashioned and unexciting. The fact that minority communities may lack the resources to fund the necessary development further reinforces the link between English and all that is modern, on the one hand, and between minority languages and all that is staid, on the other.

There are, however, some notable success stories. The Inuit Canadian film *Atanarjuat* (*The Fast Runner*), the first full-length feature film totally in an Aboriginal language (Inuktitut) and directed by an Inuk, won the Caméra d'Or award at the 2001 Cannes Film Festival. Films produced originally for Welsh-language television have also enjoyed success in the international arena. *Yr Enwog Ffred* (*Famous Fred*) received a British Academy of Film and Television Arts (BAFTA) award for Best Children's Animation and an Oscar nomination for the Best Short Animation Film in 1998.

The growth of minority-language programming on television has created a demand which is currently being met by large numbers of independent production companies. There is also growing investment in training. The Gaelic Television Training Trust, for instance, has developed a two-year course in production and craft skills in conjunction with Sabhal Mòr Ostaig College on the Island of Skye.

Minority-language publishing

There are also interesting cross-overs between the performing and creative arts. Actors, for the most part, need a script. Playwrights are authors, and authors are involved in writing of all kinds. The issues that face authors in minority languages are very similar to those that face playwrights.

In Indigenous communities, traditional systems of meaning-making – story, song, dance and art – have been joined by print only in relatively recent times. Print literacy has been embraced with considerable enthusiasm though, in most cases, it is mediated through English. There are growing numbers of world-class Indigenous authors. The Māori writer Keri Hulme, for instance, made international headlines when her novel *The Bone People* won the Booker Prize in 1985.[13] Opportunities for writing in Indigenous languages, however, are limited in terms of both the potential market and the publishing infrastructure. None the less, some support is now available. The Canada Council for the Arts provides grants for both professional and emerging Aboriginal writers and storytellers, and for the development of Aboriginal publishers and collectives. This funding is sensitive to Indigenous needs and expectations. Thus projects involving the use of stories belonging to a particular individual, family or community have to show that permission to publish has been granted; where elders are involved, it is also important to provide an honorarium, based upon the protocol of the community in question.[14] Indigenous authors are also beginning to articulate their displeasure at widespread misconceptions that can be traced to the romanticized retellings of traditional stories by non-Indigenous authors.[15]

The main demand for books in Indigenous languages currently comes from education programmes that use minority languages. In Australia, Aboriginals have been employed as literacy workers in various locations since the mid-1970s, researching and transcribing oral texts and helping to prepare class readers for bilingual programmes. The setting up of literacy production units has made it possible to exchange materials between programmes in the same language and even, in some cases, to translate and adapt materials for use by other language groups. In Aotearoa/New Zealand, Learning Media, the largest publisher of Māori books for use in schools, also produce material in five Pacific Nation languages, and international languages, such as Spanish.

The challenges facing established languages are variable. In Canada, French-language publishing is thriving. Francophones are able to access both the international literature and the extensive range of local publications. Books in Celtic languages, in contrast, are subject to the same economic constraints as those in Indigenous languages. Because the potential audience is small, the unit price of books is inevitably much higher than in larger markets. Like bilingual playwrights, bilingual authors are more likely to be attracted to writing for the more lucrative English-speaking markets. Some attempts have been made to achieve a more level playing field. The Welsh Books Council, a government-funded body, administers grants to all publishers in Wales for services in areas such as marketing, design and editorial. On average, about 500 books are published in Welsh each year.

There is also a great deal of support for Irish-language publishing. An Gúm, the government-sponsored publisher, is responsible for the production, promotion and distribution of Irish-language books, and has made an important contribution to the modern Irish literary revival since it was set up in 1926. An Gúm commissions translations of English works into Irish, as well as publishing a growing number of original works. Its activities have now been subsumed within Foras na Gaeilge, the new body responsible for the promotion of the Irish language throughout the island of Ireland.

In Scotland, the government-assisted Gaelic Books Council has served as a catalyst for Gaelic publishing since the early 1960s. Acair, a consortium chiefly for educational purposes and chiefly in Gaelic, is based in Stornoway. Approximately 100 new titles in Gaelic are produced each year by Acair and other publishers.

New immigrants, of course, are able to draw on the literatures of the home countries. They are also, in some cases, beginning to generate local works, which speak to the experiences of the new communities. The potential of the large Hispanic market is now attracting not only specialist but also mainstream publishers in the USA. HarperCollins Publishers, for instance, has launched Rayo, a new imprint that publishes titles for and about Latinos in both English and Spanish.

Responsibility for providing access to minority-language books falls to a large extent on libraries. The New York Public Library once had separate reading rooms for Slavic languages, Yiddish and Hebrew literature.[16] The Chicago Public Library used to issue special catalogues of books in other languages and even in the 1960s had impressive foreign-language collections – 20,000 books in German, 13,000 in French, 9,000 in Polish. In communities with large ethnic minority communities, English books were often in a minority. At the beginning of the twentieth century, 13,000 of the 23,000 books in the public library of Belleville, Illinois, were in German.

There is a similar history of service in Australian libraries. The Latvian community in Melbourne is reputed to have one of the finest collections of Latvian-language books in the world. The Instituto Italiano di Cultura and the Goethe Institute in this same city also have large lending libraries. For many years, specialist bookshops and 'continental reading circles' have rented folders of magazines in specific community languages to private subscribers, such as doctors, dentists and hairdressers.[17]

Libraries continue to make considerable efforts to meet the needs of the populations they serve. When staff are unable to speak the language of the inquirer, they clearly cannot respond to requests for information. If the language in question uses a different script, the cataloguing system cannot cope. The first major breakthrough for Chinese in the UK came when Westminster Charing Cross Public Library developed a computerized catalogue that held Chinese characters.[18] This inspired Helen Wong, a computing student, and Alan Seatwo, a Chinese librarian, to develop Britain's first bilingual Chinese–English system for the Liverpool Public Library Service. An added benefit of the system is that it has helped to break down barriers between Chinese users and English-speaking staff. The next phase of development is an online public access catalogue, so that Chinese users can search for information themselves.

Children's publishing

Providing reading materials for children in other languages is particularly challenging. On the one hand, books aimed at a particular age group in the home country are often too difficult for children born overseas; on the other hand, the subject matter of books that hit the right linguistic level is too childish. Growing numbers of publishers have attempted to address this problem by commissioning titles aimed specifically at a home-grown audience in a range of languages.

One interesting development has been the emergence of bilingual children's picture books, where illustrations are accompanied by English and the other language. Minority-language speakers often regard bilingual books with some suspicion. They feel that English permeates all aspects of their children's lives and that the impact of books in other languages is diminished by the addition of English; they may also fear that children will by-pass the other language and read only the English. There is evidence, however, that children use these books in a variety of ways that are highly supportive of literacy in both languages.[19] The use of two languages also means that children from different language backgrounds can share the same book, drawing on the expertise of bilingual students. Dual-language books thus have the potential to raise the visibility and status of other languages in English-speaking classrooms.

As new technologies become cheaper and easier to use, teachers are increasingly producing their own materials, often in collaboration with parents. Initially, multilingual word-processing packages for non-Roman scripts were so expensive that they were beyond the reach of school budgets. However, as prices began to drop, many teachers have been eager to experiment, sometimes to dramatic effect. In one well-documented case, a little boy who saw Panjabi on the computer in his nursery school, called out in disbelief, 'Look, that's my language on the screen!'[20]

Language, music and tradition

The rhythms, melodies and lyrics passed from one generation to the next in family events or social gatherings are strongly linked with the identity of the group. As the musician Billy Bragg points out, tradition is 'timeless and recyclable and is renewed as each generation discovers its roots'.[21] The songs that accompany the Changing Woman ceremony that marks coming of age for Apache girls reinforce identity in the same way as the singing of 'Cwm Rhondda' in Welsh international rugby matches.

In many societies, weddings are associated with an extensive repertoire of songs, serving a wide range of functions. Indian songs of solidarity, for instance, are sung at ceremonies held on the evening before the wedding. Their aim is to draw together the various members of the family, heal any rifts and present a united front before the actual ceremony. Songs of insult draw on a tradition that can be traced back to the Sanskrit court.[22] They take place during the actual ceremony up to the critical point where the bride and groom walk round the fire and are considered man and wife. The tensions that surround a wedding in any culture are intense. Songs of insult thus serve as a release valve for this tension, at the same time as providing entertainment. When the climax of the wedding ceremony is reached, the mood changes from teasing and taunting to conciliation. No longer do the women mock and ridicule the other side. Rather they entreat the bride to behave in a way that will bring honour on their family and they appeal to the groom's side to treat her with kindness. The songs thus provide a framework to ease the transition of the bride and groom from their unmarried states. They reassert family identity and provide a valuable release.

Folk songs also help cement the identity of a group. Corridos, for instance, are an important part of the ballad tradition of Mexico and the US. These epic poems are composed by and for marginal communities.[23] While many Anglos believe that salsa is the most important Latin musical influence in America, corridos in fact represent a larger proportion of US sales. Despite the distinctly unthreatening feel of accordion-driven waltzes and polkas, comparisons have been made between corridos and gangsta rap. In the rush to assume the moral high ground, many mainstream commentators fail to grasp that corrido singers – and indeed gangsta rappers – are not so much celebrating crime as expressing a dislike of authority and big money.

Religious music is another important focus for cultural and linguistic identity. Qawwali, a form of Sufi Muslim devotional music that can be traced back to twelfth-century Persia, is particularly appreciated in the Pakistani diaspora. Repeated phrases are interspersed with passionate virtuoso singing by the qawwal or lead singer, who monitors the audience response and reacts with changes in speed and 'heat'. The tempo and volume gradually increase, transporting the audience to higher and higher states of entrancement. In the words of Rashid Din, a singer with Rizwan-Muazzam Qawwali: 'Tradition in our musical life is our culture and our identity.'[24]

Tradition, however, by no means implies 'frozen in time'. In the same way as Gujarati wedding songs use both traditional melodies and modern film music, the subject matter of corridos has varied a great deal in their 200-year history. They have celebrated the revolutionary heroes of the Mexican War of the 1840s, the tequileros who smuggled liquor during prohibition, the triumph of illegal immigrants returning home to spend their hard-gained money, and the trafficking of crack cocaine. References to contemporary concerns like alcohol and litter in traditional Aboriginal Australian song cycles about graves also make the point that, while ceremonies are rooted in the past, each generation makes them its own.

The cosmopolitan cities in the English-speaking world are a reservoir of other-language talent, providing entertainment and cultural reinforcement for minority communities at the same time as broadening the experience of the mainstream. The London Diaspora Capital project, run by the arts charity Cultural Co-operation, is designed to exploit this rich potential, raising the profile of London-based artists from different national backgrounds.[25] The main tool is an interactive database on the Internet with audio-visual profiles of performers whose life journeys have converged on the capital. Iffatara Khanam is typical. Born and brought up in Bangladesh, she performed widely on radio and television before coming to the UK in the mid-1990s. She performs a repertoire of folk, modern, devotional and romantic songs, backed by traditional instruments.

Musical fusion

Music is, of course, not simply about cultural preservation: it is an area where the traditional feeds the contemporary and where different cultural heritages inform and enrich one another. African American music is one of many tributaries to have made their mark on the mainstream, from the minstrelsy of the early nineteenth century through ragtime, jazz, blues, rhythms and blues, country music and rock and roll to rap. African Caribbeans have also exerted a musical influence well beyond what might be expected for their numbers through calypso, ska and reggae. Black music, however, is just one source of ideas and material, which musicians can weave into new patterns and textures.

Minority communities influence, and are influenced by, many different musical traditions. Often the new strain receives far more attention than the original material. American Indian music, for instance, attracted little interest outside its traditional stronghold until its fusion with other musical influences. Mohawk Robbie Robertson achieved a notable success when his 1994 album *Music for the Native Americans* combined traditional chants and instruments with rock and electronic effects. Four years later,

Contact from the Underworld of Redboy, a highly original mix of rock, Indian sounds, hip hop and electronics, won a Grammy nomination in the world music category. Native American music was, until recently, relegated to the folk and New Age bins at record stores. However, its growing popularity was finally recognized with the introduction of a 'best Native American music album' category in the 2001 Grammy Awards.

Australian Aboriginal music has undergone a similar transformation. The Indigenous Arts Showcase at the Perth International Arts Festival, for instance, now features a range of contemporary music in English and in Aboriginal languages. Mervyn Mulardy is an interesting example. His music is a blend of country, reggae and rock with a strong component of traditional instrumentation. Typically the first verse of each song, delivered in Karajarri, is translated into English in the next verse. Mervyn, who lives in his traditional home, the community of Bidyadanga in Western Australia, believes that his performances provide a vital link between older and younger generations.[26]

Fusion has also attracted Celtic musicians. Clannad, the well-known Irish band, consists of two brothers, a sister and their twin uncles who grew up in an Irish-speaking village in Donegal.[27] Their passion for traditional Irish music took them to many parts of the Gaeltacht, including outlying island communities. The songs that they collected in the early 1970s served as the starting point not for a traditional band but for musicians wanting to perform their own contemporary, jazz-influenced versions of traditional material.

Commercial concerns demand that songs, like literature, should be in English to appeal to the broadest possible audience. The dilemma for minority performers is thus whether to sing in English or their first language. For instance, when Clannad won a recording contract as the first prize in the Letterkenny Folk Festival, they took the bold step of insisting that they were going to sing in Irish. Their first record was delayed by three years precisely because the company doubted the commercial viability of Irish material.

Those who have dared to defy convention have shown that the language of recording takes second place to the quality of the music, although television exposure would seem to play a vital role in this process. The success of *Music for the Native Americans* is due in no small part to the fact that it was used as background music in a TV documentary. Capercaillie achieved a hit single when 'Coisichin A Ruin', a 400-year-old Gaelic waulking song,[28] was recorded as the theme music for *A Prince Among Islands*, a programme featuring Prince Charles. Clannad achieved even greater success in 1989 with the music for *Harry's Game*, a high-profile TV drama about Northern Ireland. Based on the proverb 'Imtheochaidh siar is soir a dtáinig ariamh, an ghealach is an ghrian' (Everything that is and was will cease to be), the record reached number five in the British charts and led to a major recording contract with RCA. Nearly 10 years later the song was featured in the film *Patriot Games* and then was chosen for a nationwide US advertising campaign by Volkswagen. The impact of the music was such that hundreds of people called the company's free phone number to find out not what the car was but where they might find the background music. Irish was clearly not an impediment to commercial success.

The mixing of genres does not meet with universal approval. Clannad were surprised by the initial reaction to their newly arranged versions of local traditional tunes: 'When we started to sing these songs in the tavern, it was really funny because the visitors would clap to them, but the locals wouldn't . . . they were really quite taken aback by it.'[29] Boundaries also need to be observed: American Indian musicians carefully avoid combining sacred music with electronic sounds or even playing sacred music on the radio.

Commercial viability is a less pressing issue for musicians that form part of larger minority communities, such as the Spanish-speaking population of the USA. For many years, the rock and roll market was completely dominated by English. Yet since the 1990s Spanish speakers have been fighting back with a potent weapon: rock en Español. Performers from Spain, Latin America and the USA began filling clubs and stadiums, no doubt helped by the introduction of MTV Latino. There is now even a Grammy Award for Spanish-language rock. Chicano Groove, a home-grown genre that bridges mainstream styles such as funk and blues and Mexican American folk music, is also very popular. Take Blues Experiment, a bilingual band, fuses jam-oriented rock and roll with congas, trumpets, funky keyboards and strong vocals. Interestingly, given the highly commercialized nature of the music market, Chicano Groove is the product of independent record companies. In a radical departure from the industry norm, Son del Barrio, the leading record company in this field, is a division of Justice Matters, a non-profit social justice organization.[30] It is common for performers to show each other support by selling CDs and playing gigs together.

Another landmark in fusion music is the rise of bhangra in the Indian diaspora. Its roots lie in the traditional Panjabi music performed on festive occasions, particularly sewing and harvest celebrations. Since the early 1980s, Indians overseas have developed it into a distinctive new genre. The same percussion instruments – the dhol, dholak and tabla – which provide the rhythms for traditional bhangra form the foundation for strong melds with musical influences from the West. British bhangra is very popular with young British Indians. Since the early 1990s, however, it has also gained popularity with mainstream audiences, with bands like Apache Indian making an appearance in the UK charts.

Nitin Sawhney is another British Asian performer whose work has won mainstream critical approval. His album *Beyond Skin* was shortlisted for the Technics Mercury Music Prize, the most important arts award in British music. Sawhney blends classical Indian Qawwali singing and Urdu verse, to a musical backing of rolling drum, bass grooves and mellifluous breaks.

Minority music has embraced mainstream developments with gusto. However, the influence is by no means one-way. In the same way as rap has been appropriated by White artists, such as Eminem, the British group Kula Shaker, named after the ninth-century mystic and emperor, is heavily influenced by Indian culture. The hit song 'Tattva', for instance, has the Sanskrit refrain: 'Tattva, acintya bheda bheda tattva', while the whole of 'Govinda' is based on an ancient Indian chant. The Australian band Yothu Yindi shows a similar convergence. It consists of both Yolngu (Aboriginal) and Balanda (non-Aboriginal) musicians and embodies a sharing of cultures. The band, with their unique blend of Western and Aboriginal music, sings about their quest to unite Australians.

Music and the languages that accompany it thus offer a powerful channel for people to assert both their traditional values and their distinctiveness. It also provides a two-way source of inspiration and an unlimited supply of material, which can be shaped into rich new patterns.

Festivals

Most of the musical examples we have just considered involve solo performers, or small groups. If you put together large numbers of solo performers and small groups, maybe adding elements of other performing arts, the result is often a festival. Festivals – sacred and secular – are an important opportunity for people to come together. Sometimes they form the focus for the language and culture of a particular group. On other occasions, they are inclusive events open to all comers.

The American Indian Pow Wow, the Australian Aboriginal Corroboree, the potlatch feasts of the native people of the northwest coast of North America and many other celebrations allow participants to reassert their linguistic and cultural identity through music, dance, storytelling and other forms of artistic expression. Festivals are also an important event in the calendar of established communities. In Wales, the eisteddfod consists of competitions in all aspects of music, literature and drama. Local events are held all over Wales with winners eventually reaching the National Eisteddfod, the largest folk festival in Europe. In addition to the competitions and performances, it serves as a showpiece for Welsh cultural and commercial organizations. Very importantly, the sole language of the eisteddfod is Welsh. Parallel events for young people are organized by the Urdd Gobaith Cymru (Welsh Youth League), a voluntary organization with a membership of 47,000 children and young people.

The Royal National Mod in Scotland has much in common with the Welsh National Eisteddfod and serves as a showcase for Gaelic language and culture; so, too, does the more recent Fèis movement, which coordinates a series of Gaelic arts tuition festivals for young people. The movement came about when a group of parents on the Isle of Barra decided that the local traditions were dying out; since the schools were not teaching children the relevant skills, they needed to take responsibility themselves. As word of their success spread, many other communities began to offer similar events. Slógadh, the annual Irish-language arts festival, fulfils a similar function, attracting 30,000 visitors each year.

The Antipodes Festival, organized by the Greek community in Melbourne, is one of the more notable new minority events. It attracts an audience in excess of 150,000 to its art and craft displays, food stalls, music, street theatre and children's activities. Events are staged in venues around the city but are concentrated in the traditional Greek area of the city, in and around Lonsdale Street. The festival's success is such that the Greek Foreign Ministry uses it as a model for Greek communities worldwide.

Growing numbers of international events attest to the willingness and enthusiasm of majority populations to learn from and exchange ideas and experiences with minority communities. Peter Gabriel, the original inspiration for the WOMAD (World of Music and Dance) events which started in the UK, sees their main benefits as allowing many different audiences to gain an insight other cultures: 'Music is a universal language, it draws people together and proves, as well as anything, the stupidity of racism.'[31]

The Notting Hill Carnival in London, another notable event, has grown from a small procession of African Caribbeans in costume in 1964 to a huge multicultural arts festival, attended by up to 2 million people, second in scale only to the Rio Carnival. The event prides itself on reflecting the multicultural nature of the present-day UK, with groups participating from all over the world. According to the organizers, 'Carnival aims to celebrate the cultural heritage of its founders and at the same time be open enough to take on board evolving contemporary culture with its multiracial, multi-cultural trends.' This philosophy is neatly encapsulated in the Notting Hill Carnival motto: Every spectator is a participant – carnival is for all who dare to participate.'[32] The celebration of other cultures not only increases the vitality of minority languages, but enriches society as a whole.

Ars gratia artis

The decision of performers and writers to work in a minority language is not an easy one. The fame and fortune of those who choose to work with English inevitably eclipse those who operate in other languages, although the degree of disadvantage varies according to genre. At one end of the spectrum, musicians have enjoyed spectacular successes with recordings in minority languages; at the other end, books in other languages are accessible only to a very small readership and rarely attract the attention of mainstream publishers as potential candidates for translation.

While the financial return is more limited, work in other languages brings its own rewards. Artistic expression is a rallying point and a powerful assertion of identity for minority communities. There are growing numbers of subsidies for performance and opportunities for training and development. 'Art', says Hermann Bahr, 'does not exist to suit the moods of your majority.'[33] This sentiment is open to a rather different contemporary interpretation. The benefits of minority arts are by no means limited to minority communities. The vast array of cultural events, particularly in large cosmopolitan centres, opens up new vistas and experiences for English speakers. Increasingly, attempts are made to make productions more inclusive – either by providing translations and subtitles or by making other languages an integral element of performance.

Equally important, artistic expression does not take place in a cultural vacuum. Each generation reinterprets tradition in its own way. The refocusing of minority music through an electronic lens produces something new, complex, subtle and exciting. Bilingual theatre has emerged not only as a powerful tool for reaching wider audiences but as an exciting new art form in itself, which speaks to the experience of those who live in multilingual communities. The different languages and cultures which live side by side with English are an inspiration, an invaluable resource.

Notes

1   www.yukonstory.com
2   www.rez02.net
3   Edwards (1998).
4   Edwards and Sienkewicz (1991).
5   Johnson (2002: 25).
6   Zephaniah (undated).
7   Anon. (2003b).
8   Fishman (1966).
9   Nipp (1983).
10 Israel and Banerjee (1983).
11 Tse (2000).
12 Edwards (2000).
13 Hulme (1986).
14 Canada Council for the Arts (2002).
15 Six Nations Writers are a good example of Indigenous writers articulating their position on this and similar issues. See: www.sixnationswruters.com/snw/about_us.html
16 Fishman (1966).
17 Clyne (1991).
18 Edwards (2000).
19 Edwards and Walker (1995).
20 Edwards (1998: 32).
21 Ross (undated: 11).
22 Edwards and Katbamna (1989).
23 Wald (2002).
24 Ross (undated: 8).
25 www.culturalco-operation.org
26 Perth International Arts Festival (2003).
27 Bond (1993).
28 Waulking is a process for shrinking cloth, particularly Harris tweed, and making it more airtight.
29 Bond (1993).
30 wwww.losotros.net/about.html
31 www.womad.org/overview/index.html
32 Edwards (2000: 41).
33 Cited in Dallavia (1995).

11

Language, diplomacy and defence

This book was first conceived before the events of 11 September 2001. Few people at that time had given more than a passing thought to the role of language in diplomacy and defence. Revelations about the weaknesses in language capacity of the inner-circle countries – and, in particular, the USA – soon followed. Debate focused on issues such as the centrality of language competencies for counter-terrorism, and the critical role of second-generation migrants in this sphere. Equally important, awareness is being raised of the importance of the knowledge of other languages in ensuring justice for foreign nationals in an age of growing xenophobia.

Language and defence

In the wake of 9/11, various writers drew attention to the short-sighted nature of national policy on language teaching and its implications for defence.[1] Information which had remained in the public domain for some time without comment finally surfaced to attract a great deal of attention, particularly in the USA.

Concern was expressed, for instance, about the catastrophic shortage of translators and interpreters with security clearance. During Operation Desert Storm, only 45 of the 500,000 US military personnel had a background in any of the Iraqi languages, and only five of these were trained in intelligence operations.[2] Potentially sensitive materials often wait for months and even years to be translated by a linguist with proper security clearances, sometimes with disastrous consequences. It has been alleged, for instance, that if Arabic video-tapes and bomb-making manuals seized from Ahmad Ajaj, a Palestinian imprisoned for passport fraud, had been translated before the bombing of the World Trade Center in 1993, they would have pointed clearly to the impending attack.[3]

The lessons of World War II had, it seems, been forgotten. The story of the Navajo code-talkers illustrates in dramatic terms the usefulness of competence in other languages for national defence.[4] The suggestion for a system based on Navajo is reputed to have been made first by Philip Johnston, the son of a Protestant missionary who grew up on a Navajo reservation. Such a system would never need to be changed or written down and so would solve the urgent need for new codes. The Marine Corps eventually recruited over 400 Navajos. A list of the most frequently used words in the military lexicon was constructed; proper names and words not included in the list were spelled out using the Navajo alphabet. The code was never broken by enemy forces and remained secret until declassified in 1968. Although credited with saving thousands of lives and helping to end the war, official recognition for this Navajo achievement came only with the presentation of the Congressional Gold medal to 29 of the original recruits in 2001. The story captured the public imagination with the release of *Windtalkers*, a full-length Hollywood movie and – the ultimate accolade – a Navajo Code Talker GI Joe doll, complete with seven recorded Navajo phrases, from Hasbro Toys.

Present-day threats to security are, of course, of a different order. Some simple statistics illustrate US vulnerability. It is estimated that on 11 September there were no more than 200 non-Arab Americans with professional-level proficiency in Arabic, the fifth most widely spoken language in the world.[5] There were also fewer than 10 students of Uzbek, Turkmen and Tajik, and none of the minor languages of Afghanistan were studied in the US educational system at all.[6]

The link with defence is, not, of course, a new development. The 1958 National Defense Education Act set out to address the national security needs of the USA by focusing on the study of modern foreign languages and, in particular, less commonly taught languages. In 1985, the US Department of Education published a list of 169 'critical languages' deemed important for scientific research and national security. Support for post-secondary programmes in less commonly taught languages comes from various agencies of the US Department of Defense; and the Defense Language Institute Foreign Language Center in Monterey, California, has been at the centre of developments. Following 11 September 2001, enrolments in Arabic and other Middle Eastern language courses have been rising at government language-learning institutions, universities and schools.[7]

The armed forces play a role in language teaching in other inner-circle countries, too. The military institute, known today as the Australian Defence Force School of Languages, was established at Point Cook in World War II and currently offers training in 20 different languages. In the UK instruction is available in 46 different languages at all levels from colloquial to graduate.[8] Following 9/11, however, the sudden rush of advertisements for posts in government departments concerned with security, designed to attract speakers of Arabic, Farsi, Pashto and Tajik, would suggest that British capacity in lesser-used languages falls far short of requirements.[9]

National needs are not limited to the terrorist threat. In a Senate hearing in September 2000, for instance, the language deficiencies in US federal agencies were deemed to have reached crisis proportions.[10] This conclusion was by no means unreasonable. An estimated 80 federal agencies need proficiency in nearly 100 foreign languages in order to deal with threats from drug trafficking and communicable diseases, as well as to advance economic and diplomatic interests.

Intelligence gathering

In spite of serious weaknesses in language competency, the UK and the USA provide a high standard of service in the monitoring of foreign-language media. The BBC Monitoring Service was set up in 1939 to provide news and intelligence to all government departments, with a direct link to Winston Churchill and the War Cabinet. In 1947, an alliance was forged with the Foreign Broadcast Information Service (FBIS) of the Central Intelligence Agency (CIA). Today the BBC covers Europe, the Middle East and Africa while the FBIS covers China, Korea and Russia. Together they gather information from 140 countries in 70 languages for government and military analysts, academics, businesspeople and journalists. In the early years, monitors listened to short-wave radio; today their sources include satellite television and newspapers on the Internet. Online services have now replaced the hard-copy reports that used to be sent by mail. Yet attitudes to the usefulness of services of this kind remain ambivalent. Stringent cuts to the FBIS budget proposed in 1997 were only halted by protests from the Federation of American Scientists.[11]

Language and diplomacy

Languages are also important for diplomacy. The recent surge in anti-American feeling has served as a catalyst for the Diplomatic Readiness

Strategy at the US Department of State.[12] Language training is an important element in an initiative designed to increase the numbers of diplomats significantly by 2004. Proficiency in other languages is seen as a central plank of effective UK foreign policy and the Diplomatic Service Language Centre offers training in 84 languages, with plans to extend its services to a wider range of government agencies.[13] The Language Centre at the University of London School of Oriental and African Studies is another important training centre, offering part-time classes in 52 languages to 1,200 students each term; most classes have waiting lists.[14]

British membership of the European Union has also helped to heighten awareness of the importance of other languages. According to Eryl McNally, a Member of the European Parliament, the most effective politicians are those who speak several languages: 'Even though translation and interpreting services are available for official meetings, it's in the corridors, cafeterias and members' offices that the real business is done, the compromises reached and the amendments drawn up.'[15]

Historically, Australia was unable to supply the demand for language resources for diplomacy and foreign relations from within.[16] Alan Watt, ambassador to the USSR and Japan in the 1940s and 1950s, bemoaned the fact that his staff had to study the local language in their own time with no support from government. A parliamentary question in 1968 established that only nine Asian-based Australian diplomats were able to speak the relevant languages. A 1984 Australian Senate report noted with concern that 70 per cent of Foreign Service positions were staffed by English monolinguals, and embassies made heavy use of local nationals for interpreting.

One approach to these shortcomings is to improve foreign-language teaching in schools. Another is to harness the existing skills of minority-language speakers. The latter course of action has much to recommend it. Most people who regularly use a language with family and friends have native or near-native pronunciation and fluency. They have extensive vocabulary and a good knowledge of the cultural norms surrounding language use. They may lack the specialist vocabulary and structures required for subjects such as philosophy and politics, which they would be more likely to discuss in English. They may also have low levels of literacy in the heritage language. None the less, their accomplishments are significant: by the age of 5, for instance, many Korean children have achieved a higher level of proficiency than adult graduates of an intensive Korean-as-a-second-language programme run by the US military.[17]

Language and justice

Concerns following the events of 9/11 have had predictable consequences for minority communities and their languages. In an atmosphere reminiscent of the xenophobia around the time of World War I, incidents involving hostility to speakers of other languages are very much on the increase. Muslims have not been the only targets. The refusal of President Jacques Chirac to back the war in Iraq has led to considerable bad feeling towards French speakers in the USA, even in Louisiana, a traditional bastion of the language. It was reported, for instance, that two teachers talking French in a restaurant were challenged by a waiter, even though in fact they came from Belgium. Francophiles have been called 'un-American' and Francophones dubbed 'traitors'.[18]

Ignorance of other languages can also lead to serious miscarriages of justice. The UK and Australia both use language analysis to screen asylum seekers where there are 'objective reasons' for doubting the nationality of a claimant.[19] Australian linguists have, however, raised serious concerns about this practice. As is clearly illustrated by the example of the French-speaking Belgian teachers, it is simply not possible to determine nationality on the basis of language.

The Australian linguists studied 58 cases involving language analysis. Of these, several were based on minimal and unconvincing evidence, which drew on folk views about language rather than principled linguistic analysis. Most involved challenges to applicants' claims of Afghan nationality. According to one expert, the use of the English word *camp* with an Urdu accent was evidence that the claimant was from Pakistan and not from Afghanistan. The person in question had in fact come to Australia via a Pakistani refugee camp, where it is likely that this pronunciation would have been the norm. In another case, a claimant was deemed to be Pakistani because he used one Urdu word, one Iranian word and two other words – *Afghanistan* and *dollar* – spoken with an Urdu accent. The reliance on a few words or a person's pronunciation to demonstrate nationality or ethnicity is extremely worrying. In reality, words spread from one language to another; pronunciation changes over time; and we all accommodate the way we speak to the audience.

The validity of 'expert' analysis has been questioned on various fronts. Linguists contend that any language that is subject to scrutiny for immigration purposes needs to have been studied in great depth. In the case of the border area between Afghanistan and Pakistan, our knowledge of the linguistic situation is in fact very limited. While the experts used are generally native speakers, they are not trained linguists; their transcriptions are of a 'rough-and-ready' nature and fail to engage in the detailed phonetic analysis necessary to make a convincing case.

There is also concern about inconsistencies in the ways in which the Australian government is applying language analysis. Members of refugee review tribunals vary in the importance they attach to language analysis. Some recognize the weaknesses of current practice and disallow expert evidence; others are less critical. As a result, claimants are clearly receiving unequal treatment. It has also been pointed out that applicants who engage their own linguistic experts have more favourable outcomes. Australia is not, of course, the only inner-circle country making use of language in the processing of asylum claims. The UK government has used a similar approach for claimants from Afghanistan, Somalia, Sri Lanka and Iraq.[20]

Language, politics and protest

America Online, the world's largest Internet service provider, recently found itself at the centre of a political controversy when it attempted to control the use of other languages in its news and comment forums.[21] AOL-UK posted a message banning any use of the Irish language on a 'Peace in Ireland' forum in response to complaints from Unionists: 'This board is designed for English speakers, and Gaelic [sic] postings are not allowed. Continuation of this type of posting will result in a warning to the account. [P]osts in Gaelic will be removed without further recourse to the person who posted it [sic].' Even taglines containing 'Happy New Year' in Irish were deemed inadmissible.

Predictably, the ban triggered considerable protest. AOL quickly withdrew the policy, and announced that it intended to recruit an Irish-language speaker to monitor Irish-language posts for content. The incident clearly demonstrated that assumptions and stereotypes have the potential to sway policy; a knowledge of the language in question would have made it possible to avoid inflaming still further an already sensitive situation.

Wake-up call?

The events of 9/11 have been hailed as a wake-up call, the moment when the Western world finally realized its vulnerability and the need to be more vigilant. For many people, the central role of language in this wake-up process comes as something of a surprise. A review of current approaches to language teaching is well overdue. There is no shortage of evidence to suggest, for instance, that two-way bilingual programmes produce the best results. Yet programmes of this kind receive considerably less support than the US Defense Language Institute, in spite of the fact that the more traditional foreign-language teaching techniques employed here seldom allow learners to achieve native-speaker proficiency.

In attempting to safeguard the values which are often hailed as the hallmark of Western democracies, it is essential to maintain a balanced view. Knowledge of other languages is not simply a tool to help protect us from potential aggressors; it is also a tool to protect innocent bystanders from the worst excesses of xenophobia.

Notes

1 For an overview, see Morrison (2001).
2 Congressional finding of the Foreign Language Economic Enhancement Act, HR 5442, 102d Congress, reported by Crawford (1997).
3 Fesperman and Gibson (2001).
4 Paul (1973); Tohtsoni (undated).
5 Peyton and Ranard (2001).
6 Nunberg (2001).
7 Peterson and Morrison (2003).
8 Connell (2002).
9 Connell (2002).
10 US Senate (2000).
11 Kempster (1997).
12 US Department of State (2002).
13 Connell (2002).
14 www.soas.ac.uk/languagecentre/home.htl
15 Nuffield Languages Inquiry (2000: 17).
16 Ozolins (1993).
17 Campbell and Lindholm (1987).
18 Burdeau (2003).
19 Eades et al. (2003).
20 Anon. (2003a).
21 Sheridan (1999).

12

Is life really too short to learn German?

The traditional strongholds of the English language differ in history, demography and organization. Australia, Aotearoa/New Zealand and, to a lesser extent, Canada remained resolutely Anglo-Celtic until the 1960s, largely retaining British institutions; the USA steered an independent course. The UK and Ireland were the main source of migrants for the remaining British colonies until after World War II, at which point the UK turned to labour from the New Commonwealth to fuel economic growth. Canada, the USA, Australia and Aotearoa/New Zealand, however, continued resolutely with their all-White immigration policies until the late 1960s. Aotearoa/New Zealand and Ireland, much smaller than the other inner-circle countries, have remained more homogeneous; Ireland only became a destination for migrants following entry to the European Union in 1973.

The different histories have shaped different linguistic landscapes. Indigenous peoples make up over 14 per cent of the population of Aotearoa/New Zealand but only 1.5 per cent of that of the USA. Aotearoa/New Zealand has just one Indigenous language; Australia, Canada and the USA have many different languages. Two inner-circle countries have a 'majority minority'. In the USA, 29 million people speak Spanish in the home, far more than any other minority language; in Canada, Francophones make up a quarter of the population. In the remaining countries, no single language predominates. Some languages, however, are accorded greater rights than others. This is the case, for instance, for the Celtic languages in the British Isles, Māori in Aotearoa/New Zealand, French in Canada, and Inuktitut in Nunavut.

Yet a central tenet of this book is that the similarities between the inner-circle countries are more striking than the differences. So what conclusions can we draw about the other languages of North America, the British Isles, Australia and Aotearoa/New Zealand?

An obvious starting point is to acknowledge the nature and extent of diversity. It is true that the shift from minority language to English can be rapid: in a process which is sometimes complete within two to three generations, children today may have only a passive understanding of the heritage language. But it is no longer possible to sustain the myth that other languages are simply vestigial or play a transitory role. In the case of Spanish in the USA, for instance, repeated waves of migrants have ensured that the minority language remains a vital force. Francophones have held their ground in Quebec, an island in an ocean of English. And in the case of some Indigenous and established languages, the shift to English has been halted and even reversed, often against all odds.

One thing is certain: the range of languages spoken in the traditional strongholds of English in the twenty-first century is much wider than ever before. Although it is difficult to be precise about how many languages are spoken or the numbers of speakers, there can be no doubt that multilingualism is a normal part of life in inner-circle countries, especially in the large gateway cities. Given the extent of diversity, an obvious question is how the myth of monolingualism ever took hold.

Language, power and control

English-only policies have played a crucial role in subordination and control in all the inner-circle countries. Various weapons in the armoury of the powerful were used to achieve this end. In some cases, children were removed from their families so that they could be educated in English. The same extreme measures first used with the oldest sons of wealthy Gaels in seventeenth-century Scotland were applied to the Indigenous peoples of North America and the southern hemisphere. Removal, of course, was not enough in itself. Children in residential settings were regularly exposed to punishment and ridicule; so, too, were speakers of established languages who continued living with their families.

Last but not least, legislation was used in a pincer movement designed to enforce the will of the majority. The introduction in the nineteenth century of non-sectarian education, paid for by taxes, made the task of regulating language much easier. On this occasion, the target was not only Indigenous and established languages, but also the European languages spoken by other colonists. New laws were introduced from the late nineteenth century to limit the use of other languages in schools, in the media and in public places. Language legislation has also been invoked in recent times. Proposition 227 in California and Proposition 203 in

Arizona, for instance, have greatly reduced the number of bilingual education programmes from public schools in these states. Several failed
attempts have been made to amend the US constitution to make English
the official language.

Politicians, however, are, for the most part, pragmatists. Colonists
required an ongoing flow of human resources to allow them to extend
frontiers; industrialists needed labour for their factories; the globalization
of trade has created pools of skilled and unskilled labour in developing
countries to service the economic expansion of the West. The preference
– particularly in the case of Canada, Australia and Aotearoa/New Zealand
– was for migrants from the British Isles, followed first by northern
Europe and then by southern and eastern Europe. With the economic
recovery following World War II, the supply of European migrants could
no longer meet demands, a development which led to the dismantling of
Whites-only immigration policies. The need for labour has thus always
outweighed the desire for a linguistically and culturally homogeneous
society. In a similar way, the events of 9/11 have led to greatly increased
budgets for the teaching of Arabic and other Middle Eastern languages
in the USA.

Each new wave of migration has been resisted by the groups that
came before. Northern Europeans were extremely hostile to southern
and eastern Europeans; Europeans of all provenances are at the forefront
of attempts to limit the entry of Asians and Africans today. It is no
accident that current lobbying to restrict the use of other languages
coincides with a period of rising immigration. Recent decades have seen
the rise of campaign groups such as US English and the Alliance Quebec
in Canada. Australia has witnessed the emergence of the One Nation
Party and the UK has seen the first victories of the British National Party
in local elections. While it is no longer politically acceptable to express
deep-seated fear and mistrust of minorities in direct terms, the same
restrictions do not apply to opinions about language. It has become
increasingly clear, however, that debates which on the surface focus on
language are actually about culture, identity, power and control.

A new world order

Recent developments have greatly strengthened the position of minority
languages and made it much more difficult for supporters of English-
only policies to impose their will. The twentieth century witnessed the
disintegration of the British empire. Acts of civil disobedience by Gandhi

and his followers against the imperial administration in India, and the civil rights movement in the USA, served as catalysts for ethnic revival in many other parts of the world.

In the USA, Title VI of the Civil Rights Act was used to ensure the provision of medical interpreters and opened the way to legal challenges to the education system. The case of *Lau v. Nichols*, for instance, raised the legality of allowing children with limited English to sink or swim without support in mainstream classrooms. The judgement in the Ann Arbor case extended a similar duty of care for speakers of other dialects. The courts have also been used to challenge employers who have attempted to exclude other languages from the workplace.

Several languages have now achieved co-official status with English. In Canada, French has the same status as English in all federal institutions, and Inuktitut is one of the three official languages of the newly created territory of Nunavut. Welsh has co-official status with English in all aspects of public life. The position of Welsh, as well as that of Gaelic, Irish and Ulster-Scots, was strengthened with the ratification of the European Charter for Minority Languages by the governments of the UK and the Republic of Ireland. Māori is a co-official language in Aotearoa/New Zealand and is playing an important role in Aotearoa/New Zealanders' attempts to establish a distinctive national identity. Developments in Australia also owe a great deal to the search for a new national identity. The 1990 National Policy on Languages played a vital part in promoting the new philosophy of 'unity in diversity' adopted by all political parties since the 1970s.

The benefits of multilingualism

Mainstream media tend to focus on the assumed downsides of diversity – the additional cost of providing services in other languages, the dangers of ghettoization and so forth. It is possible to argue, however, that critics are failing to see the bigger picture. Three main groups are, in fact, beneficiaries of multilingualism: bilingual individuals who mediate between minority communities and the dominant English-speaking group; the minority communities themselves; and – most important – the wider English-speaking community.

Bilinguals are, of course, the linchpin in a range of situations. Interpreters and translators are essential in the delivery of services. In business settings, an understanding of other languages and cultures is an invaluable lubricant in transactions and negotiations. And, as the use of other languages increases, so do the opportunities in both public and private spheres for individuals who can speak, read and write other languages. Many employers reward bilingual skills with higher rates of pay.

When a language is learned through formal study, the levels achieved seldom match those of children who have acquired the language in a family setting or as part of an immersion experience. Five-year-old Māori children attending language nests, for instance, outperform 15-year-olds in state oral examinations; 5-year-old Korean children are more proficient than adult graduates of an intensive language programme run by the US military. The pervasiveness and power of English mean that families who make a commitment to transmitting the minority language often face an uphill struggle. The rewards, however, are considerable. On a personal level, bilinguals are able to move between different cultural spaces and make choices about what they find there. On a professional level, they have access to a much wider range of better-paid jobs. Individuals who speak the languages of the home are also better able to communicate with their parents, grandparents and other members of their families and communities, and are likely to have a much stronger sense of their cultural identity.

Minority communities form the second group of beneficiaries. They generate their own support structures: newspapers and other media which explore issues of interest overlooked in mainstream reporting; cultural events where people can socialize and be entertained; services in the minority language which make the customers feel more comfortable. The use of other languages is also an important aspect of cultural tourism and other activities, which bring economic benefits to groups that are often on the margins of society. The existence of these support structures, however, does not imply ghettoization. Members of minority communities are also consumers of mainstream media and services; and much minority provision also extends the range of choice for English speakers.

There is, of course, a qualitative difference between Indigenous and Celtic languages, on the one hand, and new minority languages, on the other. If Panjabi or Chinese were to disappear from the inner-circle countries, many millions of speakers would remain in the home countries. In contrast, when Indigenous and Celtic languages die, they are likely to disappear forever. Languages, like biological species, are highly adapted to their environments; they analyse the world in different ways, each with its own validity. When a language disappears, the traditional knowledge and ways of being encoded in the language die, too, and, in the process, the world becomes a less interesting place.

Many people argue that English is a unifying force and that the use of other languages leads to division and strife. Such fears are unfounded: the evidence suggests, in fact, that language is the tool and not the cause of conflict, and attempts to eliminate diversity are likely to give rise to the very tensions that advocates of English-only policies are seeking to avoid. Historically, the repression of minority languages has played a more crucial role in the alienation of their speakers than in their 'rehabilitation'.

The premise that minorities must choose between English and the minority language is patently false. Census statistics show that while the numbers who speak a language other than English in the home are increasing, so, too, are the numbers of people who also speak English. The acid test proposed by English politician Norman Tebitt – which side would British Indians or Pakistanis or African Caribbeans support in an international cricket match – succeeds only in missing the point. It is very likely that British Indians would shout for the Indian side in cricket, which has an avid following in the former British empire. However, they would be equally likely to support England in soccer, a game that failed to achieve the same popularity. We are dealing here with multiple – not unitary – identities.

The third group of beneficiaries consists, of course, of English speakers. The possibilities created by a multilingual population are unlimited. In international trade, there is now much better understanding of the ways in which bilingual intermediaries, trusted by both parties, are able to offer a competitive edge. As companies realize that minority communities represent important markets in themselves, bilinguals are proving invaluable in reaching these new markets in appropriate ways. Bilingual skills are equally important in the fields of diplomacy and defence.

English speakers also benefit by being able to access an astonishing range of cultural experiences: musical performances, subtitled films and drama, dual-language books, to name just a few. But perhaps the most exciting by-product of diversity is the creativity it generates. Traditional art forms are not static. Each new generation reinterprets artistic expression in its own unique way. However, when a traditional genre is transported to a new setting or finds itself alongside other cultural traditions, the opportunities for cross-fertilization are boundless. Bilingual theatre is not simply a ploy to allow actors and playwrights to reach a wider audience; it is a new and different genre with its own devices and its own aesthetics. In the same way, the addition of electronic and other influences to traditional music results in exciting new fusions, each with its own inherent merits.

There is, of course, the worrying issue of double standards. On the one hand, English-speaking countries have systematically excluded other languages from schools and are often reluctant to confer status and recognition on minority groups. On the other hand, there is a growing appreciation that the promotion of other languages is not simply a minority interest; rather it is a matter of national self-interest, especially in areas such as commerce, diplomacy and defence. Symptomatic of this tension is the fact that, while Hispanic speakers in the USA are switching to English at an unprecedented speed, Spanish is the most popular foreign language on the school curriculum.

Two steps forward, one step back

The second half of the twentieth century saw a paradigm change from assimilation to multiculturalism. On a rhetorical level, minority languages are far more secure than at any point in centuries. Critics of the multi-cultural policies which have been a feature of all the inner-circle countries, however, argue that this approach to diversity is superficial and palliative and fails to address the underlying racism in society.

There is no shortage of evidence to support this position. If we take the situation in Aotearoa/New Zealand, for example, English speakers are happy to use Māori words such as 'kia ora' for hello and identify with the Māori chant delivered at the start of All Blacks rugby matches. They even argue that Māori is helping to create a distinctive Aotearoa/New Zealand identity. However, Indigenous peoples are still struggling to gain full control of their children's education and have had only minimal influence on the development of Māori-language media. Despite its status as a co-official language, the first dedicated Māori television channel was launched only in 2002, years after minority-language broadcasting was in place in all the other inner-circle countries.

The situation of American Indian languages is even worse. The passing of the 1975 Indian Self-Determination and Education Act was greeted with a rhetorical flurry. President Richard Nixon announced 'a new era in which the Indian future is determined by Indian acts and Indian decisions', and described this new policy as 'a matter of justice and a matter of enlightened social policy'.[1] The first meaningful support for Indigenous languages came when the 1968 Bilingual Education Act was extended to include American Indian and Alaska Native languages. However, the use of Indian languages in school was limited, in the main, to the teaching of basic vocabulary and greetings for a few hours each week. The 1990 Native American Languages Act was intended to preserve, promote and protect American languages. However, no funding was provided and the only positive effect of this legislation was that American Indians were able to resist the growing momentum in the wider society to bring bilingual education to an end.

Funding has been a critical issue in many other situations. Support from the Canadian government in the form of the Native Communication Program in the 1980s served as a catalyst for a wide range of Indigenous publishing initiatives. Following the sudden withdrawal of funding in 1990, less than half the publications set up as part of this initiative have survived. Funding decisions have had an even greater impact in the Northern Territory of Australia. Here bilingual education was axed in 1998 on the grounds of alleged poor standards in English literacy in bilingual schools, in comparison with English-only schools. No evidence, however, was offered to support this claim; nor was there support for this new policy from Aboriginal peoples.

Nowhere is the political dimension clearer than in the erosion of the 1968 Bilingual Education Act in the USA in the 1990s and its eventual dismantling in 2002. The fact that relatively few children have ever been involved in bilingual programmes has, for the most part, been overlooked. Nor has the failure of English submersion programmes to produce improved outcomes for minority students led to the reinstatement of bilingual education. Title III of No Child Left Behind, the legislation which replaces the BEA, places sole emphasis on the rapid acquisition of English. The 'measurable achievement objectives' that will accompany it are a cause for particular concern, since the failure to show progress in annual English assessments will be punished. Many opponents of this new legislation fear that it will be used as a mechanism for eliminating native-language programmes, in much the same way as the system of payment by results in the schools of nineteenth-century Wales contributed to the decline of Welsh.

So is life too short to learn German?

The experience of the late twentieth century throws interesting light on the comment attributed to Richard Porson, the eighteenth-century British classicist, that life is too short to learn German. Knowledge of other languages is not a matter of rationing or prioritization. Educators have shown convincingly that young children can be educated through the medium of other languages at no cost to their achievements in English.

Thanks to the efforts of minority communities to keep their languages
alive, the inner-circle countries have a competitive edge in international
trade. The coexistence of different languages and cultures leads to the
cross-fertilization of ideas in all kinds of artistic expression. Bilingual,
bicultural individuals, able to mediate between minority and majority
populations, are the potential cornerstone for a more harmonious society.
Life, it would seem, is quite long enough for us to acquire a collective
knowledge of German, Chinese, Urdu and many other languages.

The view that languages are the pedigree of nations – an asset and
resource rather than a problem to be solved – has underpinned many of
the achievements of recent times. It would be naïve, however, to ignore
the voices which contest these gains. History has shown how dominant
groups strive to safeguard their power base, often with unfortunate consequences for minorities. At a time when immigration has once more
become a burning issue, it is predictable that the attitudes of English
speakers towards other languages should once more become more hostile.
What is less predictable, however, is the extent to which these attitudes
will prevail.

Note

1   Nixon (1970).

References

Journal articles without page numbers have been consulted online.

Adams, K. and Brink, D. (eds) (1990) *Perspectives on Official English: The Campaign of English as the Official Language of the USA.* Mouton de Gruyter, Berlin and New York.

Age Concern (2003) *A Beginner's Guide to the Internet.* Panjabi and Urdu versions. Age Concern, London.

Ager, D. (2001) *Motivation in Language Planning and Language Policy.* Multilingual Matters, Clevedon.

Anderton, A. (1997) The Wordpath show. In: J. Reyhner (ed.) *Teaching Indigenous Languages.* Northern Arizona University, Flagstaff, AZ.

Andrews, P. (1991) The Irish language in the education system of Northern Ireland: some political and cultural perspectives. In: R. Pritchard (ed.) *Motivating the Majority: Modern Languages in Northern Ireland.* University of Ulster with CILT, London.

Anon. (1999) Hawaii debates use of Pidgin English in classroom. *News Tribune Online Edition* 28 November. Retrieved from: www.newstribune.com/stories/112899/wor_1128990826.asp

Anon. (2003a) 'Iraqi' refugees to face language checks. *Guardian Unlimited.* Retrieved from: www.guardian.co.uk/Refugees_in_Britain/Story/0,2763,912106,00.html

Anon. (2003b) Radio-Canada. *The Encyclopedia of Canadian Theatre.* Retrieved from: www.canadiantheatre.com/dict.pl?term=Radio-Canada

Applied History Research Group (1997) *The Peopling of Canada: 1891–1921.* University of Calgary, Calgary.

Armstrong, C. (2001) Some representations of America and their diffusion in Elizabethan England: *O Strange New World* reassessed. *Eras Online Journal* 2.

Atkins, J. (1887) *Annual Report of the Commissioner of Indian Affairs to the Secretary of the Interior for the Year 1887.* Government Printing Office, Washington, DC.

Auld, L. J. (2001) *A Review of the Criminal Courts of England and Wales*: Retrieved from: www.criminal-courts-review.org.uk

Australia (1991) *Australia's Language: The Australian Language and Literacy Policy*. DEET, Canberra.

Australia (1994) *Creative Nation: Commonwealth Cultural Policy*. Retrieved from: www.nla.gov.au/creative.nation/tourism.html

Avison, S. and Meadows, M. (2000) Speaking and hearing: Aboriginal newspapers and the public sphere in Canada and Australia. *Canadian Journal of Communication* 25(3) .

Baker, C. (1997) Bilingual education in Ireland, Scotland and Wales. In: J. Cummins and D. Corson (eds) *Encyclopedia of Language and Education: Bilingual Education*. Kluwer, Dordrecht.

Baker, C. (2000) *A Parents' and Teachers' Guide to Bilingualism*. Multilingual Matters, Clevedon.

Baker, C. (2001) *Foundations of Bilingual Education and Bilingualism*. Multilingual Matters, Clevedon.

Baker, C. and Prys Jones, S. (1998) *Encyclopedia of Bilingualism and Bilingual Education*. Multilingual Matters, Clevedon.

Baker, P. and Mohieldeen, Y. (2000) The languages of London's schoolchildren. In: P. Baker and J. Eversley (eds) *Multilingual Capital*. Battlebridge, London.

Baldauf, S. (1997) Children say 'Oui' to foreign languages. *Christian Science Monitor* 13 June.

Baron, D. (1990) *The English-Only Question: An Official Language for Americans?* Yale University Press, New Haven, CT.

Baron, D. (2001) Language legislation and language abuse: American language policy through the 1990s. In: R. Gonzalez and I. Melis (eds) *Language Ideologies: Critical Perspectives on the Official English Movement*. NCTE and Lawrence Erlbaum Associates, Urbana.

BBC (British Broadcasting Corporation) (2000) Hotel bans staff from speaking Welsh. *News Online* 2 October. Retrieved from: http://news.bbc.co.uk/1/hi/wales/952693.stm

BBC (British Broadcasting Corporation) (2002) UK students lose out on Euro jobs. *BBC News Online* 25 November. Retrieved from: http://news.bbc.co.uk/1/hi/education/2504201.stm

Beasley, K. (1999) Aboriginal bilingual education in the Northern Territory. *Australian Language Matters* 7(4).

Beckett, F. (2002) Dumbing down. *Education Guardian Weekly* 5 November. Retrieved from:http://education.guardian.co.uk/egweekly/story/0,5500,825611,00.html

Bélanger, C. (2000) The three pillars of survival. *Events, Issues and Concepts of Quebec History*. Retrieved from: www2.marianopolis.edu/quebechistory/events/pillars.htm

Bender, M. (2002) *Signs of Cherokee Culture: Sequoyah's Syllabury in Eastern Cherokee Life*. University of North Carolina Press, Chapel Hill.

Benton, R. (1996) Language policy in New Zealand: defining the ineffable. In: M. Herriman and B. Burnaby (eds) *Language Policies in English-Dominant Countries: Six Case Studies*. Multilingual Matters, Clevedon.

Beresford, Q. and Omaji, P. (1998) *Our State of Mind: Racial Planning and the Stolen Generations*. Freemantle Arts Centre Press, Freemantle.

Berk-Seligson, S. (2000) Interpreting for the police: issues in the pre-trial phases of the judicial process. *Forensic Linguistics* 7(1), 213–38.

Berry, J., Kalin, R. and Taylor, D. (1977) *Multiculturalism and Ethnic Attitudes in Canada*. Ministry of Supply and Services, Ottowa.

Bond, L. (1993) Clannad and Máire Brennan. *Dirty Linen* 47(August/September).

Boswell, J. (1785) *The Journal of a Tour to the Hebrides with Samuel Johnson*. Charles Dilly, London.

Bourdieu, P. (1986) The forms of capital. In: J. Richardson (ed.) *Handbook of Theory and Research for the Sociology of Education*. Greenwood Press, New York.

Bourne, J. (1989) *Moving into the Mainstream: LEA Provision for Bilingual Pupils in England and Wales*. NFER-Nelson, Windsor.

Bowe, F. (1991) *Approaching Equality*. TJ Publishers, Silver Spring, MD.

Bowes, A. and Meehan Domokos, T. (1997) Pakistani women, general practitioners and health visitors: communication and service access. In: A. Bowes and D. Sim (eds) *Perspectives on Welfare: The Experience of Minority Ethnic Groups in Scotland*. Ashgate, Aldershot.

Branswell, B. (2000) Bilingualism in Canada. *Linguist* 40(1).

Brecht, R. D. and Ingold, C. W. (1998) *Tapping a National Resource: Heritage Languages in the United States*. ERIC Clearinghouse on Languages and Linguistics, Washington, DC. Retrieved from: www.cal.org/ericcll

British Sign Language Info-Web (undated) *Milan Era*. Retrieved from: www.bsl-infoweb.org/milan.htm

Broome, R. (1982) *Aboriginal Australians*. Sydney: George Allen and Unwin.

Buchtmann, L. (1999) Digital songlines: the use of modern communication technology by an Aboriginal community in remote Australia. Communications Research Forum. Retrieved from: www.dcita.gov.au/crf/paper99/lydia.html

Bullock, S. A. (1975) *A Language for Life*. HMSO, London.

Burdeau, C. (2003) Anti-French feelings crop up in Louisiana, too. *News 2 Louisiana* 2 April. Retrieved from: www.wbrz.com

Burnaby, B. (1996) Language policy in Canada. In: M. Herriman and B. Burnaby (eds) *Language Policies in English-Dominant Countries: Six Case Studies*. Multilingual Matters, Clevedon.

Burstall, C., Jamieson, M., Cohen, S., et al. (1974) *Primary French in the Balance*. NFER, Windsor.

Business in the Community (2003) About RfO. Retrieved from: www2.bitc.org.uk/programmes/programme_directory/race_for_opportunity/rfo_about.html

Buti, A. (2001) Responding to the legacy of Canadian residential schools. *E Law* 8(4). Retrieved from: www.murdoch.edu.au/elaw/indices/title/buti84_abstract.html

Campbell, R. and Lindholm, K. (1987) *Conservation of Language Resources.* University of California Center for Language Acquisition and Research, Los Angeles.

Canada Council for the Arts (2002) *Grants to Aboriginal Writers, Storytellers and Publishers.* Canada Council for the Arts, Ottowa.

Canadian Heritage (1999) Myths and realities. Retrieved from: www.pch.gc.ca/progs/lo-ol/publications/mythes/english/mythes.html

Carbin, D. (1996) *Deaf Heritage in Canada: A Distinctive, Diverse and Enduring Culture.* McGraw-Hill Ryerson, Whitby, Ontario.

Carreira, M. and Armengol, R. (2001) Professional opportunities for heritage language speakers. In: J. Peyton, D. Ranard and S. McGinnis (eds) *Heritage Languages in America.* Center for Applied Linguistics, Washington, DC.

Casles, S. and Miller, M. (eds) (1998) *The Age of Migration: International Population Movements in the Modern World.* Palgrave, Basingstoke.

Cenoz, J. and Genesee, F. (eds) (2001) *Trends in Bilingual Acquisition.* John Benjamins, Amsterdam and Philadelphia.

Chandrasekar, S. (1990) Building the Asian television network. *Polyphony* 12, 47–52.

Chang, H. and Pulido, D. (1994) The critical importance of cultural and linguistic continuity for infants and toddlers. *Zero to Three* (October/November), 13–17.

Chao, T. H. (1997) *Chinese Heritage Community Language Schools in the United States.* ERIC Clearinghouse on Languages and Linguistics, Washington, DC. Retrieved from: www.cal.org/ericcll/digest/chao0001.html

Churchill, S. (1986) *The Education of Linguistic and Cultural Minorities in the OECD Countries.* Multilingual Matters, Clevedon.

Claus, H. (1997) Court interpreting: complexities and misunderstandings. *Alaska Justice Forum* 13(4).

Clyne, M. (1991) *Community Languages: The Australian Experience.* Cambridge University Press, Cambridge.

Clyne, M. and Kipp, S. (2002) Australia's changing demography. *People and Place* 10(3), 29–35.

Coelho, E. (1988) *Caribbean Students in Canadian Schools.* Carib-Can Publishers, Toronto.

Colin, J. and Morris, R. (1996) *Interpreters and the Legal Process.* Waterside Press, Winchester.

Commins, P. (1988) Socio-economic development and language maintenance in the Gaeltacht. In P. Riagáin (ed.) *Language Planning in Ireland. International Journal of the Sociology of Language* 70, 11–18.

Connell, T. (2000) Languages and the square mile. In: P. Baker and J. Eversley (eds) *Multilingual Capital: The Languages of London's School Children and their Relevance to Economic, Social and Educational Policies.* Battlebridge, London.

Connell, T. (2002) *Languages and Employability.* Languages National Training Organisation, London. Retrieved from: www.languagesnto.org.uk/pdf/nuff1h/pdf

Conrad, R. (1979) *The Deaf School Child.* Harper and Row, London.

Council of Europe (1977) *Council Directive on the Education of the Children of Migrant Workers* (77/48b/EEC). 25 July. Council of Europe, Strasbourg.

Crawford, J. (1990) Language freedom and restriction: a historical approach to the official language controversy. In: J. Reyhner (ed.) *Language Education Practices and Native Language Survival.* Retrieved from: http://jan.ucc.nau.edu/~jar/NALI2.html

Crawford, J. (1997) Issues in US language policy: English plus. Retrieved from: http://ourworld.compuserve.com/homepages/JWCRAWFORD/engplus.htm

Crawford, J. (1999) *Bilingual Education: History, Politics, Theory and Practice.* Fourth edition. Bilingual Education Services, Los Angeles.

Crawford, J. (2000) *At War with Diversity: US Language Policy in an Age of Anxiety.* Multilingual Matters, Clevedon and Buffalo.

Crost, L. (1994) *Honor by Fire: Japanese Americans at War in Europe and the Pacific.* Presidio Press, Novato, CA.

Crystal, D. (2001) *Language and the Internet.* Cambridge University Press, Cambridge.

Cumming, A. (2000) Second language education in schools in Canada. Modern Language Centre, Ontario Institute for Studies in Education, Toronto. Retrieved from: www.oise.utoronto.ca/MLC/pufahlrep.pdf

Cummins, J. (1996) *Negotiating Identities: Education for Empowerment in a Diverse Society.* First edition. California Association for Bilingual Education, Ontario, CA.

Cummins, J. (1998) Rossell and Baker: their case for the effectiveness of bilingual education. *Journal of Pedagogy, Pluralism and Practice* 3(1).

Cummins, J. (2001) *Negotiating Identities: Education for Empowerment in a Diverse Society.* Second edition. California Association for Bilingual Education, Ontario, CA.

Cummins, J. and Danesi, M. (1990) *Heritage Languages: The Development and Denial of Canada's Linguistic Resources.* Our Schools/Ourselves and Garamond Press, Toronto.

Da Pidgin Coup (1999) Pidgin and education: a position paper. University of Hawai'i. Retrieved from: www.hawaii.edu/sls/pidgin.html

Dallavia, R. (1995) Ars gratia artis. *Jump!* XV(i). Retrieved from: http://web.wm.edu/so/jump/fall95/index.html

Dana, J. and McMonagle, S. (1994) Deconstructing 'criminalisation': the politics of collective education in the H-Blocks. *Irish Political Prisoner Information.* Retrieved from: http://wwwvms.utexas.edu/~jdana/ira_ed.html

Davies, J. (1993) *A History of Wales.* Penguin, London.

Day, C. S. (1935) *Life with Father*. Alfred A. Knopf, New York.

Day, R. (2001) The Irish language and radio: a response. In: H. Kelly-Holmes (ed.) *Minority Language Broadcasting: Breton and Irish*. Multilingual Matters, Clevedon.

Del Valle, S. (2003) *Language Rights and the Law in the United State: Finding our Voices*. Multilingual Matters, Clevedon.

DENI (Department of Education for Northern Ireland) (1998) *Education Reform in Northern Ireland: The Way Forward*. DENI, Bangor.

Department for Work and Pensions (2003) Government recognition and £1 million boost for British Sign Language. *News Release CSD1803-Sign*. Department for Work and Pensions, London.

Department of Education (1987) Te reo Māori in school libraries. Retrieved from: www.trw.org.nz/He-Puna/three.htm

Department of Immigration (1960) *First Report on the Progress and Assimilation of Migrant Children in Australia*. Department of Immigration, Canberra.

Díaz Soto, L., Smrekar, J. and Nekrovei, D. (1999) Preserving home languages and cultures in the classroom: challenges and opportunities. *Directions in Language Learning* 13. Retrieved from: www.ncela.gwu.edu/ncbepubs/directions/13.htm

Dicker, S. (1996) *Languages in America: A Pluralist View*. Multilingual Matters, Clevedon.

Dillard, J. (1972) *Black English*. Random House, New York.

Dion, S. (1991) Will Quebec secede? Why Quebec nationalism is so strong. *Brookings Review* 9(4), 14–21.

Döpke, S. (1992) *One Parent, One Language: An Interactional Approach*. John Benjamins, Philadelphia.

Eades, D. (1992) *Aboriginal English and the Law: Communicating with Aboriginal English Speaking Clients: A Handbook for Legal Practitioners*. Queensland Law Society, Brisbane.

Eades, D. (2002) The politics of misunderstanding in the legal system: Aboriginal English speakers in Queensland. In: J. House, G. Kasper and S. Ross (eds) *Misunderstanding in Spoken Discourse*. Longman, London.

Eades, D., Fraser, H., Siegel, J., et al. (2003) Linguistic identification in the determinaation of nationality: a preliminary report. Retrieved from: www-personal.une.edu.au/-hfraser/forensic/LingID.pdf

EC (European Commission) (1984) *Report on the Implementation of Directive 77/486/EEC on the Education of Children of Migrant Workers*. EC, Brussels.

EC (European Commission) (2001) *Europeans and Languages: A Eurobarometer Special Survey*. EC, Brussels.

Education Alliance at Brown University (2003a) *Robert F. Kennedy School, AMIGOS Two-Way Immersion Program*. Retrieved from: www2.lab.brown.edu/NABE/portraits.taf?_function=detailandData_entry_uid1=18

Education Alliance at Brown University (2003b) *Madawasks Elementary School and Gateway Elementary School, L'Acadien du Haut St Jean*. Retrieved from: www2.lab.brown.edu/NABE portraits.taf?_function=detailandData_entry_ uid1=10

Edwards, V. (1998) *The Power of Babel: Teaching and Learning in Multilingual Classrooms.* Trentham Books, Stoke-on-Trent.

Edwards, V. (2000) *Multilingual UK.* British Council, London.

Edwards, V. (2001) Community languages in the United Kingdom. In: G. Extra and D. Gorter (eds) *The Other Languages of Europe.* Multilingual Matters, Clevedon.

Edwards, V. and Katbamna, S. (1989) The wedding songs of British Gujarati women. In: D. Cameron and J. Coates (eds) *Women in their Speech Communities.* Longman, London.

Edwards, V. and Sienkewicz, T. (1991) *Oral Cultures Past and Present: Rappin' and Homer.* Blackwell, Oxford.

Edwards, V. and Walker, S. (1995) *Building Bridges: Multilingual Resources for Children.* Multilingual Matters, Clevedon.

EEOC (Equal Employment Opportunity Commission) (2000) Court speaks: English only rule unlawful; awards EEOC $700,000 for Hispanic workers. Retrieved from: www.eeoc.gov/press/9-19-00.html

EEOC (Equal Employment Opportunity Commission) (2001) EEOC settles English-only suit for $2.44 million against University of Incarnate Word. Retrieved from: www.eeoc.gov/press/4-20-01.html

EEOC (Equal Employment Opportunity Commission) (2002) EEOC sues diner for national origin bias against Navajos and other Native Americans. Retrieved from: www.eeoc.gov/press/9-30-02-c.html

Euromosaic Project (1996) *Gaelic in Scotland: The Production and Reproduction of the Minority Language Groups in the European Union.* EC, Brussels.

Eversley, J. (2000) Section II: a brief history. In: P. Baker and J. Eversley (eds) *Multilingual Capital.* Battlebridge, London.

Fesperman, D. and Gibson, G. (2001) Evidence is plentiful, but translators aren't. *Baltimore Sun* 20 September.

Fishman, J. (1966) *Language Loyalty in the United States.* Mouton, The Hague.

Fishman, J. (2001) 300-plus years of heritage language education in the United States. In: J. Peyton, D. Ranard and S. McGinnis (eds) *Heritage Languages in America.* Center for Applied Linguistics, Washington, DC.

Fitzpatrick, F. (1987) *The Open Door.* Multilingual Matters, Clevedon.

Fletcher, J. (1989) *Clean, Clad and Courteous: A History of Aboriginal School Education in New South Wales.* Southwood Press, Sydney.

Fradd, S. and Lee, O. (1998) *Creating Florida's Multilingual Global Work Force: Policies and Practices in Assessing and Instructing Students Learning English as a New Language.* Office of Multicultural Student Language Education, Tallahassee.

Francis, N. and Reyhner, J. (eds) (2002) *Language and Literacy Teaching for Indigenous Education: A Bilingual Approach.* Multilingual Matters, Clevedon.

Freeman, R. (1998) *Bilingual Education and Social Change.* Multilingual Matters, Clevedon.

Gaelic Broadcasting Taskforce (2000) Report. Scottish Executive, Edinburgh. Retrieved from: www.scotland.gov.uk/library3/heritage/gbtf-00.asp

Gaglioti, F. (1999) Aboriginal bilingual education axed in Australia's Northern Territory. *World Socialist* 10 April. Retrieved from: www.wsws.org/articles/1999/apr1999/educ-a10.shtml

Georgiou, M. (2003) Consuming ethnic media – constructing ethnic identities – shaping communities: the case study of Greek Cypriots in London. In: R. A. Lind (ed.) *Race/Gender/Media: Considering Diversity Across Audiences, Content and Producers.* Allyn and Bacon, Boston.

Gibson, H., Small, A. and Mason, D. (1997) Deaf bilingual, bicultural education. In: J. Cummins and D. Corson (eds) *Encyclopedia of Language and Education,* vol. 4: *Bilingual Education.* Kluwer, Dordrecht.

Glazier, I. and De Rosa, L. (eds) (1986) *Migration across Time and Nations: Population Mobility in Historical Contexts.* Holmes and Meier, New York.

Gobbo, J. (2000) Opening to the 18th conference for the Interpreter and Translator Educators' Association of Australia. Retrieved from: http://lis.eu.rmit.edu.au/gobbo.htm

Gonzales, A. (1922) *The Black Border: Gullah Stories of the Carolina Coast.* State Company, Columbia, SC.

Goodwin, N. (1998) Aboriginal English in education. Master of Applied Linguistics Project, Northern Territory University. Retrieved from: www.ntu.edu.au/education/csle/student/goodwin/goodwin0.html

Goodz, N. (1994) Interactions between parents and children. In: F. Genesee (ed.) *Educating Second Language Children: The Whole Child, the Whole Curriculum, the Whole Community.* Cambridge University Press, Cambridge.

Graddol, D. (1999) The decline of the native speaker. In: D. Graddol and U. Meinhof (eds) *English in a Changing World. AILA Review* 13, 57–68.

Greymorning, S. (1999) Running the gauntlet of an Indigenous language program. In: J. Reyhner, G. Cantoni, R. St Clair and E. Yazzie (eds) *Revitalizing Indigenous Languages.* Northern Arizona University, Flagstaff, AZ.

Guinnane, T. (1997) *The Vanishing Irish: Households, Migration, and the Rural Economy in Ireland, 1850–1914.* Princetown University Press, Princetown, NJ.

Hale, K. (2001) Strict locality in local language media: an Australian example. In: L. Hinton and K. Hale (eds) *The Green Book of Language Revitalization in Practice.* Academic Press, San Diego.

Hall, N. (2003) The child in the middle: agency and diplomacy in language brokering events. In: G. Hansen, K. Malmkjaer and D. Gile (eds) *Claims, Changes and Challenges in Translation Studies.* John Benjamins, Amsterdam.

Hanson, A. M. (undated) What's in a name? Nanavut '00: changing the map of Canada. Retrieved from: www.nunavut.com/nunavut99/english/name.html

Harris, J. (1991) Kriol – the creation of a new language. In: S. Romaine (ed.) *Language in Australia.* Cambridge University Press, Cambridge.

Hartley, P. (2000) *The Go-Between*. Penguin, Harmondsworth.

Hawai'i State Supreme Court Committee on Equality and Access to the Courts (2001) *Immigrant Access to the Courts: Final Report*. Honolulu: Hawai'i State Supreme Court.

Herriman, M. (1996) Language policy in Australia. In: M. Herriman and B. Burnaby (eds) *Language Policies in English-Dominant Countries: Six Case Studies*. Multilingual Matters, Clevedon.

Hickey, T. (1997) *Early Immersion Education in Ireland: na Naíonraí*. Institiúid Teangeolaíochta Éireann, Dublin.

Higham, J. (1988) *Strangers in the Land: Patterns of American Nativism, 1860–1925*. Rutgers University Press, Piscataway, NJ.

Hinsliff, G. (2002) Blunkett tells British Asians. *Observer* 15 September. Retrieved from: http://politics.guardian.co.uk/homeaffairs/story/0,11026,792497,00.html

Hinton, L. (1999) Involuntary language loss among immigrants: Asian-American linguistic autobiographies. ERIC Clearinghouse on Languages and Linguistics, Washington, DC. Retrieved from: www.cal.org/ericcll/digest/involuntary.html

Holmes, C. (1988) *John Bull's Island: Immigration and British society, 1871–1971*. Macmillan, Basingstoke.

Hosmer (1999) *American Indians in the Marketplace: Persistence and Innovation among the Menominees and Metlakatlans, 1870–1920*. University Press of Kansas, Lawrence, KS.

House of Representatives Standing Committee on Aboriginal and Torres Strait Islander Affairs (1992) *Language and Culture: A Matter of Survival: Report of the Inquiry into Aboriginal and Torres Strait Islander Language Maintenance*. Australian Government Publishing Service, Canberra.

HREOC (Human Rights and Equal Opportunity Commission) (1997) *Bringing them Home: Report of the National Inquiry into the Separation of Aboriginal and Torres Strait Islander Children from their Families*. HREOC, Sydney.

HREOC (Human Rights and Equal Opportunity Commission) (2002) Bringing them home: study guide. HREOC. Retrieved from: www.hreoc.gov.au/info_for_teachers/rabbit_proof/bth_guide/effects.html

Hulme, K. (1986) *The Bone People*. Viking, London.

Hutchins, D. (1999) Creoles and comprehension in the courtroom. *Dissertation Abstracts International, A: The Humanities and Social Sciences* 60(4), October, 1105-A.

Ignace, M. (1998) *Handbook for Aboriginal Language Program Planning in British Columbia*. First Nations Education Steering Committee, North Vancouver, BC.

IRR (Institute of Race Relations) (2000) The dispersal of xenophobia: special report. *European Race Bulletin* 33/34. Retrieved from: www.irr.org.uk/2000/august/ak000002.html

Israel, M. and Banerjee, K. (1983) Bengali Theatre in Toronto. *Polyglot* 5(2).

Istituto di Scienze e Tecnologie della Cognizione (undated) The Milan Congress in 1880. Retrieved from: istc.cnr.it/mistralis/eng/pannello14.htm

ITC (Independent Television Commission) (undated) *ITC Notes: Gaelic Broadcasting*. Retrieved from: www.itc.org.uk/itc_publications/itc_notes/view_note.asp?itc_note_id=32

Jackson, S. (1993) The first language. In: W. Ihimaera (ed.) *He whakaatange o te ao*. Reed Books, Aukland.

Johnson, L. K. (2002) *Mi Revalueshanary Fren: Selected Poems*. Penguin, Harmondsworth.

Johnston, B. (1990) One generation from extinction. In: W. H. New (ed.) *Native Writers and Canadian Writing*. UBC Press, Vancouver.

Jones, M. (1998) *Language Obsolescence and Revitalization: Linguistic Change in Two Sociolinguistically Contrasting Welsh Communities*. Clarendon Press, Oxford.

Jupp, J. (ed.) (1988) *The Australian People*. Angus and Robertson, Sydney.

Kachru, B. (1985) Standards, codification and sociolinguistic realism: the English language in the outer circle. In: R. Quirk and H. Widdowson (eds) *English in the World*. Cambridge University Press, Cambridge.

Kamin, L. (1977) *The Science and Politics of IQ*. Penguin, Harmondsworth.

Katbamna, S., Bhakta, P., Parker, G., Baker, R. and Ahmad, W. (2002) Supporting South Asian carers and those they care for: the role of the primary health care team. *British Journal of General Practice* 5(2), 300–5.

Kaur, S. and Mills, R. (1993) A young child learns English. In: R. Mills and J. Mills (eds) *Bilingualism in the Primary School*. Routledge, London.

Kazoulis, V. (2001) What did you bring with you to school? Foreword. In: J. Cummins, *Negotiating Identities: Education for Empowerment in a Diverse Society*. Second edition. California Association for Bilingual Education, Ontario, CA.

Kempster, N. (1997) Academia mounts fight to save a CIA program. *Los Angeles Times* 14 January.

Kilner, J. (2003) *Australia and the Refugee/Asylum Seeker Issue*. New Age, Melbourne.

Kim, J. G. (1982) Korean language press in Ontario. *Polyphony* 4(1).

Kirk, J. and Ó Baoill, P. (2001) Introduction: language policies for the Gaeltacht and the Scotstacht. In: J. Kirk and P. Ó Baoill (eds) *Linguistic Politics: Language Policies for Northern Ireland, the Republic of Ireland, and Scotland*. Queen's University, Belfast.

Kloss, H. (1998) *American Bilingual Tradition*. Center for Applied Linguistics and Delta Systems, Washington, DC.

Kolchin, P. (1995) *American Slavery: 1619–1877*. Penguin, Harmondsworth.

Krapp, G. (1924) The English of the Negro. *American Mercury* 2, 190–5.

Krashen, S. (1992) Sink-or-swim success stories and bilingual education. In: J. Crawford (ed.) *Language Loyalties: A Source Book on the Official English Controversy*. University of Chicago Press, Chicago.

Kublu, A. and Mallon, M. (1999) Our language, ourselves. *The Nanavut Handbook*. Retrieved from: www.nunavut.com/nunavut99/english/our.html

Labov, W. (1982) Objectivity and commitment in linguistic science: the case of the Black English trial in Ann Arbor. *Language in Society* 11(2), 165–202.

Ladd, P. (2003) *Understanding Deaf Culture: In Search of Deafhood*. Multilingual Matters, Clevedon.

Land, A. (2000) Languages speak volumes for global business. In: P. Baker and J. Eversley (eds) *Multilingual Capital: The Languages of London's School Children and their Relevance to Economic, Social and Educational Policies*. Battlebridge, London.

Lane, C., McKenzie-Bridle, K. and Curtis, L. (1999) The right to interpreting and translation services in New Zealand Courts. *Forensic Linguistics* 6(1), 115–36.

LEBA Ethnic Media (undated) The ethnic market. Retrieved from: www.leba.com.au

Lester, K. (2002) Aboriginal cultural tourism – what is it and where is it going? *Environment South Australia Magazine*.

Levine, M. (1991) *The Reconquest of Montreal: Language Policy and Social Change in a Bilingual City*. Temple University Press, Philadelphia.

LexisNexis Academic and Library Solutions (undated) Records of the American Council for Nationalities Service, 1921–1971. Retrieved from: www. lexisnexis.com/academic/2upa/Ai/AmericanCouncilNationalitiesService.asp

Ley, D. and Murphy, P. (2001) *Immigration in Gateway Cities: Sydney and Vancouver in Comparative Perspective*. Pergamon, Oxford.

Links North (undated) The history of Canada: native peoples' issues. Retrieved from: www.linksnorth.com/canada-history/native.html

Lo Bianco, J. (1987) *National Policy on Languages*. Australian Government Publishing Service, Canberra.

Lund, J. (1994) Boundaries of restriction: the Dillingham Commission. *University of Vermont History Review* 6. Retrieved from: www.uvm.edu/~hag/histreview/vol6/lund.html

Mac Póilin, A. (1997) *Irish-Medium Television in Northern Ireland*. Ultacht Trust, Belfast.

MacKinnon, K. (2000) Scottish Gaelic. In: G. Price (ed.) *Languages in Britain and Ireland*. Blackwell, Oxford.

Malchow, H. (1979) *Population Pressures: Emigration and Government in Late Nineteenth-Century Britain*. Society for the Promotion of Science and Scholarship, Palo Alto, CA.

Malcolm, I. (1995) *Language and Communication Enhancement for Two-Way Education*. Edith Cowan University in collaboration with the Education Department of Western Australia, Perth.

Malcolm, I. (2002) Coming to terms with diversity: educational responses to linguistic plurality in Australia. *Gesellschaft fuer Australienstudien (GASt) Newsletter* 16, 17–30.

Manne, R. (1988) Stolen generations. In: P. Craven (ed.) *Australian Essays*. Melbourne: Bookman.

Markus, A. (1979) *Fear and Hatred: Purifying Australia and California 1850–1901*. Hale and Ironmonger, Toronto.

May, S. (2000) Accommodating and resisting minority language policy: the case of Wales. *International Journal of Bilingual Education and Bilingualism* 3(2), 101–28.

May, S. (2001) *Language and Minority Rights: Ethnicity, Nationalism and the Politics of Language*. Longman, London.

McBroom, P. (1995) California's Native Americans are in a race against time. *Berkeleyan*. Retrieved from: www.berkeley.edu/news/berkeleyan/1995/0301/tribal.html

McCarty, T. (2002) *A Place to be Navajo: Rough Rock and the Struggle for Self-Determination in Indigenous Schooling*. Lawrence Erlbaum Associates, Mahwah, NJ.

McPake, J. and Johnstone, R. with Lo Bianco et al. (2002) *Translating, Interpreting and Communication Support Services Across the Public Sector in Scotland: A Literature Review*. Scottish CILT, Stirling.

McQuillan, J. and Tse, L. (1996) Does research really matter? An analysis of media opinion on bilingual education, 1984–1994. *Bilingual Research Journal* 20(1), 1–27.

Meadows, M. (1995) Ideas from the bush: Indigenous television in Australia and Canada. *Canadian Journal of Communication* 20(2).

Mears, T. (1997) Miami Hispanics losing their Spanish. *Boston Globe* 5 October, A6.

Meriam, L. (1928) *The Problem of Indian Administration (The Meriam Report)*. Johns Hopkins University Press, Baltimore, MD.

MHA (Midwest Hospitality Advisors) (1992) *Indian Gaming in the State of Minnesota: A Study of the Economic Benefits and Tax Revenue Generated*. MHA, Minneapolis, MN.

Ministry of Education (2000) *A Report on the Compulsory Schools Sector in New Zealand*. Ministry of Education, Wellington.

Mintz, D. (1998) Hold the phone: telephone interpreting scrutinized. *Proteus* 7(1).

Mirzoeff, N. (1995) *Silent Poetry: Deafness, Sign and Visual Culture in Modern France*. Princeton University Press, Princeton, NJ.

Mitchell, R. and Karchmer, M. (2004) Chasing the mythical ten percent: parental hearing status of Deaf and hard of hearing students in the United States. *Sign Language Studies* 4(2).

Modood, T., Berthoud, R., Lakey, J., et al. (1997) *Ethnic Minorities in Britain: Diversity and Disadvantage*. Policy Studies Institute, London.

Monaghan, F. (2003) Entering the list: campaigning for bilingual education on the net. *Language and Education* 17(4), 281–302.

Morrison, S. (2001) 9/11 brings U.S. defense language needs into focus. *Language Link* December. Retrieved from: www.cal.org/ericcll/langlink/deccurrent2.html

Morrison, S. (2003) Arabic language teaching in the United States. *Language Link* June.

Morrow, P. (1993) A sociolinguistic mismatch: Central Alaskan Yup'iks and the legal system. *Criminal Justice* 9(2).

Morrow, P. (1994) Legal interpreting in Alaska. *Alaska Justice Forum* 10(4).

NAD (National Association for the Deaf) (1994) Erroneously jailed Deaf man wins important discrimination case. Retrieved from: www.nad.org/infocenter/newsroom/nadnews/chisolmcase.html

New Zealand Immigration Service (undated) *History of New Zealand Immigration*: Retrieved from: www.immigration.govt.nz/workshop/hist.htm

Nicholls, C. (2001) Reconciled to what? Reconciliation and the Northern Territory's bilingual education program, 1973–1998. In: J. Lo Bianco and R. Wickert (eds) *Australian Policy Activism in Language and Literacy*. Language Australia, Melbourne.

Nichols, P. (1981) Creoles of the USA. In: C. Ferguson and S. B. Heath (eds) *Language in the USA*. Cambridge University Press, Cambridge.

Nicholson, R. and Garland, R. (1991) New Zealanders' attitudes to the revitalization of the Māori language. *Journal of Multilingual and Multicultural Development* 12(5), 393–410.

Nicolau, S. and Valdivieso, R. (1992) Spanish language shift: educational implications. In: J. Crawford (ed.) *Language Loyalties: A Source Book on the Official English Controversy*. University of Chicago Press, Chicago.

Nipp, D. (1983) Toronto Chinese drama associations. *Polyphony* 5(2).

Nixon, R. (1970) Special message on Indian affairs, July 8. In: *Papers of the Presidents of the United States: Richard Nixon*. National Archives 11, College Park, MD.

Nuffield Language Inquiry (2000) *Languages: The Next Generation*. London: Nuffield Foundation.

Nunberg, G. (2001) The answer is on the tip of our many tongues. *Washington Post* 7 December.

Ó Dochartaigh, C. (2000) Irish in Ireland. In: G. Price (ed.) *Languages in Britain and Ireland*. Blackwell, Oxford.

Ó hIfearnáin, T. (2001) Irish language broadcast media: the interaction of state language policy, broadcasters and their audiences. In: H. Kelly-Holmes (ed.) *Minority Language Broadcasting: Breton and Irish*. Multilingual Matters, Clevedon.

Ó Riagáin, P. (1997) *Language Policy and Social Reproduction: Ireland 1893–1933*. Clarendon Press, Oxford.

O'Brien, G. and Plooij, D. (1973) *Culture Training Manual for Medical Workers in Aboriginal Communities*. Converted to hypertext by Hugh Nelson: School of Social Sciences, Flinders University, South Australia, 1995. Retrieved from: www.medicineau.net.au/AbHealth/16.HTM

O'Bryan, K., Reitz, J. and Kuplowska, O. (1976) *Non-Official Languages*. Supplies and Services Canada, Ottowa.

O'Malley, M. and Bowman, J. (2001) Language in Quebec. *CBC News Online* June. Retrieved from: http://cbc.ca/news/indepth/language

OAD (Ontario Association of the Deaf) (1999) Deaf protest Dr. Daniel Ling's statements in *The Globe* and *Mail*. Press release 27 September. Retrieved from: www.deafontario.org/info/news/press/ling.htm

One News (2002) Māori may boycott their channel. *One News* 19 March. Retrieved from: http://onenews.nzoom.com/onenews_detail/0,1227,88427-1-7,00.html

Ortiz, J. (2003) Man ordered to speak English to daughter. Retrieved from: www.salon.com/news/wire/2003/10/14/spanish/print.html

Ozolins, U. (1993) *The Politics of Language in Australia*. Cambridge University Press, Cambridge.

Ozolins, U. (1998) *Interpreting and Translating in Australia: Current Issues and International Comparisons*. Language Australia, Melbourne.

Pagden, A. (2001) *Peoples and Empires: Europeans and the Rest of the World from Antiquity to the Present*. Weidenfeld and Nicolson, London.

Palmer, H. (ed.) (1975) *Immigration and the Rise of Multiculturalism*. Copp Clark Publishing, Toronto.

Panetta, L. (undated) Foreign language education: if 'scandalous' in the twentieth century, what will it be in the twenty first century? Retrieved from: http://language.stanford.edu/about/conferencepapers/panettapaper.pdf

Paul, D. (1973) *The Navajo Code Talkers*. Dorrance, Philadelphia.

Payton, P. (2000) Cornish. In: G. Price (ed.) *Languages in Britain and Ireland*. Blackwell, Oxford.

Peach, C. (1978) *West Indian Migration to Britain: A Social Geography*. Oxford University Press, Oxford.

Pease-Alvarez, L. (2003) Transforming perspectives on bilingual language socialization. In: R. Bayley and S. Schecter (eds) *Language Socialization in Bilingual and Multilingual Settings*. Multilingual Matters, Clevedon.

Peate, M., Coupland, N. and Garret, P. (1998) Teaching Welsh and English in Wales. In: W. Tulasiewicz and A. Adams (eds) *Teaching the Mother Tongue in a Multilingual Europe*. Cassell, London.

Peddie, R. (2003) Languages in New Zealand: population, politics and policy. In: R. Barnard and T. Glynn (eds) *Bilingual Children's Language and Literacy Development*. Multilingual Matters, Clevedon.

Perry, T. and Delpit, L. (eds) (1997) *The Real Ebonics Debate: Power, Language, and the Education of African-American Children*. Special issue of *Rethinking Schools*. Retrieved from: www.rethinkingschools.org/publication/ebonics/ebotoc.shtml

Perth International Arts Festival (2003) Mervyn Mulardy. Retrieved from: www.perthfestival.com.au/Festival/index.cfm/fuseaction/events.bio_mervyn

Peterson, L. (1997) Tuning in to Navajo: the role of radio in native language maintenance. In: J. Reyhner (ed.) *Teaching Indigenous Languages*. Northern Arizona University, Flagstaff, AZ.

Peterson, L. and Morrison, S. (2003) Federal interagency language roundtable links communicative goals and pedagogical knowledge. *Language Link* October. Retrieved from: www.cal.org/ericcll/langlink/sep03feature.html

Peyton, J. and Ranard, D. (2001) We can't squander language skills. *Los Angeles Times* 5 November.

Place, M. (1969) *Gold Down Under: The Story of the Australian Gold Rush.* Crowell Collier Press, Sydney.

Poplack, S. (1980) 'Sometimes I'll start a sentence in Spanish y termino en español': toward a typology of code-switching. *Linguistics* 18(7/8), 581–618.

Price, G. (2000) Prehistoric Britain. In: G. Price (ed.) *Languages in Britain and Ireland.* Blackwell, Oxford.

Pufahl, I., Rhodes, N. and Christian, D. (2000) Foreign language teaching: what the United States can learn from other countries. Center for Applied Linguistics, Washington, DC. Retrieved from: www cal.org/ericcll/countries.html#EXEC

Pye, C. (1992) Language loss among the Chilcotin. *International Journal of Sociology of Language* 93, 75–86.

Ramirez, J., Yuen, S. and Ramey, E. (1991) *Final Report: Longitudinal Study of Structured English Immersion Strategy, Early Exit and Late-Exit Transitional Bilingual Education Programs for Language Minority Children.* US Department of Education Contract No. 300-87-0156. Sguirre International, San Mateo, CA.

Read, A. (1937) Bilingualism in the middle colonies, 1725–1775. *American Speech* 12, 93–9.

Refugee Status Appeals Authority (2001) *Refugee Appeal Nos 72766/2001, 72767/2001, 72768/2001.* Retrieved from: www.refugee.org.nz/Fulltext/72766-01.htm

Reyhner, J. (1990) A description of the Rock Point community school bilingual education program. In: J. Reynher (ed.) *Effective Language Education Practices and Native Language Survival.* Native American Language Issues, Choctaw, OK.

Rippley, L. (1976) *The German-Americans.* Twayne, Boston.

RNID (Royal National Institute for the Deaf) (1999) *Can You Hear Us? Deaf People's Experience of Social Exclusion, Isolation and Prejudice: Breaking the Sound Barrier Report.* London: RNID.

Robins, K. (2001) *Beyond Imagined Community? Transnational Media and Turkish Migrants in Europe.* Goldsmiths College, University of London, London.

Romaine, S. (1991) Introduction. In: S. Romaine (ed.) *Language in Australia.* Cambridge University Press, Cambridge.

Romaine, S. and Nettle, D. (2000) *Vanishing Voices: The Extinction of the World's Languages.* Oxford University Press, Oxford.

Ross, J. (ed.) (undated) *New Routes: A World of Music from Britain.* British Council, London.

Rossell, C. and Baker, K. (1996) The effectiveness of bilingual education. *Research in the Teaching of English* 30, 7–74.

Royal Commission on Bilingualism and Biculturalism (1967) *Report of the Royal Commission on Bilingualism and Biculturalism: General Introduction and Book 1, The Official Languages.* Queen's Printers, Ottowa.

Runciman, L. (1993) *Royal Commission on Criminal Justice in England and Wales.* HMSO, London.

Sacks, O. (1989) *Seeing Voices.* University of California Press, Berkley and Los Angeles.

Saini, F. and Rowling, L. (1997) 'It's more than literacy': the assimilation effect of the translation model. *Ethnicity and Health* 2(4).

Samson, C., Wilson, J. and Mazower, J. (1999) *Canada's Tibet: The Killing of the Innu.* Survival, London.

SASLI (Scottish Association of Sign Language Interpreters) (1997) *Provision of Communication Support Services for Deaf, Deafblind and Hard of Hearing: A Framework.* SASLI, Edinburgh.

Sato, C. (1985) Linguistic inequality in Hawaii: the post-creole dilemma. In: N. Wolfson and J. Manes (eds) *Language of Inequality.* Mouton, Berlin.

Schellekens, P. (2001) *English Language as a Barrier to Employment, Education and Training.* Departments for Education and Employment, London.

Scher, A. (2001) The ethnic press explosion of New York City. Independent Press Association, New York. Retrieved from: www.indypressny.org/epexplosion.html

Shebala, M. (1999) Council slams door on 'English only'. *Navajo Times* 22 July.

Sheridan, K. (1999) AOL Anti-Irish controversy. *Irish People* 9 January.

Shnukal, A. (1991) Torres Strait creole. In: S. Romaine (ed.) *Language in Australia.* Cambridge University Press, Cambridge.

Smith, G. (1997) *The Irish Language Revival among Post-Famine Immigrants in America.* Scattering Conference, Irish Centre for Migration Studies, University College, Cork.

Smith, J. (2000) Scots. In: G. Price (ed.) *Languages in Britain and Ireland.* Blackwell, Oxford.

Smith, R. (1999) *Schools, Politics and Society: Elementary Education in Wales, 1870–1902.* University of Wales Press, Cardiff.

Smitherman, G. (1986) *Talkin and Testifyin: The Language of Black America.* Wayne State University Press, Detroit.

Sproull, A. (1996) Regional economic development and minority language use: the case of Gaelic Scotland. *International Journal of the Sociology of Language* 121, 93–117.

Stalker, P. (2002) *The No-Nonsense Guide to International Migration.* New Internationalist in association with Verso, London.

Stiles, D. (1997) Four successful Indigenous language programs. In: J. Reyhner (ed.) *Teaching Indigenous Languages.* Northern Arizona University, Flagstaff, AZ.

Swann, Lord (1985) *Education for All.* HMSO, London.

Tam, P. (2002) Ethnic media muy popular in California. *Marketplace* 23 April, B1.

Taskforce on Public Funding of Gaelic (2000) *Revitalising Gaelic: A National Asset.* Scottish Executive, Edinburgh.

Teixeira, C. (2001) Building an ethnic economy in Toronto, Canada. *Scripta Nova: Revista Electrónica de Geografía y Ciencias Sociales* 94.

Teschner, R. (1995) Beachheads, islands, and conduits: Spanish monolingualism and bilingualism in El Paso, Texas. *International Journal of the Sociology of Language* 114, 93–105.

Thomas, H. (1998) *The Slave Trade: The History of the Atlantic Slave Trade, 1440–1870.* Macmillan, Basingstoke.

Thomas, N. (1997) *Sianel Pedwar Cymru: The First Year of Television in Wales.* International Symposium on Contact and Conflict. European Centre for Multilingualism, Brussels.

Thomas, W. and Collier, V. (2002) *Summary of Findings across All Research Sites: A National Study of School Effectiveness for Language Minority Students' Long-Term Achievement.* Final Report: Project 1.1. Center for Research on Education, Diversity and Excellence, University of California, Santa Cruz, CA.

Tohtsoni, N. J. (undated) A celebration of Diné language. *Navajo Times* online edition. Retrieved from: http://thenavajotimes.com/Opinion/Notebook1/notebook1.html

Truckenbrodt, A. and de Courcy, M. (2002) *Implementing a Bilingual Programme.* Association of Independent Schools of Victoria, Melbourne.

Tse, D. (2000) *Bilingualism in British Theatre.* Blueprint Conference on Bilingualism and Theatre for Young People, Half Moon Theatre, London.

UK Government (1999) *Report Submitted by the United Kingdom Pursuant to Article 25, Paragraph 1 of the Framework Convention for the Protection of National Minorities.* Retrieved from: www.humanrights.coe.int/Minorities/Eng/FrameworkConvention/StateReports/1999/uk/uk.htm

University of Aukland Library (undated) *Niupepa: Māori Newspapers Digital Collection.* Retrieved from: www.lbr.auckland.ac.nz/databases/learn_database/public.asp?record=niupepamaori

US Department of State (2002) *Diplomatic Readiness: The Human Resources Strategy.* US Department of State, Washington, DC.

US General Accounting Office (1987) *Bilingual Education: A New Look at the Research Evidence.* US General Accounting Office, Washington, DC.

US Senate (2000) *The State of Foreign Language Capabilities in National Security and the Federal Government: Hearing before the International Security, Proliferation, and Federal Services Subcommittee of the Committee on Governmental Affairs.* 106th Congress, 2nd session. US Senate, Washington, DC.

van Aalst, I. and Daly, C. (2002) *International Visitor Satisfaction with their New Zealand Experience. The Cultural Tourism Product Market: A Summary of Studies 1990–2001.* Tourism New Zealand. Retrieved from: www.tourisminfo.govt.nz/documents/ IV_Cultural_report02.pdf

Vidal, M. (1998) Telephone interpreting: technological advance or due process impediment? *Proteus* 7(3).

Waitangi Tribunal (1986) *Findings of the Waitangi Tribunal relating to Te Reo Māori and a Claim Lodged by Huirangi Waikerepuru and Nga Kaiwhakapumau i Te Reo Incorporated Society.* Wellington: Government Printer.

Waite, J. (1992) *Aoteareo: Speaking for Ourselves.* Learning Media, Wellington.

Wald, E. (2002) *Narcocorrido: A Journey into the Music of Drugs, Guns, and Guerrillas.* Rayo, New York.

Walsh, M. (1999) Interpreting for the transcript: problems in recording Aboriginal land claim proceedings in northern Australia. *Forensic Linguistics* 6(1).

Weinick, R. and Drauss, N. (2000) Racial and ethnic differences in children's access to care. *American Journal of Public Health* 90(11), 1771–4.

Welsh Language Board (1999) *Welsh for Adults Strategy.* Welsh Language Board, Cardiff.

Welsh Language Board (2002) Bilingualism enhances business at Portmeirion. Retrieved from: www.bwrdd-yr-iaith.org.uk/en/welsh_language.php?cID =43andxID=90andsID=15

West Highland Free Press (2002) Parliament officer quits over 'anti-Gaelic' civil servants. Retrieved from: www.whfp.com/1570/main.html

Whitaker, R. (1991) *Canadian Immigration Policy Since Confederation.* Keystone Printing, Saint John, NB.

Williams, C. (1984) More than tongue can tell: linguistic factors in ethnic separatism. In: J. Edwards (ed.) *Linguistic Minorities, Policies and Pluralism.* Academic Press, New York.

Wilson, M. (1993) *Mental Health and Britain's Black Communities.* King's Fund, London.

Withers, C. (1988) *Gaelic Scotland: The Transformation of a Culture Region.* Routledge, London.

Wolk, S. and Schildroth, A. (1986) Deaf children and speech intelligibility: a national study. In: A. Schildroth and M. Karchmer (eds) *Deaf Children in America.* College-Hill Press, San Diego.

Wong Fillmore, L. (1991) When learning a second language means losing the first. *Early Childhood Research Quarterly* 6, 323–46.

Zentella, A. C. (1997) *Growing Up Bilingual.* Blackwell, Oxford.

Zephaniah, B. (undated) Oral poetry. Retrieved from: www.benjaminzephaniah.com/truth.html

Zhou, M. (2001) Progress, decline, stagnation? The new second generation comes of age. In: N. Smelser, W. Wilson and F. Mitchell (eds) *America Becoming: Racial Trends and their Consequences.* National Academy Press, Washington, DC.

Index

Aboriginal English 7, 24, 66, 105, 129–31
Aboriginal Language Initiative 88
Aboriginal Peoples Television Network (APTN) 174
Aboriginal and Torres Strait Island (ATSI) languages 116
Aboriginal Voices Radio (AVR) 174
Acadians 8
Adamson, Peter 107
African American Vernacular English 26, 126
African Americans 25–6, 105, 126, 200
African Caribbeans 105, 190–1
Aha Pūnana Leo movement 109
Alaska 48
Alice Springs Aboriginal English 129
Alliance for the Preservation of the English Language 40
Alliance Quebec 216
America Online 212
American Indians *see* Native Americans
American Protective Association 100
American Sign Language (ASL) 7, 8, 126, 131, 132
Ann Arbor case 127, 217
Antipodes Festival 204

Aotearoa/New Zealand
  bilingual signage 71
  colonization 21
  cultural tourism 160
  education policies 106, 117
  foreign-language teaching 141, 142–3
  immigration 29, 31, 32, 42, 214, 216
  Indigenous language 24, 214
  Indigenous population 6, 214
  interpreter services 52–3, 59, 68
  linguistic diversity 9, 10, 39
  majority language 3
  minority media 169, 176–7, 196
  national languages policy 39, 45, 117
  see also Māori
Aotearoa/New Zealand Sign Language 7–8
Arabic 10, 85, 208, 216
Arrente 6
arts 188–205
  authorship and publishing 195–8
  benefits of minority arts 205
  cross-fertilization 200–3, 219
  music 198–205
  oral poetry 190–1
  storytelling 188–90
  subsidies 205
  theatre 191–5

arts (*cont'd*):
  and tradition 205
  see also media
Asian Television Network 184–5
Assembly of First Nations (AFN)
  108
assimilation 5, 6, 38, 44, 96, 122,
  220
asylum seekers and refugees 35, 43,
  79–80, 211–12
  language analysis 211–12
Atkins, J. D. C. 98
Auslan 7, 8, 40, 126, 131, 132
Australia
  Aboriginal English 7, 24, 66,
    105, 129–31
  arts 196, 201, 203, 204
  asylum seekers 211, 212
  business and foreign-language
    skills 156–7
  colonization 21
  content-based teaching 139, 144
  creoles 24
  criminal justice system 60
  cultural tourism 160
  Deaf community 132
  diplomacy and defence 210
  education policies 95, 97, 101,
    106–8, 114, 116–17, 120,
    123, 125, 139, 140, 221
  eugenics movement 30–1
  foreign-language teaching 140
  immigration 28, 29–30, 31, 32,
    34, 42, 214, 216
  Indigenous economies 150
  Indigenous languages 6, 23, 24
  Indigenous peoples 6, 23
  interpreter services 52–3, 68
  language skills deficit 48
  linguistic diversity 9, 10, 21–2
  linguistic intolerance 28–9
  majority language 3
  minority market 158
  minority media 168, 171,
    175–6, 179–80, 182, 185
  multilingualism 21–2, 39, 86,
    137, 154

  national languages policies 39,
    116, 125, 217
  population censuses 5, 9
  public libraries 197
  'stolen generations' 30–1, 36, 97
  translation services 70
  Whites-only policy 29, 214
Australian Aboriginals
  Aboriginal English 7, 24, 66,
    105, 129–31
  arts 196, 201, 203, 204
  and the criminal justice system
    60, 64, 65
  culture 160
  education 97, 106–7, 108
  'stolen generations' 30–1, 36, 97

Babel Tree project 70
Banerjee, Kalyan 193
BBC Monitoring Service 209
Beasley, Kim 106–7
Bell, Alexander Graham 31
Bengali 10, 85, 193
bhangra 202–3
Bilingual Family Newsletter 90
bilingualism
  bilingual education 95, 102, 108,
    110, 111, 115–16, 117–21
  Canada 38–9, 137, 138, 154,
    161–2
Black English 7, 126–8
Black English Vernacular 26, 126,
  127
Blunkett, David 43
Brigade d'Autodéfense du Français
  (French Self-Defence Brigade)
  73
Britain *see* United Kingdom (UK)
British empire 13, 216
British National Party (BNP) 43,
  216
British Sign Language (BSL) 7, 8,
  40, 41, 45, 53, 126, 131, 142
Brittonic 14
Broadcasting in Remote Aboriginal
  Communities Service (BRACS)
  175

Broken (Broken English) *see* Torres
  Strait Creole

Cajuns 8
Canada
  Aboriginal Languages Initiative
    (ALI) 36–7
  Allophones 112, 113, 115
  arts 191–2, 193, 195–6
  bilingual signage 71–3
  bilingualism 38–9, 137, 138, 154,
    161–2
  cultural tourism 160
  Deaf community 132
  education policies 96, 98, 108,
    112–13, 115, 120–1, 122–3,
    124, 125, 126, 138, 141–2,
    149
  foreign-language teaching 141–2,
    143
  Francophones 8, 38, 39, 40,
    112–13, 149, 151, 214, 215,
    217
  immigration 32, 33–4, 40, 42,
    214, 216
  Indigenous languages 23, 36–7,
    88
  Indigenous peoples 6, 11, 22–3,
    36–7
  interpreter services 53, 59–60
  language skills deficit 48
  linguistic diversity 9, 10
  majority language 3
  'majority minority' 214
  minority economies 150, 151,
    153–4
  minority media 169, 170, 171,
    172, 174–5, 177, 180, 181,
    182, 183–4, 221
  monolingual backlash 40, 73
  national languages policies 38–9,
    40, 45, 113, 125
  population censuses 5, 9
  Quiet Revolution 38, 84, 113, 151
  workplace issues 161–2
Canadian Translators and Interpreters
  Council (CTIC) 53

Canadians for Language Fairness
  40
Cape Breton 97
Capercaillie 201
Caribbean creoles 66
Cartier, Jacques 20, 49
Celtic languages 7, 13–14, 214,
  218
  Celtic-language broadcasting 184
  Celtic-language publishing 196
  Celtic-language theatre 192
  see also Cornish; Gaelic; Irish;
    Welsh
Celtic music 201–2
Central Australian Aboriginal Media
  Association (CAAMA) 150,
  181, 182, 183
Champlain, Samuel de 20
Charter of the French Language
  71–2
Chicano Groove 202
Chilcotin 81
Child Migrant Education Program
  114
children
  child interpreters 51–2, 83
  childcare provision 90
  children's publishing 198
  Deaf children 88
  hearing children of Deaf
    parents 88
  mixed-language households
    80–1, 82–3, 84, 86–7, 218
  mixed-race children 30
  New Commonwealth children
    114
  removal from families 6, 30–1,
    96, 215
  see also education
Children of Deaf Adults (CODA)
  88
China 3
Chinese 9, 10, 155, 172, 182,
  197, 218
  Chinese theatre 192–3
  Chinese-language education 121,
    122, 123

Chinese communities 31–2, 118, 153
Chinese Scholars' Association 124
Chirac, Jacques 211
Chisolm, Ronald 60–1
Clannad 201–2
Claus, Haydee 61–2
code-switching 87, 126
colonization 6, 13, 19–23, 94
  colonial languages 8, 21
  linguistic consequences 23
Comhluadar 89
Community Interpretation Services Program (CIS) 52, 55
community languages see new minorities – languages
Content and Language Integration Project (CLIP) 139
Cook, Dr Cecil 31
Cook, Captain James 21
Cornish 7, 14, 44
corridos 199, 200
Council for the Advancement of Communication with Deaf People 53
court interpreters 53, 59, 60, 61–7, 68
Court Interpreters Act 59
Crawford, James 43
creoles 7, 10, 24, 25, 26–7, 66
  Australia 24
  Caribbean creoles 66
  decreolization 26
  Hawai'ian Creole English (HCE) 7, 27, 105, 128–9
Croatian 10
Cuban Americans 9, 117, 149, 193
cultural tourism 158–61, 218
Cylchoedd Ti a Fi (You and Me Circles) 89, 110

Day, Clarence Shepard 144
Deaf community 40
  access to health services 54, 55
  cochlear implants, opposition to 44, 132

and the criminal justice system 60–1
  as cultural and linguistic minority 44, 132
  Deaf children 88
  economic issues 152–3
  education 95, 97, 99, 101–3, 131–2
  and the eugenics movement 31
  hearing children of Deaf parents 50, 88
  lip-reading 131
  medicalization of deafness 44
  Oralism 101–3, 131, 132
  radio and television broadcasting 178–9
  social partnerships 97
  theatre 194
  Total Communication policy 131–2
  see also sign languages
diplomacy and defence 207–13
  foreign-language learning 208–9, 210, 213
  intelligence gathering 209
  language competencies 207–8, 209, 210
  miscarriages of justice 211
  political controversy 212
Diplomatic Readiness Strategy 209–10
dual-language immersion 139–40, 144
dub poetry 190
Dutch 10

Eagle, Maria 41
Ebonics 7, 26, 126, 127–8
economic issues 149–65
  cultural tourism 158–61
  economic value of multilingualism 149, 154–5, 164, 217–18
  foreign-language skills in business 156–7
  global markets 155–7, 219
  language in the workplace 161–4
  media role 157, 160, 183

minority economies 150–5
minority markets 157–8, 164,
    219
education 94–145
    adult education 142
    bilingual education 95, 102, 108,
        110, 111, 115–16, 117–21
    challenges to the status quo
        102–3
    community-based language
        teaching 106, 109, 116,
        121–4
    content-based teaching 139,
        144
    corporal punishment and ridicule
        97–9
    Deaf community 95, 97, 99,
        101–3, 131–2
    dual-language immersion
        programmes 139–40
    English-only policies 6, 96,
        97–101, 102, 116, 119, 120
    established languages 109–13
    foreign-language teaching 140–3,
        208–9, 210, 213
    immersion education 102, 105,
        108, 119, 133, 138–9, 149
    indigenous language education
        105–9
    language competence 134, 137,
        143
    legislation 100–2
    linguistic oppression 95–103
    linguistic tolerance 94–5
    missionary activity and 94–5
    new minority languages 113–17,
        121–5, 133
    pidgins in education 128–9
    pre-school provision 110
    professional development and
        accreditation 124–5
    sectarian issues 100, 122, 215
    segregated schooling 26
    'sink or swim' strategies 113–15
    see also under Deaf community –
        Deaf children; individual
        countries and minorities

eisteddfodau 204
England see United Kingdom
Englisc 17
English
    estimated numbers of English
        speakers 5
    as foreign language 3
    as global language 3
    as majority language 3
    for 'official' purposes 3
    roots 18–19
English Plus 42
English-only policies 219
    education 6, 96, 97–101, 102,
        116, 119, 120
    workplace 163–4
established languages 7–8, 109–13
eugenics 29–31, 43
European Charter for Regional or
    Minority Languages 38, 45,
    217
European Union 50, 140, 144,
    152, 210

Failte project 160
families and bilingualism 79–92
    career advantages 86, 218
    communication and
        relationships 82–3
    cost-benefit analysis 80, 91–2
    culture and personal identity
        83–4, 91, 218
    intellectual issues 85–6
    isolated families 90–1
    language loss 80–1, 82–3, 84
    mixed-language households
        80–1, 82–4, 86–7, 218, 219
    patterns of language use 86–8
    religious life 84–5
    support for bilingual families
        88–91
festivals 203–5
film, video and DVD 194–5
First Nations 5, 11, 36, 71
    education 96, 108
Fishman, Joshua 121–2, 133, 171
Foras na Gaeilge 38

Foreign Broadcast Information
    Service (FBIS) 209
foreign-language teaching 140–3,
    208–9, 210, 213
Franklin, Benjamin 22, 71, 171
French 8, 17, 142, 143, 214
    Canadian Francophones 8, 38,
        39, 40, 112–13, 149, 151,
        214, 215, 217
    co-official status (Canada) 38,
        39, 45, 217
    French-medium education 95,
        112–13, 122
French colonialism 20, 21

Gabriel, Peter 204
Gaelic 16, 71, 97
    arts 192, 196–7, 204
    culture 159–60, 204
    Gaelic-medium education 110,
        111
    Manx Gaelic 7, 14
    media 178, 183, 184
    Scottish Gaelic 7, 16–17, 37,
        44, 80, 84, 90, 97, 110, 111,
        152
    see also Irish
Gaelic in the Community Scheme
    90
Gaelic Energy Centres 90, 152
Gaelic Television Training
    Trust 195
Gaeltacht 15
German 10, 22, 121
    German-language press 171
    German-medium education 95,
        100, 101
German communities 27–8
ghettoization 218
global markets 155–7, 219
globalization viii, 9, 13, 34–5, 86,
    144, 216
Glór na nGael 89–90
Goddard, Henry 29
Goidelic 14
Good Friday Agreement 44, 112
Greek 10, 122, 172

Greek community 204
Gujarati 10, 85
Gullah 27

Hakluyt, Richard 19
Hawai'i 69, 94–5, 101, 109
Hawai'ian Creole English (HCE)
    7, 27, 105, 128–9
Hawai'ian Pidgin English (HPE)
    128
health care
    access to 54
    carers 55–6
    cultural construction of
        health 56–8
    elderly patients 55
    medical interpreting 50, 52,
        54–8
    misunderstandings and
        misdiagnosis 55
Hearing Mother-Father Deaf
    (HMFD) 88
Heritage Language Initiative 123
Heritage Language Program 122
heritage languages 11, 83, 121
    see also minority languages
Hindi 10
Hinglish (Hindi-English) 87
Hinono'eitiit Hoowu' (Arapaho
    Language Lodge) 89
Hispanics 8–9, 80, 120, 141,
    220
    arts 193, 197
    education 115
    media 172
    minority market 157
    socioeconomic and workplace
        issues 149, 163
    see also Spanish
Huguenots 153
Hulme, Keri 195
human rights concerns 34, 103

identity
    language and 44, 83–4, 217
    multiple identities 219
Ilocano 69

immersion education 105, 119,
    138–9, 144
  dual-language immersion
    139–40, 144
India 3
Indian immigrants 33, 34
Indian Service Summer School
    102
Indians see First Nations; Native
    Americans
Indigenous economies 150–1
Indigenous languages 6, 218
  education in 105–9
  Indigenous-language publishing
    168–9
Indigenous peoples
  assimilation 5, 6, 44, 96
  colonization 6, 13, 19–23, 94
  dispossession 23
  ethnic revival 103
  marginalization 6
  see also individual peoples
Innu 63, 83, 89, 90
Institute of Linguists (IOL) 53
intelligence gathering 209
International Covenant on Civil and
    Political Rights 59
Internet
  e-commerce 155
  family resources 91
  multilingual resources 70
  web publishing 167, 181, 186
interpreting 49–69
  advocacy and cultural mediation
    role 52
  child interpreters 51–2, 83
  consecutive interpretation 62
  cultural challenges 62–5, 68
  de facto interpreters 50–1, 53
  improving service quality 68–9
  legal challenges to 65–7
  legal interpreting 59–69
  medical interpreting 54–8
  miscommunication potential 62,
    66–7
  professionalization of interpreters
    52–3

simultaneous interpreting 39–40,
    50, 59, 60, 61–2
  telephone interpreting 53–4, 157
Intertribal Wordpath Society
    (IWS) 176
Inuit 6, 11, 37, 90, 176, 183–4,
    195
Inuktitut 36, 37, 81, 195, 214,
    217
Ireland 14–16
  arts 192, 196, 201–2, 204
  bilingualism 137
  cultural tourism 158–9
  economic issues 151–2
  education 15, 97–8, 102, 110,
    111, 133, 152
  immigration 9, 214
  majority language 3
  mass migration, effect of 15
  media 184, 177–8
  population censuses 5
  see also Northern Ireland
Irish 7, 14–16, 71
  co-official status 37–8, 152
  early history 14–15
  in education 111–12
  Irish speakers (numbers) 7, 15
  language oppression 98
  language promotion 15, 89–90
  in the New World 15
  redefined as minority language
    15–16
Isle of Man 7, 14
Italian 10, 122

Japan 3, 149
Japanese 10, 149
Japanese communities 32
Jefferson, Thomas 21, 22
Jewish communities 84–5, 153, 154
Johnson, Linton Kwesi 190–1
Johnson, Samuel 3
Johnston, Basil 98
Jones, Griffith 94

Karajarri 201
Khanam, Iffatara 200

Kina, Robyn 66–7
King, Mackenzie 33
King, Martin Luther 35
Know-Nothing Party 100
Koori English 129
Korean 10, 69, 210
Korean Schools Association 124
Kriol 24
'Ksan Performing Arts Group 191
KTNN Radio 176, 182, 183
Kula Shaker 203
kura kaupapa Māori 106

La Trobe, Charles 22
language analysis 211–12
language legislation 215–16
Language Line 53
language loss 80–1, 82–3, 84, 218
language-learning ability 142
langue des signes de Québec (LSQ)
    126, 131
Latin language 17
Lau Remedies 118, 217
law
    accommodating cultural
        difference 68
    legal interpreting 39–40, 51, 52,
        53–4, 58–69
    miscarriages of justice 66–7, 211
    vulnerability of non-English
        speakers 60, 68
Lebanese 10
Lewis, Saunders 37
libraries 197
Lincoln, Abraham 26
Linguistic Availability Performance
    Allowance (LAPA) 86
linguistic imperialism 22
linguistic tolerance 94–5
Louisiana Creole 27
Loya, Olga 189–90

Macedonian 10
Maddrell, Ned 14
Manx Gaelic 7, 14
Māori 9, 24, 39, 44, 149, 214,
    218, 220

co-official status 36, 45, 59, 149,
    217
culture 160
education policies 106, 117, 220
legal interpreting 59, 68
literary production 195, 196
media 176–7, 220
populations 23
marginalized languages 126–32
master-apprentice programmes 89
McNally, Eryl 210
media 167–86
    digitization and satellite
        technology 167, 180–1, 184,
        185
    issues and challenges 183–5
    minority press 157, 167–72,
        173
    radio and television broadcasting
        167, 173–81
    resistance to ethnic media 183–5
    role of ethnic media 181–3
    sign-language broadcasting
        178–9
    state role 167, 173
    technological proliferation 186
    telemarketing 157
    see also arts
medical interpreting 50, 52, 54–8
Menominees 150
Mentrau Iaith (Language
    Initiatives) 89
Métis 6, 11
Metlakatlans 150
Meyer, Robert 100–1
Michif 37
migration 13, 27–8, 216
    asylum seekers and refugees 35,
        43, 79–80, 211–12
    contemporary migration 34, 35
    early twentieth-century
        migration 27, 28–30, 32
    hostility towards migrants 28–32,
        216
    and labour demand 27, 33, 214,
        216
    urban phenomenon 42

minority economies 150–5
  benefits of bilingualism 154–5
  established economies 151–3
  Indigenous economies 150–1
  minority markets 157–8, 164,
    219
  new minority economies 153–4
minority languages
  educational policies 105–17
  repression 219
  see also individual languages
minority press 157, 167–72,
    173
  established language press 169,
    171
  Indigenous press 168–9
minority rights 35–40
monolingual backlash 40, 42–4,
    73, 120
monolingual myth 3, 5, 79, 215
Mudiad Ysgolion Meithrin (Nursery
    Education Movement) 110
Mulardy, Mervyn 201
multiculturalism 38, 220
multilingualism
  benefits 217–20
  extent of 5–10
  financial implications 49
Murray, Alan 41
music 198–205
  festivals 203–5
  folk songs 199
  fusion music 200–3, 219
  religious music 199
  tradition and 198–200
  wedding songs 199
Muslim family celebrations 85

National Accreditation Authority
    for Translators and Interpreters
    (NAATI) 52
National Association for the
    Advancement of Colored
    People 35
National Register of Public Service
    Interpreters 53
nationalism 5

Native Americans 11, 24–5, 35–6,
    71
  arts 188–9
  education 96, 98, 102, 108–9,
    220–1
  Indigenous economy 150–1
  languages 220–1
  master–apprentice programmes 89
  media 176
  music 200–1, 202
  populations 23
  special status 35–6
Navajo 83, 108, 176, 181, 183
Navajo code-talkers 208
Nebrija, Antonio de 23
Neville, A. O. 31
New Commonwealth 33, 114
new minorities
  arts 192–3
  economies 153–4
  education 113–17, 121–5, 133
  languages 8–10, 218
new world order 216–17
New Zealand *see* Aotearoa/New
    Zealand
Nga Tamatoa 106
Nicholas, Joseph 49
9/11 207, 208, 209, 212, 216
Nishnawbe-Aski Nation 174–5
Nixon, Richard 35–6, 220
non-standard languages *see*
    marginalized languages; sign
    languages
North America
  colonial languages 8, 21
  European colonialism 6, 13,
    19–22
  immigration 27–8
  indigenous languages 6
  see also Canada
Northern Ireland
  education 102, 111–12
  Irish language status 37–8
  Irish speakers (numbers) 7
  Irish-language media 178
  population censuses 5
  Ulster-Scots 7, 17, 38, 44, 171

Northern Native Broadcast Access
    Program (NNBAP) 174
Notting Hill Carnival 204–5
Nunavut 36, 81, 169, 217

Oakland resolution 127–8
O'Henley, Alex 44
One Nation Party 42, 45, 48,
    216
Operation Desert Storm 207
oral poetry 190–1

Pacific Pidgin English 24
Pakistani immigrants 33
Panjabi 10, 85, 194, 202, 218
Patois 8
Pennsylvania 22
Pentreath, Dolly 14
Philip, Arthur 21
Pidgins 23–4, 25, 128–9
    Hawai'ian Pidgin English (HPE)
        128
    Pacific Pidgin English 24
    Pidgin dialectalism 129
Pioneer Fund 43
Pitjantjatjara 57
Polish 10
population censuses 5–6
Portmeirion 158
Portuguese 10
Project Akamai 129
Project Holopono 129
publishing
    authorship 195–8
    bilingual authors 196
    children's publishing 198
    dual-language books 198
    minority-language publishing
        195–8
Puerto Ricans 87
Pye, Clifton 81

Qawwali 199, 203
Quebec (Lower Canada) 8, 20, 21,
    38, 71, 73, 89, 95, 112, 113,
    120–1, 149

Race for Opportunity (RfO) 157
radio and television broadcasting
    173–81
    destructive potential of
        mainstream media 173–4
    established language broadcasting
        177–9
    Indigenous broadcasting 173–7
    new minority language
        broadcasting 179–81
    state control 173
    style of production 175–6
rap 190, 199, 203
Reagan, Ronald 42, 119
refugees see asylum seekers and
    refugees
religious institutions, education
    and 94–5, 122
religious observance 84–5
Rez02 project 188–9
Riley, Richard 140–1
ritual significance of language 84–5
Robertson, Robbie 200
Roop Singh 189
Rough Rock Demonstration School
    108
Royal National Institute for Deaf
    People (RNID) 55
Royal National Mod 204
Russian 10, 122

Sacajawea 49–50
Samoan 9, 10
Sands, Bobby 111
Sawhney, Nitin 203
schooling see education
Scotland 16–17
    arts 152, 192, 196–7, 204
    bilingual signage 71
    cultural tourism 159–60
    economic issues 152
    education 97, 110, 111, 142,
        152
    Gaelic 7, 16–17, 37, 44, 80, 84,
        90, 97, 110, 111, 152
    Highland Clearances 16

language activism 37
language promotion 37, 90
linguistic oppression 96
mass migration 16–17
media 171, 184
monolingual backlash 44
Scots 7, 17, 37
Scots 7, 17, 37
    Ulster-Scots 7, 17, 38, 44, 171
September 11 terrorist attacks,
    2001 see 9/11
service provision 48–74
    childcare provision 90
    information provision 70
    interpreting 49–69
    translation 69–73, 157
sign languages 7–8, 40, 88, 126,
    131–2
    American Sign Language (ASL)
        7, 8, 126, 131, 132
    Aotearoa/New Zealand Sign
        Language 7–8
    Auslan 7, 8, 40, 126, 131, 132
    British Sign Language (BSL) 7,
        8, 40, 41, 45, 53, 126, 131,
        142
    sign interpreters 50, 53
slave languages 25
slave trade 24–6
Slógadh 204
Smith, Andrew 41
social Darwinism 29, 97
social inclusion see service provision
socioeconomic inequality 149
Somali 10
South Africa 3
Spanglish 87
Spanish 8–9, 10, 84, 85, 86, 98,
    215
    in education 95, 122, 140
    foreign-language teaching 121,
        141, 142, 144, 220
    linguistic repression 87, 99
    see also Hispanics
Spanish colonialism 20
status issues 86

Statutes of Iona 16, 96
storytelling 188–90
Sylheti 85

Tagalog 9, 10
Taha Māori programmes 106
Tajik 208
Tate, Frank 101
te kohanga reo 106
teaching standard English as a
    second dialect (TSESD) 130
Tebitt, Norman 219
telemarketing 157
telephone interpreting 53–4, 157
Tex-Mex 87
theatre 191–5
    bilingual theatre 193–4, 205,
        219
    film, video and DVD 194–5
    new minority communities
        192–3
    other-language theatre 191–3
    theatre-in-education companies
        194
Tilden, Douglas 95
Tongan 10
Torres Strait Creole (Broken, or
    Broken English) 24
Trail of Tears 23
translation 69–73, 157
    arguments against 69–70
    bilingual signage 71–3
    Internet resources 70
    standard of 70
Treaty of Waitangi 36
Trudeau, Pierre 49
Turkish 10, 182, 185
Turkmen 208
Twf (Growth) project 89

Ullans see Ulster-Scots
Ulster-Scots 7, 17, 38, 44, 171
Ulster-Scots Agency 38
United Kingdom (UK)
    arts 189, 193–4, 203, 204–5
    asylum seekers 211, 212

United Kingdom (UK) (*cont'd*):
  Black English 126
  colonialism 19–20
  cultural tourism 158, 160
  diplomacy and defence 209, 210
  education policies 114, 115–16,
    124–5, 139, 140, 142, 143
  established languages 7
  immigration 9, 19, 32, 33, 35,
    214
  interpreter services 53
  linguistic diversity 10
  majority language 3
  minority economies 153, 154
  minority markets 157
  minority media 171, 172, 177–8,
    180–1, 184, 185
  monolingual backlash 43
  multilingualism 40, 140, 142,
    143
  and multinationals 155–6
  population censuses 5
  public libraries 197
United Nations 50, 103
United States of America (USA)
  Americanization movement 28,
    100
  arts 189–90, 202, 203–4
  Black speech 7, 26, 126–8
  civil rights movement 34, 35,
    103, 115, 217
  creoles 26–7
  Deaf community 132
  dual-language immersion
    programmes 139–40, 144
  education policies 95, 96, 98,
    99, 100–1, 102, 108–9,
    114–15, 117–22, 123, 125,
    139–41, 144, 221
  foreign-language teaching 140–1,
    142, 143
  immigration 31, 32, 34, 35, 42,
    123, 214
  Indigenous languages 23
  Indigenous peoples 6, 214
  interpreting services 52, 53–5,
    59

  language legislation 215–16
  language skills deficit 48
  linguistic diversity 9, 10, 21
  majority language 3
  'majority minority' 214
  minority economies 150–1, 153
  minority markets 157
  minority media 171, 172, 176,
    179, 181, 182, 184–5
  monolingual backlash 42–3
  multilingualism 39–40, 154–5
  national security issues 207–8,
    209–10
  public libraries 197
  workplace issues 163–4
  see also African Americans; Native
    Americans
Unz, Ron 119–20
Urdu 10, 69, 203, 211
US English (organization) 42, 43,
  45, 48, 216
Uzbek 208

video-conferencing 176, 182
videophones 54
Vietnamese 10

Waitangi Tribunal 36, 59, 68
Wales 17–18
  Anglicization of the gentry 18
  arts 192, 193, 195, 196, 204
  bilingual signage 71, 72, 158,
    159
  cultural tourism 158
  economic issues 152, 183
  education 94, 98, 99, 100,
    110–11
  language activism 37
  media 171, 178, 183
  mixed-language households 80–1
  monolingual backlash 43–4
  national languages policy 18, 45
  nationalism 18
  workplace issues 162
  see also Welsh
Warlpiri 6, 175–6
Watt, Alan 210

Wawatay Communications
    Society 175
Welsh 7, 69, 84, 142, 149
    bilingual signage 71, 72, 158,
        159
    co-official status 18, 59, 149,
        217
    early history 17–18
    in education 89, 110–11
    language oppression 98
    language promotion 18, 37,
        48–9, 89
    in public life 59
    Welsh speakers (numbers) 7
Welsh Books Council 196
Welsh Courts Act 59
Welsh Language Acts 59
Welsh Language Board 89
Welsh Language Society 37, 71

Western Australian Aboriginal
    English 129
Widd, Thomas 95
WOMAD (World of Music and
    Dance) 204
workplace issues 161–4
World War II 32, 208

xenophobia 28–9, 45, 100, 101,
    211

Yellow Earth Theatre 193–4
'Yellow Peril' 32
Yoruba 10
Yothu Yindi 203
Yukon Storytelling Festival 188
Yup'ik community 48, 60, 63–5

Zephaniah, Benjamin 191